Our Lady of the Exile

✳ *Our Lady of the Exile*

Diasporic Religion at a
Cuban Catholic Shrine in Miami

THOMAS A. TWEED

OXFORD
UNIVERSITY PRESS

OXFORD
UNIVERSITY PRESS

Oxford   New York
Auckland   Bangkok   Buenos Aires   Cape Town   Chennai
Dar es Salaam   Delhi   Hong Kong   Istanbul   Karachi   Kolkata
Kuala Lumpur   Madrid   Melbourne   Mexico City   Mumbai   Nairobi
São Paulo   Shanghai   Singapore   Taipei   Tokyo   Toronto

Copyright © 1997 by Thomas A. Tweed

First published in 1997 by Oxford University Press, Inc.
198 Madison Avenue, New York, New York 10016

First issued as an Oxford University Press paperback, 2002

www.oup.com

Oxford is a registered trademark of Oxford University Press, Inc.

Library of Congress Cataloging-in-Publication Data
Tweed, Thomas A.
   Our lady of the exile : diasporic religion at a Cuban Catholic
shrine in Miami / Thomas A. Tweed.
      p.   cm.—(Religion in America series)
Includes bibliographical references and index.
ISBN 0-19-510529-X; 0-19-515593-9 (Pbk.)
   1. Cuban American Catholics—Religious life—Florida—Miami.
2. Cubans—Florida—Miami—Religion.   3. Caridad, Virgen de la—
Cult—Florida—Miami.   4. Ermita de la Caridad (Miami, Fla.)
I. Title.   II. Series: Religion in America series (Oxford University
Press)
BX1407.C83T84   1997 2002
282'.759381—dc21   96-51082

9 8 7 6 5 4 3 2 1

Printed in the United States of America
on acid-free paper

To Kevin and Bryn

Acknowledgments

One of the pleasures of finishing a book is that the author gets the chance to thank some—though never all—of the people who helped along the way. Because I did fieldwork as well as archival research for this five-year project, my debts are many.

Most important, I am extremely grateful to the pilgrims at Our Lady of Charity's shrine in Miami, who were so generous with their time. Teresita and Miguel Núñez and Kitty and Juan Barturen were exceptionally kind. Juan even read most of the manuscript, offering encouragement and suggestions. I hope that all of the Virgin's devotees who took the time to tell me stories and answer my questions feel that their efforts were worthwhile. I know that I could not have written this book without their extraordinary willingness to talk so openly about their lives on the island and in exile.

I also owe a large debt to the Most Reverend Agustín A. Román, auxiliary bishop of Miami and director of the shrine. He talked with me often and at great length. I would never have had the same access to sources or responsiveness from local Catholics without his unfailing support. For reasons that I still do not understand—although I am deeply grateful—Bishop Román seemed to trust me from the start. That does not mean that he will agree with all of my interpretations in this book. When I reflect on that, I am comforted by an exchange we had several years ago at the shrine. At Bishop Román's request, I spoke about my project to a group of Cuban young adults there. Afterward, I sensed that I had not said exactly what he would have liked. As we walked from the shrine together, he said only: "It takes many voices." I took that as confirmation of my initial judgment that I had surprised (or disappointed) him and as further evidence of his charity and gentleness. If there are passages in the book that again surprise or disappoint, I hope that he can forgive me.

Other clergy and staff at the shrine and in the Archdiocese helped too. The Reverend Francisco Santana, the Reverend Romeo Rivas, and other priests who have served at the shrine provided information. The lay volunteers and Daughters of Charity of St. Vincent dePaul, who work diligently at the shrine office, put up with my many stupid questions and odd requests. Bishop Román's secretary, Norma T. Molina, gave me crucial material and passed on countless messages. Araceli M. Cantero, executive editor of the Archdiocese's Spanish monthly, *La Voz Católica*, allowed me access to their files, published a notice about my project, and granted me permission to use photographs. The Reverend Tomás M. Marín, chancellor of the Archdiocese of Miami, permitted me to see the official files about the shrine, which contained some key documents. The taped interviews I did with Monsignor Bryan O. Walsh, who played a leading role in the Archdiocese during the 1960s, confirmed my hunches and filled in gaps in the printed sources. Many other local priests helped as well, including the Reverend Pedro Luís Pérez, the Reverend Michael J. McNally, the Reverend Felipe J. Estévez, and the Reverend Juan Sosa. Father Sosa also read most of the manuscript, offering insightful comments.

Some local Miamians who worked on the construction of the shrine spoke with me and provided documents and photographs, including Donald W. Myers, the contractor, and Teok Carrasco, the muralist. Manolo Reyes, who helped raise funds for the temporary shrine, provided indispensable information.

A number of friends and research assistants helped with the project. My friend and former coworker Ada Orlando cared deeply about the book and sometimes even accompanied me to the shrine and the celebrations. She also read the entire manuscript. Next to Bishop Román, Ada did more to help than anyone. I am very grateful. Her mother, Emilia Aguilera, also helped, providing a perspective from another generation. Carmen Watson checked the manuscript for errors. Two other friends took some of the photographs in the book: John Jessup and Michael Carlebach. B. J. and Richard Cole and Thomas Goodman provided comfortable lodging, bag lunches, and lively conversation during some of my return visits to Miami. Gladys Ramos at the Cuban Archives at the Richter Library of the University of Miami went beyond the call of duty. I also am grateful to Ivonne Hernandez, Hilda Mateo, and David Sosa, three undergraduates at the University of Miami who helped with research. My research assistants at the University of North Carolina helped with the bibliography and other matters: Sean McCloud, Elizabeth Miller, Lynn Neal, Robert Waller, and Jennifer Wojcikowski. Together with the other students who enrolled in my graduate seminar in fall 1995, they also commented insightfully on the manuscript.

Without financial support I would not have been able to finish the fieldwork or the writing. After I moved to North Carolina in 1993, the University of North Carolina awarded me research grants to complete the fieldwork in Miami, and the National Endowment for the Humanities Fellowship for University Professors in 1994–95 provided me with time to write.

Many scholars read portions of the manuscript and improved it in countless ways, including Ruth Behar, George Brandon, Juan Clark, John Dixon, Arnold Eisen, Matthew Glass, Helen Hills, Patricia O'Connell Killen, John Kirk, Daniel Levine, Robert Levine, Laurie Maffly-Kipp, Colleen McDannell, Joseph Murphy, David Morgan, Caroline V. Prorok, Christian Smith, Anthony M. Stevens-Arroyo, Jack Sasson, Yi-Fu Tuan, Peter W. Williams, and Sandra Zimdars-Swartz. Mercedes Sandoval, Raúl Cañizares, and Ann Braude offered helpful suggestions. Professor Enrique López Oliva of the University of Havana provided information about contemporary religious life on the island. Participants in the Young Scholars in American Religion Program, which was sponsored by the Pew Charitable Trusts, carefully and critically read an early summary of the project. Audiences at the University of Florida, the University of Tennessee at Knoxville, Duke University, and the University of Notre Dame asked good questions. So did my former colleagues at the University of Miami and my current colleagues at the University of North Carolina, where I presented summaries of the project in public lectures. The Geography Department at UNC also invited me to share my research in a public lecture, and their questions and comments helped me to refine my thinking. My friends in the reading group on Religion and Cultural Studies at Duke and Carolina —especially Elizabeth Clark, Dale Martin, and Tomoko Masuzawa—provided a stimulating setting for exploring theory, some of which found its way into this book indirectly or directly.

A few friends who teach U.S. religion, Catholic studies, or Cuban history read most or all of the manuscript and offered detailed comments and probing questions: R. Scott Appleby, Catherine Brekus, Robert A. Orsi, and Louis A. Pérez Jr. I owe them a great deal. Ann Taves was remarkably supportive and generous. We commiserated by electronic mail regularly during the year that I drafted this book, and she gave appreciatively critical readings along the way. I am grateful for her friendship.

To thank people is not to assign responsibility. I listened carefully and respectfully to comments from Cuban Catholics, Miami clergy, and diverse scholars. Sometimes, although always after sustained reflection, I decided not to follow the counsel of those who were kind enough to read the manuscript in draft form. I tried to be especially sensitive to the responses from Cuban laity and clergy, often revising the manuscript as they had suggested or, when we disagreed, acknowledging their dissent in the notes or the text. Still, *I* wrote the book, and the mistakes are mine.

Finally, I want to thank my family, who helped in many ways. My mother, Janet Tweed, cultivated in me a respect for the beauty and power of Marian devotion. If I have managed to understand the piety of Cuban devotees of the Virgin, my mother deserves some credit. My wife, Margaret L. McNamee, is the kindest person I know. I am profoundly grateful for her continuing love, support, and encouragement. My children, Kevin and Bryn, are the greatest source of joy in my life, and I never could hope to repay them for that. In any case, this book is for them.

Chapel Hill, North Carolina T. A. T.
August 1996

Contents

Illustrations

Figures

Maps

Tables

Our Lady of the Exile

Introduction

A small sign in Spanish—Ermita de la Caridad—announces the location of a shrine in Miami that rests on Biscayne Bay just south of the downtown skyscrapers. The conical shrine dedicated to the patroness of Cuba, Our Lady of Charity, sits several hundred yards from the road that leads to the downtown area (figure 1). Most non-Latino residents do not know it exists, yet it is the sacred center of the Cuban Catholic community in exile. It was dedicated on 2 December 1973, and it has attracted increasing numbers of visitors since then, the majority of them mature, middle-class whites of Cuban descent. By the 1990s, it had become the sixth largest Catholic pilgrimage site in the United States, annually attracting hundreds of thousands of pilgrims. In this book I analyze devotion to Our Lady of Charity at this urban shrine.[1]

I first encountered the shrine in 1991. I had been researching the history of religion in Miami, and in my travels around the city to uncover sources I stumbled upon it. I was perplexed and intrigued. Who was this Virgin to whom the building was dedicated? Why were she and the shrine so important to the visitors? Who were these visitors anyway? If they were mostly Cubans, as it seemed, how did the symbols function in their lives?

This book began as an attempt to answer these and other questions. In this task I was helped by my early religious experience. I was raised in an Irish Catholic family in Philadelphia, and the power of popular devotions to virgins and saints was made clear to me at an early age. I had watched the women of my church moving their lips, their eyes filling with tears, as they knelt beneath the image of Mary to offer personal petitions. At the kitchen table my mother told stories of saints, as some families—those with more respectable lineages, I suppose—tell tales about living relatives and dead ancestors. Saint Francis, Saint John Bosco, and Saint Anthony were more familiar to me than my aged Aunt May, my grandmother's sister, whom we visited every other year or so, mostly—it seemed to me—to gorge ourselves on butterscotch candies.

Having read about the history of Catholicism in Europe and Latin America, I also

Figure 1. The Shrine of Our Lady of Charity in Miami.

was somewhat familiar with the function of the cult of the saints in forming collective identity. I knew, for instance, that Polish and Mexican Catholics had their
national Virgins; but nothing I had read or experienced prepared me for the intensity of nationalistic feelings I would find at the shrine in Miami. Even on that first
visit to the shrine a hunch began to form: maybe this has something to do with
Cuban exiles' attachment to their homeland. That is embarrassing to confess now,
since the signs were everywhere, as I learned on subsequent visits. As early as the
second visit I noticed—how had I missed it the first time?—that a Cuban flag was
painted on stones to the left of the shrine exterior, a bust of the leader of Cuban
independence watched Castro's Cuba from a pedestal on the rear exterior wall, and
the large mural inside narrated Cuban political, military, and religious history.

As I visited the shrine regularly and read widely in Cuban and Cuban American
history, I became convinced that a study of devotion at the shrine in Miami might
allow me to see things that had been obscured when I stood at other locales. Narrators always stand at a particular geographical site and social space as they tell their
stories. Positioned at that immigrant shrine in a diverse city, a city of exiles, near
the geographical center of the Americas, new sights opened for me. I began to see
more clearly the significance of locality for identity and religion.

This book, then, is about religion, identity, and place. I hope to make several contributions. First, some scholars have begun to compare the religious history of the
United States with that of other nations in the Atlantic world, the Pacific world, or
the Western Hemisphere. This can open new angles of vision. By centering my narrative in Miami, near the geographical midpoint of the Americas, and considering

developments in Cuba, I indirectly contribute to scholarly attempts to situate religious developments in the United States in a wider geographical context. Second, scholars in a number of fields have been concerned with how groups form collective identity, including nationalistic forms of it. Here I consider the complex relations between collective identity and place, focusing on the identity of the involuntarily displaced, or "diaspora nationalism." Finally, I explore the interconnections of religion, identity, and place by studying the religion of the displaced. More narrowly, I add to the literature on "new" immigrants, in this case Latino Catholics. Robert A. Orsi, Jay Dolan, Paula M. Kane, James S. Olson, and others have authored insightful studies of Catholic immigrants, although none of them have focused on the theme of displacement as fully as I do here. Latino Catholics have received more attention in recent years. Only one history of the Latino church in the United States has appeared, yet two new book series on Latino religion help fill some gaps. Part of one of those volumes focuses on Cuban American Catholics, but for the most part Cubans remain understudied. Cubanists have underemphasized religion, especially Catholicism; and Americanists have underemphasized Catholicism and overlooked Cubans. More broadly, a few scholars have speculated about religion and displacement, including cultural geographer Yi-Fu Tuan and religion scholar Jonathan Z. Smith. For all the recent concern for international migration, and more specifically the new Latino and Asian migration to the Americas, surprisingly little has been written about transnational religion. This case study, I suggest, offers insights about—to introduce terms I develop later—diasporic religion and its transtemporal and translocative symbols.[2]

Sources and Methods

Authors care more about what they did than readers do. That makes sense. I have spent five years of my life trying to understand the shrine and the people who go there. Unless you are a Cuban from Miami, you probably just now have begun your encounter with the Virgin and her shrine. Yet most readers want to know something about the author's sources and methods—but not too much—so that they can form judgments about the trustworthiness of the account. For that reason, and others, I think it is helpful to volunteer just a bit about what I did and why, to say something about why I feel confident enough about my interpretations to write a book.

I had the chance to live in Miami for five years while I taught at a local university, so for three of the five years of this project, which I began in 1991, I had easy access to sources and abundant opportunities for interaction. After I moved to North Carolina in the summer of 1993, I returned regularly for research, with stays that lasted from several days to several weeks. While I lived in the southwest section of metropolitan Miami from 1988 to 1993 I listened to Spanish-language radio, read Spanish-language periodicals, forked *arroz blanco y frijoles negros* in Little Havana, and chatted with Cuban exiles, whom I saw regularly at my office and in my neighborhood. Much of this did not directly inform this book. However, it shaped it indirectly by helping me place activities at the shrine in a wider cultural context.

As I began to study devotion at the local shrine, which was about fifteen miles from my home and six from my office, I turned for help first to those I knew and then to the prominent lay and clerical members of the Cuban community. Excited and perplexed by what I saw at the shrine, I asked Cuban American students, professors, and secretaries at my university what they knew about it. One of my coworkers, an administrative assistant who had migrated from Cuba as a teenager, became an important conversation partner. I asked neighbors, acquaintances, and strangers. The father of one of my son's friends had been exiled as a child, and as we watched our young sons chase balls around the soccer field he gave me my first clues about how important the Virgin was, even to those who did not affiliate formally or attend mass regularly. Another man I met in a Spanish-language bookstore in Little Havana provided a number of useful leads. Early on I interviewed the auxiliary bishop who has responsibility for the shrine, The Most Reverend Agustín A. Román, and I also talked with him many times after that. Other clergy, too, volunteered stories and analyses about Cuban American religiousness. I contacted the lay leaders of the Confraternity of Our Lady of Charity, who offered their own perspectives. I also read everything I could find. After months of this research, I became increasingly aware of the distance between me and those I wanted to understand. That meant, I decided, that I was ready to begin.

As I started more systematic study, I decided that I would use both historical and ethnographic methods and consider a wide range of sources. To quantify what might be quantified, I looked at census figures, documentary records, and survey data about Cubans and Cuban Americans. Those figures told me, for example, how many exiles lived in Miami and how many went to mass in prerevolutionary Cuba. It did not tell me what religion has meant to them. For that, I consulted the more traditional sources of historians. Those included periodicals and pamphlets published by the shrine and the Archdiocese as well as newspapers, poetry, nonfiction, and fiction. I also read devotional letters written to the shrine from Cuba and the United States, although all of those written before 1992 were lost when Hurricane Andrew washed Biscayne Bay into the storage area in the shrine's basement.

These textual sources highlighted beliefs, as most scholarship on religion in the United States has, yet I was convinced that artifacts also inscribe meanings. For this reason I studied the community's material culture as well—architecture, yard shrines, photographs, paintings, key chains, holy cards, and plastic statues—for clues about how those express and shape attitudes about religion and place.

Scholars of American religion also have privileged beliefs over behaviors. To understand what devotees at the shrine *did*, and what that might have meant to them, I drew on participant observation and conducted interviews. I observed and participated in every type of ritual practice at the shrine—masses, rosaries, blessings, vigils, and processions. My fieldnotes, which I constructed from the field jottings scribbled on small notepads during the day, record my experiences at these rituals and my recollections of informal conversations participated in and overheard at the shrine. I consulted these bound and indexed fieldnotes again and again as I wrote this book. I also did taped unstructured interviewing, sitting down with lay followers and clergy to talk for an hour or more, but without any fixed list of questions.[3]

Most important, I conducted 304 structured interviews in which visitors to the shrine were asked to respond to twenty questions on a questionnaire. I conducted research at all days and times. I stood outside on the steps near one of the three exits. As visitors left the shrine I told them that I was writing a book about devotion to the Virgin at the shrine, and I asked if they had time to answer some questions. This method did not assure a random sample, of course, even though it yielded responses from a diverse group in terms of gender, region, and age (see tables 3.1, 3.2, and 3.3); but it did provide rich detail about how some visitors understood devotion at the shrine. That supplemented what I learned from textual sources, material culture, and participant observation. Except in the few instances when visitors preferred English (all of those informants were under age thirty), the questionnaires and the conversations were in Spanish. At one point, I stopped carrying the English version of the questionnaire because it had been six months since anyone had asked for it. Even when visitors would turn to English along the way, as some did, they often returned to their native language to express a deeply held belief. Half of the twenty questions they answered, in Spanish or English, were open-ended (appendix B). I asked, for example, not only about their arrival date and native region but also about their impressions of the mural and the reasons for their devotion. Most of these questionnaires were self-administered, but occasionally those who were infirm, aged, or illiterate asked me to read the questions to them. In either case, I stood beside them as they answered. This allowed me to clarify ambiguities in the questions and encouraged them to explain their answers. It also led to a very high response rate. As we went along I often asked them for elaboration or clarification, and often they volunteered more than I requested, sometimes telling long, and usually sad, stories about their life in Cuba and their exile in America. After they finished answering the standard questions I asked visitors if they had time to talk further. Many did. I spoke with most pilgrims once, except the members of the confraternity whom I saw very often; and the conversations lasted approximately thirty minutes. Some were shorter, as devotees rushed home to make dinner, scurried to gather relatives, or hurried back to the office. Other conversations lasted much longer, even several hours.

Throughout the project I identified myself and my purpose and was welcomed with uncommon generosity, although at first a few pilgrims wondered about my political views and personal motives. Although there are differences of viewpoint among them, the overwhelming majority of visitors to the Miami shrine are political conservatives, fervent anticommunists who despise Fidel Castro and support the U.S. blockade and all other policies to isolate and weaken the socialist government on the island. As Spanish-language talk radio and periodicals in Miami indicate, however, there are passionate disagreements between the anticommunist exiles who predominate (in the city and at the shrine) and those Cubans (or "Anglos") who advocate— as one group of Cuban and Cuban American intellectuals put it—building "bridges to Cuba." It is in this political context that some pilgrims initially were suspicious of me. And, in fact, my political views are to the left of most pilgrims at the shrine. Yet I was interested not in condemning Cuban exiles' political culture but in understanding their religious practice. To my surprise, the pilgrims I spoke with eventually seemed to be convinced of that. For example, one middle-aged woman I encountered on a weekday afternoon seemed wary until she inspected the questions and concluded that I did not openly profess any worrisome political views. In particular, she seemed relieved to find that my questions did not imply that I advocated "dialogue" with the government of Castro (although they did not condemn it either). Like many other visitors with whom I spoke, after she satisfied herself about my motives—that I was trying to understand devotion to the Virgin at the shrine—she freely volunteered story after story. Considering the passionately held political views of shrine visitors and the history of ethnic tension in Miami, some pilgrims' initial suspicion did not surprise me. In fact, that was one reason I not only promised them anonymity, as is usual in such studies, but also refrained from recording the names of those who participated in the structured interviews.[4]

As I became more and more welcomed by the clergy and laity over the years, I found that warm reception more curious than their initial skepticism. Some of the Cuban pilgrims' openness seems to have been grounded in simple human kindness. With my name badge, university affiliation, and imposing clipboard, I also must have looked authoritative and thus elicited the usual responses to authority. After several years of thinking and inquiring about the high level of cooperation I received, I concluded that at least four other factors also informed it. In a city that has had its share of ethnic tensions, many Cubans appreciated that *any* representative of the Anglo community cared enough to ask them about their patroness and shrine, or about anything. They also appreciated that I asked them in their native language, however imperfectly I did so at times. As studies of interviewing indicate, middle-class informants in the United States with higher levels of education tend to be more willing to participate in interviews, and many of the visitors fit that social profile. Finally, they knew that I was writing a book that would record part of their history, for them and their descendants.[5]

We had our reasons for interacting, then, and both the observer and the observed were changed in the process. No matter how sensitive, unintrusive, and empathic I might like to think I was, Cuban visitors were bound to notice an Anglo professor with name badge and clipboard incessantly asking and scribbling. My presence changed things in participant observation in ways that are hard to document, although that was much less significant in rituals that draw thousands of participants, like the annual festival. Also, as studies on interviewing show, differences in the age, gender, ethnicity, and class of the interviewer yield differences in informants' responses. This is unavoidable.[6]

As the years passed, my presence and its effects on the Cuban devotees became more visible. For instance, at the first annual festival I attended in 1991 I sat toward the top of an outdoor stadium, making my jottings in a sea of anonymity. By the 1994 festival mass, however, I sat on the main aisle five rows back from the stage, behind the confraternity leaders and in front of the seminarians, as the photographer I brought with me crouched conspicuously on stage by the altar to record the event for this book. My position changed further, and my visibility grew, when Bishop Román asked one member of the confraternity to describe my project at one of their regular meetings. Spanish-language archdiocesan communication systems— newspaper and radio—also described my project. In subsequent visits to the shrine a few Cubans indicated that they had noticed the announcements, and some seemed even more eager to help, now that official Catholic sources had appeared to give the project their imprimatur.

Not only had I changed some visitors in unintended ways; gradually my experiences at the shrine shaped me too. I often found myself trying to fight back tears as I listened to compelling tales about exile from older men and women, prompting me to reflect on the effects of displacement in all of our lives. Those emotional encounters also led me to be much less concerned with the political differences between us, and more sympathetic to Cuban pilgrims' struggles to ease their sadness and explain their loss through religion. I was affected in other ways too. I was surprised and moved when the Cuban-born bishop told me in 1993 that he had prayed for me on a recent trip to the Vatican, handing me a small crucifix blessed by the pope that he had carried from Rome. I became entangled in the emotional lives of two visitors when I observed, and later interviewed, a mother who pushed her ten-year-old daughter in a wheelchair to the Virgin's altar to ask for help because the doctors had told her that none was available. More than a decade earlier I had stopped practicing Catholicism, but I felt the emotions of my childhood piety stir as I watched extended families kneeling at the altar on Sunday afternoons and scrubbed children processing in spring's subtropical sun, with the Virgin leading the way.

One incident brought home to me how much I had been shaped by years of participation, reading, and conversation. Three years into the project I had been attending a conference in Washington, D.C., and decided to visit Our Lady of Charity at the Basilica of the Immaculate Conception, a national center of American Catholicism that enshrines more than seventy national saints and virgins linked with immigrant groups. As I located the familiar white marble image, I found myself—spontaneously and inexplicably—praying in Spanish to Our Lady of Charity for the liberation of Cuba: "Virgen Santísima, salva a Cuba." Even after thinking about the religious and political implications of this for some time now, I am not sure what I did and why I did it. Had I "gone native," at least for that one moment, identifying with a political viewpoint that I did not share? Had my childhood piety resurfaced temporarily? Was it simply an act of respect and empathy for those who had been so kind to me and told me so many sad stories? Readers might have more clues than I. In any case, I had to let go of any notion of myself as an unengaged and immutable observer.[7]

That does not mean, however, that ethnographic knowledge is unwarranted or unreliable. As one philosopher of science has argued persuasively, all knowledge is "situated." It is always a sighting from a particular location, but it not less warranted for that reason. In fact, self-conscious reporting of what an observer can see from a particular site is as much knowledge as is available to us. My reports from the shrine are not views from everywhere at once or nowhere in particular; but, then, no observer's writings ever have been that. This text, however, is one imaginative yet disciplined construction of the meanings of devotion at the shrine, as reported by a male, middle-class, Anglo professor with a particular life history.[8]

Nor does letting go of notions of an unengaged and immutable observer mean that ethnographies are, or ought to be, nothing more than autobiographies, although they are that too. By trying to be reflexive—the root meaning of the word is "capable of turning or bending back"—I can do as much as possible to be aware of the effects of my experiences on my research. That awareness can, and sometimes should, enter the text as I report on the engaged interactions of fieldwork, or even the situated knowledge constructed from reading. In this introduction, and in what follows, I sometimes include personal narrative. Sometimes my reaction, or the interpersonal context, seemed important to convey. Generally, however, I have tried to pull back from unrestrained autobiography. At this historical moment, when many interpreters in the humanities and social sciences are advocating first-person narratives as a way of acknowledging that they are engaged and mutable observers who report located knowledges, it is also helpful to consider the ways in which our interpretations can—and ought to—be more than diary. The confessional mode, too, introduces epistemological and moral problems. It claims authority just as it pretends to undercut it. It does so by implying that the author has privileged information about his or her own motives and location, persuading the reader that the writer has come clean. My autobiographical referents in this introduction, for instance, obscure as much as they illumine. They might give the impression that I am self-conscious about how I am located as an observer. I try. But what have I not told the reader? What is inaccessible to me? No matter how forthright and vulnerable authors might appear in such confessional passages, more always remains hidden—to author and reader. That is inevitable. That does not mean that persuasive interpretation is impossible or the autobiographical voice is inappropriate. I already have shown that I do not mean that. Yet personal narrative in the confessional mode is not the solution to all the epistemological or moral problems facing interpreters. It, too, has its limits.[9]

Interpreters, then, are engaged participants in the construction of the situated knowledges reported in books like this one, but one of the aims of ethnography, and history, surely ought to be to report what we see, not just who we are and where we stand. As one cultural anthropologist, Robert J. Smith, has reminded us, "The subjects of ethnographies, it should never be forgotten, are always more interesting than their authors." I find Cubans at the shrine interesting; I am less sure about me. This has implications for research and writing. "If we are to continue to do ethnography at all," Smith has argued persuasively, "I cannot see that we have any other option than to listen carefully to what people say, watch what they do, and keep our voices down."[10]

Argument and Organization

Keeping my voice down most of the time, in this book I argue that exiles struggle over the meaning of symbols, but almost all Cuban American visitors to the shrine in Miami see it as a place to express diasporic nationalism, to make sense of themselves as a displaced people. There, exiles map the landscape and history of the homeland onto the new urban environment. Focusing on the ways they do this in rituals and artifacts, I suggest that through transtemporal and translocative symbols at the shrine the diaspora imaginatively constructs its collective identity and transports itself to the Cuba of memory and desire.

My argument unfolds in six thematically organized chapters. In the opening chapter I trace the history of Cuban and Cuban American devotion to Our Lady of Charity, emphasizing its locative or nationalistic character (figure 2). I suggest that the

Figure 2. The interior of the Miami shrine, with the small statue of Our Lady of Charity in the center. The statue rests on a pedestal above the altar and below the painted image of the Virgin on the mural.

majority of prerevolutionary Cubans were relatively "unchurched," especially in rural areas. Popular devotion to the Virgin, however, has been strong since the seventeenth century, and she has been intimately linked with national identity since the nineteenth-century wars for independence from Spain. Devotion to the patroness of Cuba intensified in exile as the diaspora turned to her to help them make sense of who they were, now that they were displaced from the places that shaped their identity. The shrine of Our Lady of Charity in Miami is one site in the urban landscape that has special significance in this regard. I offer an overview of the exodus to Miami and the founding of the American shrine.[11]

In the second and third chapters I emphasize the *contested* meanings of symbols at the shrine. In chapter 2 I suggest that laity and clergy struggle over meanings. The clergy (and lay elite) have seen the shrine as a place to "evangelize" the nominal Catholics in the exile community. They hope to "purify" Catholicism by removing the residue of Santería, the Afro-Cuban religion that survives in popular devotions. Lay followers also struggle among themselves over the meaning of symbols, and in chapter 3 I consider the diversity of people and practices at the shrine. Although race, class, and region are less important sources of difference among Cuban pilgrims than they were in the homeland, gender and age do divide visitors in important ways. The mature, white, middle-class Cubans who visit the shrine in the greatest numbers offer prayers and make vows for a variety of reasons—especially for healing, childbirth, and family.

In the final three chapters I turn to the heart of my argument as I identify the *shared* meaning of the translocative and transtemporal symbols. In chapter 4 I provide a theoretical framework for the chapters that follow. I sketch the outlines of a theory of religion and place that emerges from the Cuban American case, emphasizing some common features of diasporic or transnational religion. The religion of the displaced draws on transtemporal and translocative symbols that transport followers to another time and bridge the homeland and the new land. In chapter 5 I consider how diasporic nationalism is inscribed in artifacts at the shrine. In the sixth and final chapter I show how Cuban exiles express diasporic nationalism in several organized rituals. Summarizing what we can learn from the Cuban case and drawing on examples of other diasporic groups, in the postscript I speculate about the wider implications of this study for narrating the religious history of the Americas and understanding the religion of displaced peoples.

I ✳ *Devotion to Our Lady of Charity*

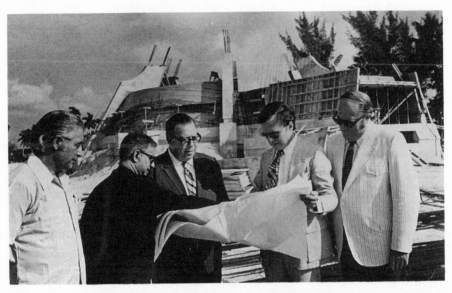

Figure 3. Planners examine the architectural drawings for the new shrine in 1972, a year before the building was dedicated: *from left to right*, Teok Carrasco, the muralist; the Reverend Agustín A. Román, the shrine director; José Miguel Morales Gómez, a leading lay Catholic; Maurice Ferré, a Puerto Rican–born businessman who donated concrete and later would serve as Miami's mayor; and Robert C. Saunders of Standard Dry Wall Products, who donated materials. (Courtesy *The Voice*; photo by Tony Garner.)

1 ✳ *The Virgin's Exile*

The Cuban Patroness and the Diaspora in Miami

The story of Cuban exile Catholicism begins on a rainy Friday in 1961 as Our Lady of Charity travels from an airport in Havana to a baseball stadium in Miami on her feast day, 8 September, a day when the Cuban patroness herself would become an exile. The statue of Our Lady of Charity that journeyed from Havana to Miami had sacred power for her dispersed devotees, even though it was not the original image, which remained in the shrine in the easternmost province of Cuba. It was a replica that had been pedestaled in a parish church in Guanabo Beach, a section of Havana. In other years that same diminutive Virgin had been carried from the church in the annual processions on her feast day. That day in 1961, however, concealed in a small suitcase, she traveled by airplane across the Straits of Florida to be reunited with the Cuban diaspora.[1]

The events that led to the Virgin's exile began a month earlier, in August 1961, when Cubans in Miami contacted Italy's ambassador to Cuba. Agreeing to their request, he granted asylum for the Virgin from Guanabo Beach. The Italian ambassador, acting on the exiles' behalf, then asked Elvira Jované de Zayas, a member of the diplomatic corps of the Republic of Panama, to smuggle that statue of Our Lady of Charity to Miami. During the first days of September, then, the image found safe haven in the Panamanian Embassy in Cuba. The Panamanian diplomat, who was linked to Cuba by profession and marriage, managed to get a safe passage for a friend's son, Luís Gutiérrez Areces, who became an unwitting participant in the Virgin's migration. After much difficulty, the diplomat from Panama gave the young man bound for Miami a satchel or valise (*un maletín*) containing the small statue of Our Lady of Charity. As he boarded the plane at the Havana airport, the diplomat told him only that he should not lose the satchel; he did not tell the young man what it contained. Meanwhile, back in Miami, an overflow crowd of 25,000 Cuban exiles—most of whom had arrived in the two years since Fidel Castro's revolutionary army had marched victoriously into Havana—congregated in a baseball stadium to celebrate her feast day. Organizers of that Catholic ritual grew more and more worried when the Virgin still had not arrived at six o'clock, an hour before the rosary and mass were scheduled to begin. Although they did not know it at the time, however, the Cuban patroness had already landed at the Miami airport. The young migrant who unknowingly had aided her escape delivered the satchel to St. Patrick's Church in Miami Beach, as he had been instructed. From there she was hurried by car to the stadium in downtown Miami. At seven o'clock, just ten minutes before the rosary would start, a Cuban migrant rushed into the stadium and handed the satchel to Father Armando Jiménez Rebollar, who had been the priest in the Virgin's home parish in Havana. The priest took the Virgin from the satchel and prepared her for the first of many festival masses that she would preside over in exile. When the Miami crowd finally could see their national patroness, they wept and waved, shouted and sang. Our Lady of Charity's new life as an exile had begun, and that night the lives of other exiles in Miami changed in important ways as well.

The passionate reception that the Virgin received makes it clear that Cuban affection for her did not begin that night in 1961. In this chapter, I trace the history of Cuban devotion to Our Lady of Charity, the national patroness, on the island and in Miami. In the first section I explore Cuban religious developments before the revolution of 1959, emphasizing the links between the national patroness and collective identity. Continuing to focus on those links, in the second section I consider the piety of Cuban Catholic exiles in Miami since 1959, tracing the beginnings of organized devotions to Our Lady of Charity and the origins of her Miami shrine, where the exiled Virgin finally found a home when the building was consecrated in 1973.[2]

Our Lady of Charity in the Homeland, before 1959

Religion outside the Churches

The Roman Catholic Church landed on Cuban shores with Christopher Columbus in 1492, but it made remarkably little progress there in some ways over the next two centuries. Just as the "Golden Age" of Cuban Catholic history (1750–1850), a century in which the Church began to establish itself on Cuban soil, was ending, most observers, native and foreign, still found the institution extraordinarily weak. In 1849, one visitor told his readers, in *The Island of Cuba*, that "the state of religion in this island is most deplorable." A year later another foreign observer noted that "at present day, in all of the churches of Cuba, a brief mass, scandalously hurried through, and witnessed by a very small portion of the inhabitants, is all that attests the Sabbath of the Lord." Interpreters of all perspectives regularly reported that the churches were few and the people "indifferent." Even Catholic officials in Cuba agreed. In 1849, upon being appointed to head the diocese in Santiago de Cuba, Father Jerónimo Usera y Alarcón pronounced that "the state of this Church is deplorable." By almost any standard, Cuba before and after this so-called Golden Age of Catholicism has been a relatively unchurched nation. Too few priests, and even fewer native ones, pastored to the people. Too few churches dotted the landscape. An institutional Catholic piety that focused on the sacraments was weak in Cuba, even compared with other nations in Latin America. And as many observers

Table 1. Religion in Cuba before the Revolution: 1954 Survey

Religious Affiliation	Percent
No affiliation	19.0
Catholic	72.5
Protestant	6.0
Jewish	.5
Spiritist	1.0
Santería	.5
Mason	.5

Belief in Existence of God	Percent
Exists	96.5
Does not exist	1.5
No opinion	2.0

Source: La Agrupación Católica Universitaria, "Encuesta nacional sobre el sentimiento religioso del pueblo de Cuba, 1954 ," in Manuel Fernández, *Religión y revolución en Cuba: Veinticinco años de lucha ateística* (Miami: Saeta Ediciones, 1984), 22.

also have reported, where it was found it thrived disproportionately among white, middle-class women and children in the cities.[3]

The situation did improve in some ways during the first half of the twentieth century, especially the 1940s and 1950s. During this period, Catholic schools did gain popularity and importance, training many of Cuba's leaders. Several middle-class lay organizations which aimed to promote ecclesiastical involvement and social justice, such as Acción Católica and Agrupación Católica Universitaria, also revitalized the Church in some ways.[4]

Yet on the eve of the revolution of 1959 and the massive emigrations that followed, many Cubans—especially in rural areas—remained outside the reach of the institutional church. In 1954, for instance, Cuba had the lowest proportion of nominal Catholics (72.5%) and practicing Catholics (5–8%) in Latin America (table 1). In 1955, there were 26,700 Cuban inhabitants for each diocesan priest on the island (table 2). Many of those who lived outside the cities had no church nearby, so their piety could not revolve around the sacraments, as most clergy would have liked. In fact, some of the most stunning evidence of Cuba's noninstitutional Catholic piety comes from two surveys of agricultural workers who were heads of household in 1956 and 1957. Four out of ten did not affiliate with any religion (41.4%), and only 52 percent identified themselves as Catholic. Almost nine out of ten (88.8%) of the Catholics reported that they had not attended mass in the

Table 2. The Unchurched Population of Prerevolutionary Cuba, 1955

Parishes	206
Inhabitants per parish	29,700
Diocesan priests	229
Inhabitants per diocesan priest	26,700

Source: "Evolución de las estadísticas religiosas de Cuba, 1945–1974," *Cuba diáspora* (1975): 25.

previous year. Most striking of all, more than half (53.5%) said that they had never even *seen* a priest.[5]

All this is *not* to say—as some interpreters have claimed—that Cubans were not religious. They simply were not linked closely with ecclesiastical institutions. It was the Church and the priests with whom many were unfamiliar; they felt quite comfortable with the Christian God and saints, many even with the African *orishas* of Santería. In 1954, an overwhelming majority of Cubans (96.5%) reported in a survey that they believed in God (table 1). That almost mirrors the statistics for the same period in the United States, which often is held up as one of the most religious eras in the history of a nation of religious affiliators and church attenders. Even though this did not surface in the 1954 Cuban survey—perhaps because it was conducted by a Catholic organization—domestic and shrine religion, both Catholicism and Santería, were vigorous.

On the eve of the revolution of 1959, and for centuries before that, Cuban Catholics worshiped in their homes and in the streets. Many of the exiles whom I interviewed in Miami were old enough to recall religious life before the revolution. Rural residents, and others too, told me that they rarely had gone to church in Cuba. Many had lived too far away for regular visits, they explained. But they fondly recalled the religion of the home. Cesar, a sixty-four-year-old man from a rural township who had rarely attended mass as a child, trembled with emotion as he told me that his strong devotion to Our Lady of Charity began in the home. Each night before bedtime, as his mother had instructed, he knelt to kiss the feet of the statue of the Virgin enshrined in their living room. Observers had noticed the pervasiveness of this domestic religion even well before the middle of the twentieth century. For instance, one writer suggested in 1856 that "the country people of Cuba as well as the other inhabitants are not very religious," but "this does not prevent, however, images of the Virgin and of saints being in every house." Domestic devotions also spilled out into the streets. As with Catholics in other Latin American nations, patronal festivals and regional pilgrimages have been the two most important collective religious rites for Cubans. One American Protestant observer in the 1880s who had little sympathy for this form of piety noted that Cubans had "a mania for processions." Even men, he reported with surprise, participated in these religious celebrations. Some of those men, now exiles in Miami, recalled devotional life in the years before the revolution. They told me that besides attending church on the feast of the Epiphany, they remembered participating in festivals and pilgrimages, especially on the feast days of the three main objects of popular devotion—Saint Barbara, Saint Lazarus, and Our Lady of Charity.[6]

The Virgin and Nationalism in Cuba

Of these three objects of popular devotion, Our Lady of Charity has been most important for the collective identity of Cubans on the island and in the diaspora. The connection between the Virgin and the nation has a long history, although the origins of devotion to Our Lady of Charity remain somewhat unclear. Cubans, and Cuban Americans, have told many stories about the Virgin. One writer in the 1930s who had traveled in Cuba and asked devotees for information found himself disoriented by the multiple historical narratives: "I was told so many conflicting stories about the origin and early career of this Virgin that it made me dizzy." He was disoriented because narrators have disagreed about how and when Our Lady of Charity arrived in Cuba, and many more minor details concerning the events during her first few decades on the island.[7]

Readers who demand natural and not supernatural explanations for events might remain dizzied, or at least dissatisfied, but one document rediscovered in the 1970s in the General Archives in Seville adds an important reconstruction of the events to the historical record. It is the sworn testimony of Juan Moreno (d. 1696), an African slave and Marian devotee, which is dated 1 March 1687. Moreno's account informed the earliest narrative of the history of Our Lady of Charity in Cuba, written in 1703 by Father Onofre de Fonseca (1648–1710), the priest who presided over the first shrine to the Virgin. The official interview with Moreno, who later served as head of the Cobre militia, did not survive in oral tradition, however; and it was overlooked by most interpreters until the 1970s, when the Cuban scholar Leví Marrero located, published, and analyzed the 1687 testimony. That document is especially significant not only because it is earliest, and thus closest to the events narrated, but also because Moreno was one of the three laborers who claimed to have discovered the statue of the Virgin. We have, then, a document that claims to be an eyewitness account.[8]

That account suggests that the first apparition of the Virgin of Charity in Cuba occurred in 1611 or 1612—not in the 1620s, as oral tradition had it, and not in the first decade of the seventeenth century, as some Cuban Catholic historians had estimated before they had a chance to read Moreno's testimony. Moreno was eighty-five years old when he answered questions for posterity's sake, which means that the interview was recorded seventy-five years after the event—if he was correct when he claimed that he was "around ten years old" when he encountered the Virgin in Nipe Bay. As he remembered it from the vantage of his old age, then, the miraculous discovery of Our Lady of Charity occurred at 5:30 on a morning in 1611 or 1612 as he and two Indian brothers, Rodrigo de Hoyos and Juan de Hoyos, rowed in a small boat off the coast of present-day Oriente province. Salt was important then in food preparation, and the three were searching for it when a storm approached. After taking shelter for some time—one version says several days—they set out again in search of salt. As they did they were startled by an object floating in the water. It was, Moreno recalled, a statue of the Virgin, which had miraculously remained dry. On a small board or tablet (*una tablita*) attached to the image were the words "Yo soy la Virgen de la Caridad," identifying it as Our Lady of Charity.[9]

The document does not offer any clues about how that statue came to be floating in Nipe Bay, but over the years devotees and historians have offered their interpretations. Some devotees, of course, have not felt the need to propose any explanation. What has mattered to them is that the three found her and that she has remained with Cubans ever since. Others have been more curious, however. Those who have pursued these questions have agreed that devotion to Mary, in some form, reaches back to the first years of Cuba's history. As one official account published by the contemporary shrine in Miami put it, "The Cuban people always have shown great love to Our Blessed Mother." Oral tradition, and the written record too, supports the common view that Alonso de Ojeda (1474–1515), who accompanied Columbus on his journey in 1493, might have brought one of the first images of Mary to Cuba. The Virgin discovered in the Bay, some have claimed, might have been Ojeda's. Or, others have speculated, perhaps another Spanish colonist brought the image there. Irene Wright, a North American historian who considered the issue in an important essay in 1922, suggested that the statue might have been transported to the New World by Captain Francisco Sánchez de Moya, who arrived on the island in 1597 to open the copper mines in eastern Cuba. Others have speculated further: maybe the image Juan Moreno encountered in Nipe Bay fell from a Spanish ship that had sailed in or near Cuban waters.[10]

These explanations, which suggest that the image originally was brought to the island by a Spanish colonist or sailor, all are plausible (although the second and third scenarios seem more likely), because a Madonna named Our Lady of Charity was popular in certain regions of Spain during the second half of the sixteenth century and the early years of the seventeenth century. Citing a letter written by the governor of eastern Cuba in 1620, Wright argued that Our Lady of Charity in El Cobre was identical to the image venerated in a hospital shrine with the same name in Illescas, a town in the province of Toledo (figure 4). That Spanish image, which is called Our Lady of Charity and bears a resemblance to the Virgin of Cobre, became a focus of devotion in that region of Spain after reports circulated that she had performed a healing miracle in 1562. One Spanish document from that period suggests that the shrine to Our Lady of Charity there was "the most visited and frequented sanctuary in all of Spain." Whether or not the Spanish pilgrimage site was that popular, Our Lady of Charity certainly had a following in the area, so it seems possible that one of the early Cuban colonists brought an image of that Virgin, probably from somewhere in that Spanish region. Making that explanation more plausible, the cardinal who gave Ojeda his image of the Virgin was a patron of the hospital at Illescas, and Sánchez de Moya hailed from the same province in Spain.[11]

Focusing on Irene Wright's claim that Our Lady of Charity was identical to the one venerated in Illescas, Cuban scholars entered a debate on the subject during the 1920s. The great Cuban folklorist Fernando Ortiz started and sustained the discussion. In the periodical he edited, *Archivos del Folklore Cubano*, Ortiz published in 1928 the first rendering of Wright's controversial thesis in Spanish. In the following few years others entered the debate in that journal—Cuban folklorists, art historians, and Catholic priests. Focusing on the iconographic representation of the two Virgins—noting, for example, that the half moon beneath the Virgin of Cobre's feet pointed downward, not upward as with the Virgin of Illescas—some Cuban interpreters emphasized the uniqueness of the Cuban Our Lady of Charity (figure 5). Others countered with contrary historical examples, confirming the main thrust of Wright's argument for Spanish parallels. Olga Portuondo Zúñiga, a Cuban historian who has systematically studied the issue more recently, has not rejected Wright's thesis, although she has (following Ortiz's unpublished notes on the subject) emphasized the hybrid character of the Virgin of Cobre: although of Spanish origin, she also is Indian, African, and creole. In the end, Wright's main point— that the Cuban Virgin of Charity had Spanish roots, probably in Illescas—seems

Figure 4. The statue of Our Lady of Charity in Illescas, Spain, which some scholars have suggested was the source of the image of the Cuban national patroness. (Courtesy *La Voz Católica*.)

reliable, although many of the details about the Virgin's passage to the New World remain uncertain.[12]

Wherever the statue of Our Lady of Charity originated and however it came to be discovered in Cuba around 1612—and, finally, we cannot be sure—Moreno's testimony suggests that it moved from place to place in the years immediately after the discovery. Moreno and the de Hoyos brothers initially took the image back to Barajagua, a small settlement nearby in the eastern province of Cuba. However, the image kept miraculously disappearing and reappearing from the first rustic altar set up there near the northern coast, so in 1613 local devotees and Sánchez de Moya,

Figure 5. The statue of the national patroness on the main altar at the Shrine of Our Lady of Charity in El Cobre, Cuba. (Courtesy *La Voz Católica.*)

who then was the leader of the copper mines near Santiago de Cuba, apparently carried the Virgin in a procession to El Cobre, a nearby town in the mountains off the southern coast, where—oral tradition suggests—a young girl, Apolonia, also had a vision of the Virgin on Cobre Hill. And there Our Lady of Charity would remain enshrined on one altar or another until this day.[13]

Although interpreters—devotees and scholars—have assumed that Our Lady of Charity was placed immediately in the shrine on Cobre Hill, recently the historian Olga Portuondo Zúñiga has argued persuasively that at first another Virgin, Nuestra Señora de Guía, Madre de Dios de Illescas, was the focus of devotion in the sanctuary. When she arrived from Barajagua around 1613, Our Lady of Charity seems to have been placed initially in the chapel of the hospital for slaves, which was adjacent to the shrine in El Cobre. By the 1640s, inventory records show, the image of Our Lady of Charity had been moved to the main altar of the newly reconstructed shrine, and since that time that Virgin has been the focus of devotion there.[14]

After the 1640s devotion to Our Lady of Charity spread. Slaves who worked in the copper mines around El Cobre seem to have venerated Our Lady of Charity during the earlier decades of the seventeenth century, in the hospital chapel and in their homes; and then during the century's final decades, when the Virgin's image was pedestaled on the main altar of the Cobre shrine, devotion to Our Lady of Charity spread among the general population of the province of Oriente. As time went on, devotion expanded further still—first to the eastern half of the island and later throughout all of Cuba. The regional protectress became the national patroness.[15]

It was during the nineteenth-century wars for independence from Spain that the Virgin of Cobre became decisive for the way that Cubans imagined themselves as a nation. Collective memory has a way of antiquating traditions, extending them into a remote time of origins. Although devotion to Our Lady of Charity did begin in the seventeenth century in Oriente, it was only during the nineteenth century that nationalist sentiment arose in Cuba—the last of Spain's colonies in the Americas to secure independence—so it was only then that the Virgin could become so closely identified with the nation. The historical record shows the identification emerging already by the first Cuban war for independence, the Ten Years War (1868–78). Most officials of the church, who were predominantly of Spanish descent, sided with the colonizers in the struggles for independence that would last more than thirty years. There were prominent exceptions, of course. As early as 1812, Father Félix Varela y Morales, a precursor of the independence movement who later was exiled to the United States for his views, had taught the right of national self-determination in an influential Havana college and seminary. When the struggle for national autonomy turned to the battlefield as the Ten Years War began in 1868, some clergy advocated freedom from Spanish control and supported *los mambises*, the creole insurgents. Many of the vocal minority of Cuba's clergy who supported the revolutionaries did so by appealing to the protection of the Virgin of Charity.[16]

During the later war for independence (1895–98), which finally proved successful, some Cuban clergy—although still not the majority—appealed to the Virgin. Mothers, daughters, and sisters who waited for *los mambises* to return from battle also petitioned her on the soldiers' behalf. More important still, the soldiers themselves sought protection from the Virgin, including prominent military leaders such as Antonio Maceo, Máximo Gómez, and Calixto García. Many of those who went off to fight wore images of Our Lady of Charity on their uniforms. Others kept the Virgin of Cobre with them by dangling medals or scapulars from their necks. Even if the majority of the priests had sided with the colonial power, then, the Virgin had not. By the time the Spanish had been defeated (in 1898), the American occupying government had departed, and an independent Cuban republic had been established (in 1902), the Virgin of Cobre had become "la Virgen Mambisa." She had become the rebel Virgin, the patriot Virgin, the national Virgin.[17]

In fact, it was the veterans of that war for independence who saw to it that the Roman Catholic Church officially recognized her as national patroness. Ten years after the republic was established, she was celebrated as "Patrona de Cuba" in an influential hymn published in a leading Cuban magazine, but she was not formally named Cuba's saint until several years later. In 1915, 2,000 veterans held a reunion in El Cobre during September, the month of the Virgin's feast day. There, in the town where their protectress was enshrined, they decided to express their gratitude for her role in the battles that had brought national freedom. To formalize their gratitude and their intimate relation with her, they wrote to the pope, Benedict XV. In that missive, dated 24 September, the soldiers explained that they had come to El Cobre to "prostrate themselves before her altar." They recalled how they, and their mothers and wives, "all had prayed before her for the attainment of victory" during the fight for independence. It would be ungrateful, they argued, to fail to raise their voices now to ask the Vatican officially to name Our Lady of Charity the patroness of the new Cuban republic. In a response dated 10 May 1916, Pope Benedict XV granted the veterans' petition, proclaiming Our Lady of Charity Cuba's national saint. Two years later, one of those veterans, the third president of the Republic (together with Marianita Seva, his pious wife), led the efforts to construct a new national shrine to the Virgin in Cobre. On the Virgin's feast day in 1927, church officials consecrated that building, which is the last of several to enshrine the patroness in that town.[18]

In the three decades that followed before Castro's revolution, pilgrims continued to walk—or crawl—up the steep steps to the Cobre shrine to petition the Virgin for health, children, or a happy marriage (figure 6). The many artifacts left there over the years in gratitude to Our Lady of Charity show that the devotees found many of their prayers answered. For example, one visitor in the 1930s noticed not only crutches, paintings, and wax limbs on the walls of the Chapel of Miracles—objects that are more common in Catholic shrines in Europe and Latin America—but also other signs of thanks: a doll, a pistol, a hat, a sponge, a pocketknife, and a Cuban flag. As that flag and other verbal and nonverbal sources indicate, Cubans also made the pilgrimage to pray for their nation and to thank "la Virgen Mambisa" for her role in securing national independence.[19]

In turn, Our Lady of Charity also traveled to see her devotees, and that further strengthened the bonds between the Virgin and the nation, especially for those who lived too far from her shrine in eastern Cuba to visit regularly. To celebrate the fiftieth anniversary of the Republic, the Catholic Church organized a fifteen-month national pilgrimage in 1951–52. The Virgin set out from El Cobre on 20 May, the date the Republic had been established. A military plane carried her to the western tip of the island, stopping at more than two hundred locations along the way. This journey began just two months after Fulgencio Batista y Zaldivar and a group of army officers overthrew the elected president of Cuba, and the Virgin traveled again just ten months after Fidel Castro and his army assumed control from Batista in 1959. That November, Our Lady of Charity journeyed to Havana to preside over the National Catholic Congress, a meeting of Catholic laity. Signaling intensifying discord between church and state, however, the event became in effect a protest against communism. The anti-Castro Catholics at that meeting claimed the national patroness for their side, chanting choruses of "Caridad" (charity) to the same rhythm that Castro's revolutionaries had cried "¡Paredón!" (to the execution wall). The Virgin again was being connected with national identity, but she came to be associated not so much with the ruling government as with protest against it, as she also had been during the struggle for independence from Spain.[20]

But that was not how it began in the first days and months after Castro's victory in January 1959. At the start, some signs indicated that Cuban Catholics and the new government might get along. The national patroness, it seemed, also might back the new regime. For example, in the "liberty issue" of the popular magazine *Bohemia*, which was published one month after Castro marched into Havana, a "Prayer for Cuba" appeared. That prayer thanked Our Lady of Charity because Cuban sons

Figure 6. The exterior of the Shrine of Our Lady of Charity in El Cobre, Cuba, which was dedicated on the Virgin's feast day in 1927. (Courtesy Cuban Archives, Otto G. Richter Library, University of Miami.)

"had returned victorious" from the bloody battles of the past year. The implication was that the national Virgin had sided with Castro's revolutionary army. Some priests had fought on the victorious side during that campaign. Many other Catholic clergy and laity were hopeful during those first months, especially since the new leader had reassured many with his now famous proclamation: "I am not a communist." But as the months and years passed, the tensions between the Church and the state grew.[21]

Those tensions peaked, and erupted into violence, outside a parish church in Havana during feast-day celebrations for the Virgin in 1961. That year Castro publicly declared that his insurrection was "socialist," and on 17 April a CIA-sponsored exile assault brigade launched a failed attack at the Bay of Pigs. The proclamation that would have been read to the Cuban people if the assault had been successful claimed "our glorious Patron Saint" for their cause: "Have faith, since the victory is ours, because God is with us and the Virgin of Charity cannot abandon her children." As the 8 September feast day of the national patroness approached, then, Castro's government and anticommunist Catholics in Havana faced each other nervously across lines that had moved continually since the first optimistic days of the revolution. This was the situation as Eduardo Boza Masvidal, auxiliary bishop of Havana and pastor at La Virgen de la Caridad parish church in the city, made plans for the annual feast-day celebrations in 1961, which would be held on 10 September. Boza recently had voiced opposition to the Castro regime, so government officials had reasons to worry about what might happen at the procession at his church.

It is difficult to reconstruct the events of that day because accounts by the government and the Church vary widely. According to Boza and several other Catholic eyewitnesses, government officials had tried to sabotage the Virgin's procession by permitting it only at seven o'clock in the morning, instead of the late afternoon, as was usual. To avoid provoking the government, Bishop Boza recalled, he canceled the procession. He even removed the Virgin's statue from the altar. Government officials remembered the events very differently. The Cuban minister of the interior vigorously repudiated Boza's version, suggesting that they had granted the permit but that Boza had tried to stir "counter-revolutionary" sentiment. Whatever happened in the preceding days and hours, it seems clear that approximately 4,000 devotees of the Virgin—most of whom apparently opposed the communist government—gathered in the late afternoon of 10 September in front of the church named after the national patroness. Carrying aloft a picture of the Virgin that he had brought from his home, Arnaldo Socorro, a member of the Young Catholic Workers, led the unsanctioned procession through the streets of Havana, as some of the marchers carried him on their shoulders. As the crowd marched on toward the presidential palace, chanting as it went, the religious procession became a political protest. In the shootout that resulted, the young Catholic was killed, presumably by a bullet from a policeman's gun. Soon after, Boza was arrested. One week later, 131 priests and religious were expelled from the island.[22]

After that the government prohibited religious processions, and those anticommunist Catholics who still had been unsure about Castro's attitudes toward their religion now believed that they had sad but indisputable evidence of the regime's hostility. Although some Catholics on the island still claimed the patroness for their revolution, by 1961 most anti-Castro Catholics in Cuba felt sure about where the Virgin stood on the issue: she stood with them, opposing Castro and socialism and advocating democracy and capitalism. During the following year almost 80,000 emigrants would join the Virgin and the other Cubans already in exile, and hundreds of thousands more would follow in the years to come.

Our Lady of Charity and Her Devotees in Miami

Migrants in the City of Migrants

Cubans started emigrating to America in the nineteenth century (table 3). Before 1868, when the wars for independence began, a small community of political exiles centered in New York. Migrants came in larger numbers after the political turmoil intensified on the island and as cigar factories flourished in Florida—in Key West and, later in the nineteenth century, Ybor City. Yet few residents of Cuban descent in the 1990s trace their lineage directly to the 230,000 immigrants who settled in New York, Key West, or Ybor City between 1859 and 1959. Most have arrived since

Table 3. Year of Arrival of Cubans in the United States

Year of Arrival	Number
1901–10	40,159
1911–20	27,837
1921–30	15,608
1931–40	4,122
1941–50	15,451
1951–60	149,777
1961–70	460,214
1971–80	246,591
1981–90	122,141
1991–94	65,000
Total	1,146,900

Source: James S. Olson and Judith E. Olson, *Cuban Americans: From Trauma to Triumph* (New York: Twayne, 1995), 93.

the socialist revolution of 1959. In 1990 almost 1,000,000 Cubans lived in the United States, and seven out of ten of those had been born on the island.[23]

The post-1959 exiles settled in New York, New Jersey, and California, but the majority awaited their imminent return to the island near their port of entry, Miami. So many settled there that by the 1990s the only city with a larger Cuban population was Havana. According the 1990 census, the metropolitan Miami area counted almost 600,000 residents of Cuban descent.[24]

Florida's connections with Cuba, a more important territory in the Spanish colonial empire, reach back to the sixteenth century. In politics, Florida was a military outpost of Havana; in religion, it effectively came under the jurisdiction of the bishop of Santiago de Cuba. A small and temporary Spanish settlement once stood near present-day downtown Miami. In 1896, when southern and northern Protestants officially founded the city of Miami as a tourist and agricultural center, small Cuban communities flourished to the south in Key West and across the Everglades in Ybor City, but not in Miami itself. The Latin influence had disappeared by the late nineteenth century. Since the colonial missions and fortresses in Florida had not been built of stone, as they were in California and Texas, not even architectural ruins could remind the new residents of South Florida's Spanish past or Cuban connections.[25]

During the middle third of the twentieth century, Cuba and Florida exchanged tourists, entertainment, and goods, but in many ways Miami remained a southern Protestant town as the Cuban influx began in 1959. That almost unprecedented migration transformed the cultural landscape of Miami. Consider that in 1960, even after some had begun to flee the island, only 3 percent of the Miami population claimed Cuban descent. By 1990, the proportion of Cubans in the urban area had reached almost 30 percent (table 4). The Cuban population had increased thirtyfold in thirty years, and the effects on all aspects of urban life were immediate and strong, and not only in Little Havana, the area of the city where the first Cuban exiles had clustered.[26]

The impact of this mass migration would have been considerable even if all else in Miami had remained static and stable; but in many ways, even before and espe-

Table 4. Cubans Living in Dade County, Florida, 1960–1990

Year	Total Dade Population	Cubans	Percent of Population
1960	935,047	29,500	3.1
1970	1,267,792	224,000	17.6
1980	1,625,781	407,000	25
1990	1,937,094	561,868	29

Source: U.S. Bureau of the Census.

cially after 1959, Miami has been a city of migrants: American Indians, European Americans, Bahamians, Haitians, Nicaraguans, and of course Cubans. The Miccosukees who live on a reservation just south of the Miami metropolitan area descend from those who, in the eighteenth and early nineteenth centuries, exiled themselves from the other Creek Indians in Georgia, the Seminoles or *Simanoli* (the "wild" or "runaway" ones). At the end of the nineteenth century, northern and southern Protestants moved to the Miami area, lured by the promise of fortune and the testimonies about climate. Since then visitors of European descent, both Protestant and Catholic, have come to the region as tourists to stay a week or a winter. The African and Jewish diasporas also have settled in the Miami area. The local African population hails not only from southern states but also from Caribbean nations. Bahamian blacks were among the early Miami residents in the years after establishment in 1896, and almost one-fifth of the entire population of the Bahamas—between 10,000 and 12,000—emigrated to Florida between 1900 and 1920. Eastern European Jewish immigrants found a place in the Miami business community during the first years of the city, and others followed them as tourists and residents during the second third of the twentieth century. South Florida, then, emerged as one of the centers of the Jewish diaspora. By 1990 Jews amounted to more than 10 percent of metropolitan Miami's population, a much higher proportion than in the nation as a whole. A decade earlier, just as Castro was opening the gates for another mass exodus of Cubans from the port of Mariel, the evening news also included daily reports about "boat people" from Haiti washing up on the beaches of South Florida. A Nicaraguan exodus followed later in the 1980s. As the Contra War wound down in 1988, thousands of Nicaraguans passed through Guatemala, Mexico, and Texas on their way to settle in Miami. By the 1990s, tens of thousands of Nicaraguans had joined hundreds of thousands of Cubans and migrants from many other Latin American nations. That meant that by then one-half of the population of metropolitan Miami claimed Latino descent. A higher proportion of residents than in any other major American city— 57 percent—spoke a language other than English at home, and an astonishing 45 percent of the area's population—almost 900,000 people—had been born outside the United States. Miami had become a city of migrants.[27]

An Anglo-Protestant establishment persisted into the 1990s in the area, even after the migrations had transformed the urban landscape, but Anglos had to construct meaning and negotiate power, like everyone else, as one group among others. In the late 1980s one local resident had complained that a Thai Buddhist community had no right to establish a new temple there because they were "not even in the mainstream of American life." But as advertisements for the *Miami Herald*'s multicultural collection of columnists proclaimed—in both English and Spanish editions of the paper—in Miami "there is no mainstream." Rather, as some sociologists noticed, "parallel social structures" had emerged in the city of migrants. Other urban areas could claim diverse populations, of course; but in an age dominated by discourse about "multiculturalism," Miami stood out. Some observers celebrated Miami's ethnic, linguistic, and religious diversity; others condemned it. Either way, the American popular imagination elevated the city as an example of all that was right—or wrong—with America.[28]

Religion and Identity: Cuban Exiles in Miami

It was in this cultural context, as migrants in a city of migrants, that Miami's Cubans struggled to make sense of their identity as a displaced community. On the island, Cubans had constructed a sense of national identity from the 1860s to the 1950s in relation to Spain on the one hand and the United States on the other, although that identity was never fixed and always contested. Cubans struggled among themselves to form collective identity in a variety of political arenas and at many cultural sites—in music halls and baseball stadiums as well as battlefields and government offices. The Catholic churches, overall, were less important in this regard. Since the clergy often sided with the Spanish colonial powers, and many people lived far from their parish, institutional Catholicism was less significant for the construction of national identity on the island—even though some priests, like Father Varela, had great influence in this regard and many devotees of Our Lady of Charity linked her with national identity after the 1890s.[29]

In Miami, too, Cubans negotiated their identity in a variety of ways. Constructing *cubanidad*, or "Cubanness," in exile meant retaining their language, foodways, architecture, institutions, and music. Even more than they had earlier in their history, Cuban migrants also turned to religion to make sense of themselves as a displaced people, as many other migrants have done. The survey data and anecdotal evidence suggest that religion, both in churches and in homes, took on increased significance for many Cubans in Miami. I do not want to give the wrong impression here: most Cuban Americans remained outside the reach of the Roman Catholic Church. At the same time, though, almost all observers agreed that religious practice had become more regular and important in exile. To the Catholic clergy's dismay—more on this in chapter 2—Santería was much more visible in the urban landscape than it had been in the homeland. So was Protestantism, even though several denominations had been active in Cuba before 1959. Most relevant to my argument here, Cubans in Miami seemed to participate more in collective worship in the Catholic Church, although it is difficult to be sure about how much more participation there has been because no study has focused directly on this issue. We are left to calculate reasonable estimates from the results of several related studies. According to one recent study, Miami's Catholics as a whole have the second lowest weekly church attendance rate in the nation (18.4%). We know from another survey that approximately 80 percent of those Catholics in metropolitan Miami were of Latino heritage. As many as half of those were born in Cuba. Forty-two percent of Span-

ish-speaking Catholics interviewed reported that they attended mass more than
twenty-five times each year, a slightly lower percentage than for non-Hispanics in
the Archdiocese. That would mean that the least institutionally religious in this sub-
group of the Latino population went to church every other week and the most pious
attended every week. Other quantitative evidence comes from another survey of
almost 5,000 Cuban exiles, 52 percent of whom live in South Florida, and those
results also confirm the impressions that the diaspora attends church more in exile
than it did in prerevolutionary Cuba. Even if we adjust the statistics to account for
the overestimates that creep into self-reports and assume that the patterns among
Cubans in Miami approximate the most pessimistic estimates for local Catholics as
a whole, approximately 15 to 20 percent are "practicing" Catholics, compared with
5 to 8 percent in prerevolutionary Cuba. Those figures might be higher. Whatever
the exact statistics for church attendance, it seems clear that Cuban Americans in
Miami are more institutionally religious than historically had been the pattern in
their island nation.[30]

Readers who are familiar with the reports of high religious affiliation and church
attendance in the United States might interpret this increase in ecclesiastical piety
as a sign of assimilation or Americanization. Perhaps. But I believe that several
other factors are at work. First, practicing Catholics came in disproportionate numbers in the earliest waves of migration from Cuba in the 1960s. One priest who
worked closely with the exiles estimated that as many as 80 percent of the first
100,000 who came in 1960 and 1961 (who were mostly urban residents) had regular contact with a parish in Cuba. These numbers are much lower for those who
have come since the 1980s; the most reliable estimates of Catholic Church participation in postrevolutionary Cuba fix that number as between 2 and 4 percent. Without further study we cannot be sure, but it seems that practicing Catholics originally
came in larger proportions. If that is right, then it is not surprising that Cubans in
Miami might be somewhat more institutionally religious. They arrived that way.[31]

Second, Cubans go to church more in Miami because they can. Churches are less
distant and more numerous in the city. Clergy—and many clergy and religious
came with the other exiles to Miami—also are more plentiful than they had been
on the island. This is most important for those who had lived in rural regions of
Cuba, although it shapes all exiles' religious experience.

Third, many exiles believe that the Cuban American clergy and the American
Catholic Church have aligned themselves with the right side on the most important
political and social issues. For much of Cuban history, Catholic officials sided with
colonial powers or remained silent during times of turmoil, which amounted to the
same thing. As most exiles see it, this pattern has been reversed to a great extent in
the United States. Many of the local Cuban clergy have solid records of resistance
to the Castro regime—and that is what being on the "right side" means to most,
although not all, of Miami's migrants. After all, many priests were forcibly exiled
by the government in 1961, and in exile most of them explicitly or implicitly have
condemned the socialist government on the island and spoken out for the "liberation" of the homeland. Further, from the start of the mass migration, the newly created Archdiocese of Miami and its leader, Bishop Coleman F. Carroll, supported the
exiles, especially in the years before the American government offered systematic

assistance. Bishop Carroll had rejected the idea of separate "national parishes" organized along ethnic lines: that idea was out of favor nationally by this time, and he wanted a different strategy to assimilate the Cubans as quickly as possible. However, that assimilationist impulse, which surfaced in some ways in the years ahead, coexisted with a firm commitment to provide aid. Under Carroll's leadership—and learning from similar efforts at outreach among Puerto Ricans in New York—in 1959 the Archdiocese opened Centro Hispano Católico to serve the needs of Spanish-speaking Catholics in Miami. They offered medical assistance, child care, and English instruction. The Catholic church also sponsored the Unaccompanied Children's Program, widely known as Operation Peter Pan, to nurture the thousands of Cuban children who had arrived without their parents. By 1962, one priest estimated, the Archdiocese had spent almost $1.5 million helping the Cuban exiles adjust to their new land. That kind of support continued. The *Marielitos*, those who were picked up in a "freedom flotilla" in 1980 from the port of Mariel in Cuba, found the Church offering help almost immediately. It produced, for instance, an "orientation" pamphlet for the refugees that offered practical advice about the transition to the new land. The Church also gained sympathy because it helped to arrange temporary housing and find jobs for recent arrivals.[32]

Finally—and this is the explanation favored by most devotees of the Virgin with whom I spoke in Miami—there is something about the disorientation and suffering of exile itself that has led them to religion. Ricardo, a layman who played a leading role in building the first temporary shrine to Our Lady of Charity in Miami (the building committee met in the Florida room of his home) told me that Cubans had turned more to religion after their dislocation. "Not a single family has not been divided by the sea, the years, the hate, or revenge." Cubans in Miami turn to religion more, he proposed, because "they have suffered more." Echoing many theorists of religion, he suggested that suffering, and crisis of various forms, inclines individuals and communities toward religion. Ada, a middle-aged devotee of the Virgin, repeated the usual assessment of religion on the island. She noted that many had repeated the familiar prerevolutionary idiomatic expression, "Yo soy católico a mi manera" (I am Catholic in my own way). Yet in exile, Ada claimed, Cubans began going to church more. When I asked why, this active lay follower of the Virgin told me that it was difficult to be an exile: "In another country we need more help."[33]

Organized Devotion to the Patroness in Miami

Just as Cuban exiles in Key West and New York had appealed to Our Lady of Charity during the tumultuous 1890s, so too both of these contemporary migrants in Miami also emphasized the significance of devotion to the national patroness for making sense of exile. Both had prayed to the Virgin in Cuba. Like many other unchurched Cubans, Ada recalled, "we had Our Lady of Charity in our home." Ricardo, also a devotee, had processed beside the Virgin of Cobre when the patroness visited Havana in 1959. Both linked her, too, with the collective identity of the Cuban diaspora and the fate of the island nation. Like most of the Virgin's devotees with whom I spoke, both suggested that "la Virgen Mambisa," who had struggled with the insurgents against another unwelcome political force, had become an even more important national symbol now as they looked back on the island from across the Straits of Florida. Around that shared symbol, they suggested, the churched and the unchurched could gather to restore the Cuban "nation" that had been dispersed when the migrations had begun in 1959.[34]

Cubans could gather around that shared symbol because—as with other national Virgins, such as Our Lady of Guadalupe in Mexico and Our Lady of Czestochowa in Poland—Our Lady of Charity had been identified with the homeland. As devotees in Miami now narrate it from the diaspora, the biography of the Virgin and the history of the nation are so connected that they seem indistinguishable. Celina, a visitor to the Miami shrine, explained when I asked about the connection: "Cuba and the Virgin are the same thing." This middle-aged woman, who was born in Havana and arrived in Miami in 1960, expressed a common sentiment among first-generation migrants. Many other exiles made the same point. Continuing and intensifying a tradition, the Cuban clergy, too, have identified the Virgin with the nation. Eduardo Boza Masvidal, the exiled bishop who had served as pastor at Our Lady of Charity parish in Havana during the 1961 procession, put it this way: "To look at the [image of] the Virgin of Charity is to think about Cuba because she has been inexorably linked with our nationality and our history."[35]

As on the island, exiles in Miami have expressed devotion to the national patroness informally in homes and in streets. Like one rafter in 1994 who triumphantly and gratefully held aloft an image of the Virgin that he had carried with him for protection as he rowed the ninety miles across the Straits of Florida (figure 7), many Cuban migrants have offered private prayers to the Virgin before they set out on their perilous journey and after they arrived on American shores. Even those who were unchurched in the homeland have done this, many Cuban exiles have told me. Once devotees of the Virgin have settled in the Miami area, many have carried her image in pocketbooks and wallets and venerated her in domestic altars and yard shrines (figure 8).[36]

This sort of informal domestic piety has continued, of course; but organized public devotions to Our Lady of Charity, which are my focus in this book, also began shortly after the first waves of migrants arrived from Castro's Cuba. Even before the Virgin's exile in 1961, the first signs of collective devotion appeared in Miami. In 1960, Cuban priests organized the first feast-day mass in exile. That first celebration was much smaller in scale than those that would follow, however. It was held at a parish church, Saints Peter and Paul, in the southwest section of city, where many exiles had begun to cluster. Approximately 800 Cubans attended that ritual. The next year, as I noted in the opening of this chapter, a large and passionate crowd—estimates ranged from 25,000 to 30,000—packed Miami Stadium.[37]

That display of devotion got the attention of church officials in Miami, who would remember that event in the years ahead as they devised strategies to spiritually nurture the new Cuban migrants. The diocese of Miami had been created in 1958, only a year before the revolution in Cuba. When Bishop Carroll assumed leadership of the diocese, his flock included few Cubans. Yet as he was still building an organizational structure, the Cuban migrations began. Almost immediately, then, the bishop faced a crucial issue: how should the Catholic Church respond? Carroll knew his history. He was aware of the strategies that other Catholic leaders had tried in

Figure 7. Like many others before them, these Cubans arrive in the waters off the South Florida coast in September 1994 after a perilous journey by sea. The man to the left holds up an image of Our Lady of Charity as the rescuers approach, signaling his sense of indebtedness to the Virgin for their safe passage. (Courtesy *The Miami Herald*; photo by Walter Michot.)

Figure 8. A small yard shrine in Little Havana. These domestic
shrines vary in size from two or three feet in height (the height of this
one) to more than six feet. Plastic flowers adorn the interior of this
shrine. A light, which is taped in place and missing the bulb in this
shrine, illuminates the image at night so that pedestrians and drivers
can see it from the street.

the United States—from ignoring ethnic and linguistic differences to establishing
distinct "national parishes" for each local group. Partly because of his earlier experience as an auxiliary bishop in Pittsburgh, Carroll was convinced that segregating
Cubans into their own parishes would slow the process of Americanization. At the
same time, he recognized that he had to find a way to reach the Cubans, who were
so unconnected with the Church and so unattached to the parish system. That was
where the national patroness came in.[38]

Although Cuban and Irish clergy who had the ear of the bishop also played a role,
it was Carroll himself who did the most to encourage organized devotions and build
a local shrine (figure 9). One highly visible Cuban American—visible because he

Figure 9. Archbishop Coleman F. Carroll poses in 1969 with a statue of Our Lady of Charity and one of the two architectural plans for the Miami shrine, which called for a more elaborate "cultural center, museum, monument, and shrine." That design was rejected later in favor of the simpler plan. (Courtesy *The Voice.*)

delivered the first daily television news program in Spanish in the city—told me that in 1965 he and several other Cubans had approached the bishop to propose that the diocese build a shrine to Our Lady of Charity. The idea for a shrine, however, does not seem to have originated in that 1965 meeting. Already convinced of the power of the Virgin for Cubans, Bishop Carroll got the idea for a local shrine after seeing a photograph of an ethnic chapel elsewhere in the United States. In a memorandum on Diocese of Miami stationary dated 7 April 1964, Carroll wrote to an exiled priest in Miami about the idea:

> Recently, I received in the mail the pictures which I am now sending to you. Evidently, a shrine has been built in a parish which, I believe, is in Albany. The thought occurred to me that perhaps somewhere in the Miami diocese there should be a shrine in honor of Our Lady of Cobre. . . . I pass this idea on to you and suggest that you sound out three

or four reliable and dependable people. . . . I would be very willing to use my influence and my office to make this a worthwhile project if you and your Cuban friends think it worthy of consideration.[39]

Many local exiles in the years that followed would come to believe that a shrine would be a worthy project, but some of the exiled priest's "Cuban friends" worried that a shrine would make the task of pastoring at the parishes even more difficult. As one local priest remembers it, the Cuban clergy were aware that their compatriots were not accustomed to regular parish participation, yet even the unchurched often had devotion to the Virgin of Cobre. If given the choice, many clergy feared, migrants would visit a shrine to the Virgin on Sundays instead of attending their local parish church. That would destablize the parish system.[40]

Despite these concerns, Bishop Carroll decided to promote the idea of a local shrine. Feast-day masses for the Virgin had continued in Miami each year since the large turnout in 1961, and at the 1966 celebration Carroll called on Cuban American Catholics to construct a shrine to Our Lady of Charity on land that the Archdiocese would donate, a plot bordering Biscayne Bay. In his remarks to the crowd of more than 25,000 that night, on the fiftieth anniversary of the consecration of Our Lady of Charity as national patroness, the Anglo bishop proposed the construction of a Cuban shrine. It was, Carroll suggested, "only appropriate that the same God-loving people who now find themselves torn away from their beloved country— exiled in a strange though hospitable land—erect a shrine attesting of their deep love for their very dear patroness, Our Lady of El Cobre." Explaining the sanctuary's official purpose, the bishop suggested that it "would be a constant reminder to all of her great powers of intercession—of her willingness to help all who honor her." He continued by pledging the diocese's "willingness to help" in this task and ended by exhorting the Cuban community to donate their money and time "so that a fitting shrine be erected on the shores of Biscayne Bay—facing the admirable land of Cuba."[41]

Surprised and delighted by the bishop's proposal, almost immediately Cubans began the work of raising the funds, organizing the devotions, and constructing the building. Within one year, by the spring of 1967, Carroll had appointed the shrine's first director, Father Agustín A. Román, who had been one of the priests exiled by Castro in 1961. In the years ahead Román would have the most influence on the development of organized devotions to the Virgin in Miami. Soon after taking on his new job as director, Román served with local lay Cubans on a committee that built a small "provisional chapel" on the site in 1967 (figure 10). With the construction of that chapel, the Virgin's devotees had a place to visit her.[42]

A year after that, in 1968, Román established the Confraternity of Our Lady of Charity of Cobre, the exile lay organization dedicated to the Virgin. According to the confraternity's bylaws, members agree to meet three obligations: "a) greet the Virgin daily; b) send a monthly donation to the Center; c) participate at the mass on the annual festivity of Our Lady of Charity (September 8)." In those first years, before the permanent shrine was constructed, thousands of Cuban Americans accepted these obligations by signing the confraternity's registry.[43]

Many of those confraternity members—and thousands of others in the exile

Figure 10. The Reverend Agustín A. Román addresses newly arrived Cuban exiles in the temporary chapel in Miami in 1967. The structure has served as the convent and administration building since the permanent shrine was dedicated in 1973. (Courtesy *The Voice*; photo by Tony Garner.)

community as well—responded to the popular shrine director's written and verbal pleas for contributions to build a permanent sanctuary. Seven years after Bishop Carroll officially had proposed the idea and six years after devotees had established a nonprofit corporation to raise money for the project, a shrine to Our Lady of Charity, La Ermita de la Caridad, was consecrated in Miami on 2 December 1973 (figure 11). Cardinal John Krol of Philadelphia joined Carroll in officiating at the mass that day on the steps outside the new shrine, as thousands of Cuban exiles crowded around to greet their national patroness, who finally had found a more permanent home in exile.[44]

In the years since its dedication, most non-Cubans in Miami have failed to notice this shrine (map 1). In 1994, for reasons that remain unclear, a European American and an African American conspired unsuccessfully to steal the Virgin's image from the shrine. On the other hand, an Anglo-American Protestant had effusively praised the shrine a few years earlier. "I'm in love," that Anglo confessed in 1983. "I'm in love with a church [*sic*]. . . . It captures a people's love for their religion." Yet because the shrine is secluded from the view of passing motorists—the only sign on the main road is in Spanish—and the local "parallel social structures" sometimes seem to run on infinitely in social space without meeting, groups in the Miami area who have negotiated power and meaning with Cubans in other urban spaces went on after the shrine's dedication as if nothing had happened. For the

Figure 11. The dedication of the Shrine of Our Lady of Charity in Miami on 2 December 1973. (Courtesy *La Voz Católica.*)

overwhelming majority of Miami's Anglos, Jews, and African Americans, nothing had.[45]

For many Cuban Catholics, on the other hand, the diaspora now had a new sacred center. Bishop Carroll and Father Román had imagined the sanctuary as a place where the Church might tend to the unchurched in the exile community. It proved even more successful in attracting Cubans than anyone had projected during the years that clergy and laity spent planning it. Tens of thousands of migrants had visited the provisional chapel each year between 1967 to 1973; but in the years after the dedication of the permanent building, more and more Cubans came to homage and petition the national patroness. Just two months after the shrine's consecration, Father Román reported an increase in devotion to the Virgin at that site. "The number of faithful who visit is three times larger than before," the shrine director wrote to an archdiocesan official in a letter dated 5 February 1974. "Even though it is hard to know exactly," Román continued, "we can assert that several thousand people visit this place each week." Just as prerevolutionary Cubans had been Catholic "in their own way," so too the pilgrims to the Miami shrine came for their own reasons. From the start, however, what seemed most important to Román, the director of the shrine since 1966, was the role the shrine might play in reaching the unchurched exiles. In that same letter in 1974, and in many subsequent sermons, interviews, and articles, Román revealed his central concern. "The large majority of our visitors," he

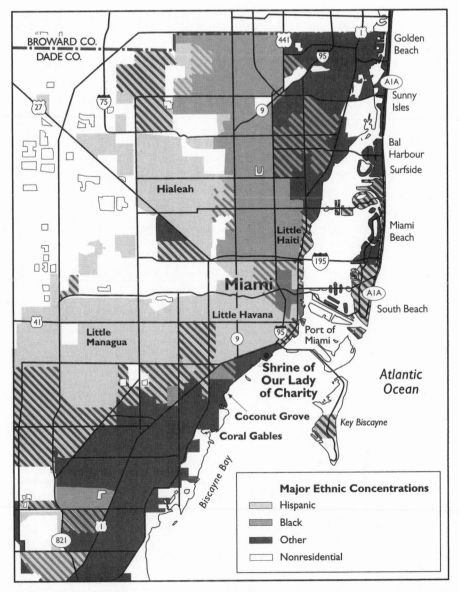

Map 1. Miami and the Shrine of Our Lady of Charity. (Adapted from *National Geographic* 181 [January 1992]: 94.)

explained to the archdiocesan official, "are estranged to a large degree from religious practice. . . . Our work is one of *evangelization*." In the next chapter, I focus on struggles between clergy and laity at Our Lady of Charity's Miami shrine, as the priests there have tried to take advantage of the opportunity to catechize the Cuban devotees who remain beyond the reach of the Roman Catholic Church.[46]

II ✳ *Contested Meanings at the Shrine*

Figure 12. The interior of a *botánica* in Hialeah. Statues of Our Lady of Charity rest on the counter to the right of several images of Saint Lazarus.

2 ✳ *Santería, Catholicism, and Evangelization*

Struggles for Religious Identity

On a warm June day a middle-aged, lower-class black woman strode to the water's edge just behind the shrine to Our Lady of Charity in Miami. This recently arrived Cuban exile, who dressed in the white of an *iyawó* or Santería initiate, placed a small faded statue of the Virgin on the concrete wall bordering the bay. Ignoring the interior of the shrine, where a priest was leading a hundred visitors in saying the rosary, Mirta faced the sea, raised both arms to the heavens, and began reciting the rosary aloud. She interspersed the stylized prayers with spontaneous and passionate "sermons" on various topics, as a crowd of twenty-five gathered around her. When she stopped, about fifty minutes later, visitors pressed in—asking her questions, writing her phone number, and thanking her enthusiastically.[1]

At first glance it is difficult to know what to make of this event. As with all religious rituals, it is polysemic, encoding multiple meanings. Some of those meanings resist recovery or expression. On one level, however, it enacts a struggle for religious identity. This parallel ritual, as I call it, created a social space outside ecclesiastical boundaries just as it drew on shared symbols—prayers, gestures, beads, and statue. In one of her brief sermons that day, Mirta expressed her anti-ecclesiastical impulses. "I take communion not in my mouth but directly from God," she said, extending her arms toward the sky, "and I take it alone." She explained further: "The Virgin, not the Church, helped me to leave Cuba last year." When I interviewed her after the crowd dispersed that day, Mirta told me that she never attends any formal rituals at the shrine, although she visits there often. Each time, however, she avoids the interior as she conducts unsanctioned rites outside. Mirta's intense devotion to the Virgin began twenty-four years earlier, when she was eighteen. Until 1993 she lived in the countryside in the province of Oriente, where the original shrine to Our Lady of Charity had been built. She often visited that shrine in Cobre, but like many other Cubans on the island, she said that she "never went to church" in her homeland. At the same time, Mirta insists that she is Catholic.[2]

The Cuban auxiliary bishop who has served as director of the shrine, Agustín A. Román, is not so sure. When I asked him about Mirta, who has become an increasingly popular local figure, the bishop told me that he personally had begun efforts to nudge her toward Catholicism. When I asked if she was a follower of Santería, he said, "Not exactly." When I asked if Mirta was Catholic, he again said, "Not exactly." That, for the bishop and the other clergy, is the problem. Some laity and clergy negotiate religious identity as they struggle over the meaning of shared symbols, especially the image of the Virgin herself. And the shrine is one important site of this contest, which involves competing notions of the meaning of "Catholic" and, more generally, "authentic" religiousness.[3]

This contest is not a simple one. It is not simply a struggle between laity and clergy at the shrine. Some laity, especially leaders in the Confraternity of Our Lady of Charity, side with the Cuban clergy on this issue. Others in the wider urban area also get involved to some extent because the struggle involves not only initiated and uninitiated Santería followers who visit the Virgin's Catholic shrine in Miami (as well as those who do not) but also clergy (and lay members) of two independent churches in the city that claim "Catholic" status but are not accepted as part of the Roman Catholic community.

This contest concerning religious identity does not preoccupy most of the lay visitors to the Miami shrine. Some Cuban American pilgrims are wholly or mostly unaware of the quiet struggles. If my hundreds of conversations with visitors at the shrine are any indication, the majority of them know that many Cubans in Miami remain unchurched and that the shrine attracts some followers of Santería. They also know that the clergy disapprove of Santería and exhort Cubans to enter the parish system. Still, that is not a central concern for most visitors. Generally, they respect the priests and listen politely to their exhortations. But they come for their own reasons—a variety of them, as I argue in chapter 3.

Further, the struggle over religious identity is not the only concern of shrine administrators. They worry about practical matters such as budgets and schedules and attend to many spiritual duties such as celebrating mass and hearing confessions. Most important, as I argue in part III of this book, the Cuban priests associated with the shrine also concern themselves a great deal with the ways in which that sacred site is a place where the diaspora makes sense of itself as an exiled community. So the struggles over *national* identity in many ways are more important than those over *religious* identity, although the two are related.

The Cuban Roman Catholic clergy, however, care a great deal about the "popular piety" (to use their term) of the unchurched visitors to the shrine. The shrine was built, in part, as a means of reaching the increasing numbers of nominal Cuban Catholics in Miami. But the meanings of the symbols at the shrine have been *contested* in some important ways. The Catholic clergy at the Shrine of Our Lady of Charity have viewed that pilgrimage destination as a place where they might "evangelize" nominal Catholics in the Cuban exile community, especially but not exclusively those who have been influenced by Santería. In turn, lay visitors have reacted variously—by endorsing, ignoring, or (as in Mirta's parallel ritual) resisting the clergy's efforts.[4]

Santería and Catholicism in Cuba

Santería is the Cuban form of a transatlantic Yoruba tradition that developed among slaves and former slaves on the island. What began as the *orisha* worship as practiced among Yoruba-speaking peoples from the West African region now known as Nigeria was transformed as it combined with Spanish Catholicism and Kardecan Spiritism, which originated in France in the nineteenth century and shaped neo-African religions in the Caribbean and South America. Santería emerged in the creole culture that formed in Cuba, combining elements from Spanish, Islamic, West and Central African, and Amerindian sources.[5]

More specifically, most scholars agree that Santería began to take its present form in the *cabildos*, or religious brotherhoods, that the Cuban Catholic Church began organizing in 1598. This Spanish institution was organized along ethnic lines in Cuba, with Africans gathering separately. The urban African *cabildos*, which were under the direction of diocesan priests, aimed to serve the Church's goal of bringing more and more Cubans within formal ecclesiastical boundaries. African religious brotherhoods in the cities, which also became centers of social life, allowed the combining of African and European forms, which the clergy encouraged initially as a strategic step toward "Christianization." It was in this social context that Santería emerged, as Yoruba *orishas* (deities) came to be associated with Catholic *santos* (saints). To the dismay of the clergy, most of whom were foreigners, few Cubans were led into institutional Catholicism, with its emphasis on the Church's seven sacraments. Instead, the *cabildos* fostered the combination of Yoruba religion and Spanish Catholicism. The Cuban Church's attitude toward these brotherhoods was ambivalent, with increasing interference and hostility from the late eighteenth century until the *cabildos* were formally banned just before the turn of the twentieth century. By then, however, Yoruba *orisha* worship and Spanish devotional Catholicism had been combined. A hybrid tradition had been formed.[6]

Struggles for Religious Identity in Miami

It is not surprising that these patterns—both the religious combinations and the noninstitutional inclinations—have endured to some extent in the religious life of the nominal Catholics who have fled to the United States since 1959. As I suggested in the last chapter, exile religion shows only modest influence of the sacramental Catholicism advocated by Church officials, although more so than in the homeland. The piety of Cuban visitors to the Miami shrine of Our Lady of Charity, although it has been shaped by their experiences in churchgoing America, still often centers in the home and street. It also often reveals African as well as European influences, always more one than the other but never without the effects of the history of cultural contact in the homeland. For instance, many of the self-identified Cuban Catholics who enshrine images of one of the unsanctioned "saints" of Santería in their yard or home remain unaware that the images signal African influences, as I learned in many conversations at the shrine and around the city.

Given all this, it is not surprising that the clergy in Miami, and at the shrine in particular, preoccupy themselves with "evangelization" of Cuban Catholics. In sermons and writings, Cuban-born priests—such as Father Juan Sosa, who worked at the shrine and has served as liturgical coordinator for the feast-day mass—explain their concern by appealing to official Catholic documents. For instance, they often cite Pope Paul VI's apostolic exhortation on the importance of starting evangelization with "popular piety." Pope Paul affirmed that there are "expressions of the search for God" among those peoples whom the Church has dismissed. Some local clergy use this officially sanctioned idea to construct a strategy for dealing with the influence of Santería among nominal Catholics that, as the priests see it, steers between the extremes of rejecting it too harshly or accepting it too uncritically.[7]

If the clergy explain their preoccupation with evangelization by appealing to official documents, it originated in their daily contacts with Cubans. They are reminded often that even though the exile community feels more positively toward the clergy—and especially Bishop Román—than prerevolutionary Cubans did, "religion as practiced" is partly in tension with "religion as prescribed."[8]

For some clergy, like Bishop Román, the concern for reaching the unchurched also arose from their own experience of being outside ecclesiastical boundaries. Unlike Father Sosa, who attended one of the Catholic schools run by Spanish priests in the city of Havana, Román grew up officially linked with a rural parish that had one pastor for a population of 28,900 parishioners. Other obstacles stood in the way too: "Due to the distance from our home to the place where the liturgy was celebrated neither my family nor those who lived around us participated on a regular basis in the worship ceremonies of our Church." As with many other Cubans with whom I have spoken, at the same time Román prayed to the Virgin and identified with Catholicism: "I never heard in my family or in those around us any manifestation that they did not belong to the Catholic Church."[9]

Román's personal bond with the unchurched explains not only his popularity—"He's one of us," many Cuban Catholics told me—but also his early training as a missionary and his long-term emphasis on "evangelization." This former missionary to indigenous peoples in southern Chile told me in our first interview in 1991 that a lack of proper "evangelization" is the main problem facing the Cuban Catholic community in Miami. He elaborated by drawing three concentric circles on note paper. The smallest circle at the center, he explained, represented the minority of exiles who are devoted members of the "liturgical community" and attend mass regularly at their parish. The next circle represented those who were nominal Catholics, the majority of Cuban Americans. The final circle, farthest from the center, represented those who were not officially Catholic. Bishop Román has been concerned especially about the second group, nominal Catholics.[10]

As Román, Sosa, and the other local clergy address nominal Catholics about the influence of Santería, they frame their discourse in terms of paired opposites—purity/impurity and knowledge/confusion. They talk, first, as if the Catholic faith had been made impure by its combining with Santería. For instance, Román remarked that "those evangelizing the Cubans need to realize that one zone in need of *purification* is that in which the influence of Santería is significant." The priests acknowledge that "popular piety" expresses a search for the sacred, yet at the same time they emphasize that popular faith has been mixed with impure elements and needs the cleansing of missionizing. To make the same point, they also characterize the influence of African elements in Cuban religious practice in terms of a lack of knowledge, for which the people are more or less responsible, depending on which local priest is offering the analysis. What tens of thousands of local Cubans need, then, is catechesis, an introduction to the "Truths of the Christian Faith," as one pamphlet distributed at the shrine puts it. Father Luís Pérez, who has said the rosary at each feast-day mass since 1961, uses this sort of language in his writings and sermons. There is much "ignorance," he said, explaining the cause and extent of Santería influence among baptized Catholics. In this characterization of the problem it is the people's lack of understanding that must be addressed by the official Church. As Román told me, appealing to the same sort of language, the real problem is to eliminate the "confusions." "Deficiencies in evangelization," the bishop argued elsewhere, "have allowed the *orishas* of Santería to be confused with the saints of Catholicism." "The number of officially initiated Santería adherents," he rightly estimated, "is rather small." Many, however, dabble: "What is rather numerous is the amount of people belonging to the baptized multitudes of our Church who sporadically visit the *santero* or minister of that religion looking for good luck, health, or protection, or wanting to know the future."[11]

Whether they employ the language of impurity or the rhetoric of confusion, the priests' concern is the same. The Cuban clergy have hoped that the shrine would provide the means to "purify" nominal Catholicism of the residue of Santería that survives in popular devotions. Using the rhetoric of confusion, Román claimed that "the shrine of Our Lady of Charity has been designed with [a] pedagogical idea in mind." The shrine is important to the clergy for many reasons, not just its usefulness as a site from which to evangelize the unchurched. It is, after all, the shrine of the *national* patroness. Still, for Román and other priests at the shrine, the sanctuary also is important because it can help in their ongoing efforts to catechize.[12]

And they are concerned about reaching the nominal Catholics because they are deeply worried about their spiritual welfare. The priests believe that although "popular piety" deserves respect as an authentic attempt to approach the divine, those Cubans who are estranged from the "liturgical community" remain in spiritual danger. The Cuban clergy at the shrine have varied to some extent—by temperament, doctrine, and practice—in how they deal with those outside the boundaries of the Church, as they draw those lines. However, they share a sincere concern to bring the exiles into the parish system and the sacramental life.

Even a casual visitor will notice the priests' efforts to evangelize. Evangelization is a prominent a theme in the sermons, artifacts, and practices at the shrine. For example, recall the pamphlet on the souvenir table that instructs the unchurched visitors in the "Truths of the Christian Faith." Aware of the hybrid and noninstitutional piety of some visitors, priests also take every opportunity to correct and catechize during personal encounters and public rituals. Before the Eucharist is distributed during most important masses, for example, the celebrant instructs the nominal Catholic devotees of the Virgin there about the several conditions that must be met in order to receive communion. That does not happen in most parishes in most places in the United States. It happens regularly at the shrine because the Cuban clergy recognize that some participants are not versed in "orthodoxy" or "orthopraxis" (as the clergy understand each), and they hope to take advantage of the chance to instruct them.

The centrality of "evangelization" at the shrine also is evident in the large number of printed sources. They not only testify to the priests' concern to reach the unchurched but also, more specifically, document their frequent appeals to the rhetoric of impurity and confusion in their writings about Santería, evangelization, and the shrine. We might examine the views of Father Sosa, Bishop Boza Masvidal, or Father Pérez. As one of many examples, consider an interview with Bishop Román that appeared in the local Catholic periodical in 1975, two years after the shrine was dedicated. In that one-page piece, "Shrine: A Place of Popular Worship," Román used the term "purify" four times as he focused on the ways that the shrine functions to cleanse the "syncretistic" popular piety of pilgrims. He explained how the people "have [Our Lady of Charity] mixed up with pagan imagery." He meant Santería and Ochún, as he indicated in that interview. "From my office sometimes," he elaborated, "I see people who come to the Shrine and who also get close to the water and throw things into it—a practice which is part of pagan rituals." In that printed interview he went on to suggest that he was glad that these pilgrims came, even if they visited as followers of Santería to throw copper pennies to Ochún. Turning to the rhetoric of ignorance, Román explained that he welcomed the opportunity to "illumine" them.[13]

The Cuban clergy's catechetical concern is expressed clearly in their attempts to distinguish Our Lady of Charity from Ochún, the Yoruba goddess of the river, with whom she is "confused." The devout associate both with water, yellow, sweets, money, and love. Santería initiates, especially devotees of Ochún, come to the Miami shrine, even though clerical and lay officials sometimes ask them to leave or encourage them to change. For example, one summer afternoon in 1994 as I waited in the shrine office to talk with one of the sisters who answers telephones there, I heard a typical exchange. A shrine priest chastised a young couple who seemed to him more aligned with Santería than Catholicism, exhorting them to baptize their son. On another day, an active lay member of the confraternity told me that when they encounter Santería initiates at the shrine, usually dressed in white and throwing pennies, they "chase them off." Some lay leaders join with clergy, then, in this struggle.[14]

Still, as the Cuban clergy and lay elite realize, those Santería followers find much that is familiar and affirming at the shrine. "For these people," Bishop Román acknowledged, "the Shrine is also a place very much their own." It is, after all, by the water. Like Ochún, the Virgin is associated with fertility and love, and prayer cards on the souvenir table petition Our Lady of Charity for a successful pregnancy. Finally, yellow rose bushes and painted yellow stones encircle the left exterior of the shrine. For those who know the references, all these elements link the Virgin and the *orisha*, despite the clergy's best efforts to separate the two.[15]

These contests for religious identity are waged in many arenas of Cuban American religious life. They are especially clear in struggles over narratives, artifacts, and rituals associated with devotion to Our Lady of Charity at the shrine and in the cityscape.

Contested Narratives

The narratives and counter-narratives about the patroness of Cuba are social sites at which Cubans negotiate identity. Two important stories illustrate this point, both of which claim to describe the origins of Our Lady of Charity/Ochún as national patroness. The "official" ecclesiastical narrative about Our Lady of Charity is repeated again and again, in print, in cassettes, and in sermons. That story, which I introduced in chapter 1, goes like this: At the start of the seventeenth century three laborers rowed a small boat in search of salt. As they paddled toward the salt mine in the Bay of Nipe, they found an image floating in the water. The image, which miraculously had remained dry, had an inscription that said, "I am the Virgin of Charity." That icon was enshrined in the easternmost province. As other miracles were attributed to her, devotion spread to the other parts of the island over the centuries. It peaked during the wars for independence from Spain during the 1890s. Veterans from those battles, who had worn her image on their shirts and prayed to her for aid, successfully petitioned the pope to name Our Lady of Charity the patroness of Cuba. On 8 September 1916 Pope Benedict XV granted their petition, and she officially became the guardian of the country.[16]

A counter-narrative, constructed in Cuba and repeated in Miami by followers of Santería, explains how Ochún, not Our Lady of Charity, became patroness of Cuba. Ochún, the Yoruba goddess, was saddened when white slave traders took many of her children to a far-off place called Cuba. Confused about what was happening, she consulted her older sister, Yemayá. Her sister explained that she could not stop the forced removal. Ochún, from her deep love for her suffering children, then decided to move to Cuba, but she didn't know anything about the island. "What is Cuba like?" she asked her sister. The climate and vegetation are much like here, Yemayá explained, but not everyone there is black like us. Ochún then asked her sister to grant her two wishes, which she did—to make her hair straighter and her skin lighter so that all Cubans, regardless of their color, could worship her.[17]

These two stories differ dramatically. The second Santería narrative is tied to Cuban national identity, as in the official Catholic version. Yet it not only substitutes the African *orisha* for the Catholic Virgin but also de-emphasizes the links with war and patriotism and highlights the significance of slavery and race. The stories, needless to say, construct different collective identities. The second narrative also explains why the object of devotion, the Spanish-looking Virgin with straighter hair and lighter skin, actually is the African *orisha*. That, in turn, invites the "confusions" that so worry the local clergy.

Contested Artifacts

Some laity and clergy also struggle over the significance of artifacts. For example, on the souvenir table at the central entrance to the shrine, small plastic bottles with the name and image of the shrine sell for ten cents each. Visitors carry armfuls of these to the nuns, priests, and volunteers in the office on the other side of the building. They then ask the officials, or lay volunteers, to fill the bottles with holy water. All this seems unspectacular. After all, water is sacred in many traditions, and holy water is common in Roman Catholic religious life. Almost every parish church in the United States has small basins of it to the left and right of the entrance to the narthex or the nave. Because Cubans are involved, however, the situation at the shrine is filled with ambiguity and tension. Some of those asking for holy water at the shrine are casual or devoted followers of Santería, and blessed water serves as an ingredient in many potions. The shrine volunteers and staff know this, of course. But they usually oblige the pilgrims' requests to fill their bottles, not always able to tell why visitors want the holy water or how they might use it.[18]

They struggle over icons as well, and the clergy's catechetical effort and devotees' quiet resistance inform the battle over the two San Lázaros, one of which stands to the right of the shrine's altar (figure 13). In Roman Catholic tradition, Lazarus of Bethany, Jesus' friend, was the brother of Martha and Mary. The author of the Gospel of John also claims that he was resurrected by Jesus (John 11–12). This is the Saint Lazarus approved by the Church hierarchy and placed in the Miami shrine. However, another Lazarus appears in one of Jesus' parables. Jesus gave the name Lazarus to a man who lay sick and miserable at a rich man's gate. In the story, Lazarus received his reward, while the rich man was condemned to eternal torment (Luke 16:19–31). Despite the use of a personal name in the parable, there is no evidence that he was a historical figure. Nonetheless, this Lazarus, who appears in the iconography with tattered loincloth and crutches, was revered in the medieval period as the patron of beggars and lepers. In Cuba he became associated with the African *orisha*, Babalú Ayé.[19]

Along with Our Lady of Charity and Saint Barbara, this officially unsanctioned Saint Lazarus is one of the three most popular objects of Cuban American devotion. The clergy knows that. Besides strategically naming a parish in a Cuban neighborhood after the saint, and enshrining the orthodox image there, Church officials have tried to remove the "confusions" in other ways. The contest goes on at the shrine too, where clergy not only installed the orthodox image but also placed a pile of pamphlets at his feet. That pamphlet, written by Father Luís Pérez, attempts to instruct shrine visitors by distinguishing the sanctioned from the unsanctioned saint. Yet at the parish named for Saint Lazarus, grateful parishioners still pile crutches beside the image, just as they do in the Santería "church" dedicated to him a few miles away. The pastor of San Lázaro Roman Catholic Church still must evangelize, he told me. Parishioners bring the unsanctioned image for him to bless, but he refuses their requests and corrects their "confusions." At the shrine, I have not seen many people read the pamphlet he wrote; some apparently do, though, because the staff has to put out more copies now and then. Yet it's difficult to know what those who do read it make of what they read. Some Cubans in Miami have followed the clergy's advice. Some have politely ignored the clergy's efforts to instruct them, as the many images of the unsanctioned Saint Lazarus in pocketbooks and yard shrines indicates.[20]

Images of Our Lady of Charity also appear throughout the urban landscape, and they encode multiple meanings in varying contexts. She is niched in Roman Catholic parish Churches where Cubans predominate, such as St. John the Apostle in Hialeah and St. John Bosco in Miami. She is enshrined in small local churches which claim the label "Catholic" but which officials from the Archdiocese of Miami

Figure 13. A female devotee touches the statue of Saint Lazarus that stands to the right of the main altar at the Miami shrine.

condemn as affiliated with Santería. Those include El Rincón, which is dedicated to Saint Lazarus, and El Santuario de Nuestra Señora de la Caridad del Cobre, which is defiantly named for the original shrine to the patroness in Cuba. Our Lady of Charity adorns graves in Woodlawn Cemetery in Little Havana, on Calle Ocho (figure 14). She is the subject for many local artists—writers, composers, filmmakers, and painters. One primitive oil painting commissioned by a Cuban American in Miami in 1969, for example, portrays an ebony-faced Virgin holding a white-faced Jesus in her arms. The more traditional Spanish-looking Virgin appears on holy cards tucked unseen in wallets and pocketbooks, while motorists with keen eyes can spy her four-inch image on the bumpers of devotees' cars.[21]

She also resides in domestic spaces in Cuban neighborhoods, both interior home altars and exterior yard shrines. From my conversations with yard shrine owners, mostly women, it seems that many are built to fulfill a vow made to the Virgin in a time of need. One local yard altar enshrines an icon that Dorita brought with her from Cuba when she arrived twenty-six years earlier (see figure 8). She did it to fulfill a promise. "In Cuba, there was a terrible hurricane and my son was injured and almost died. At that moment I fell to the floor on my knees and promised to enshrine

Figure 14. A large statue of Our Lady of Charity on a gravestone in Woodlawn Cemetery in Little Havana.

her and devote myself to her [if she healed my son]." An eighty-three-year-old woman from Havana, Elsa, built a four-foot concrete and stone shrine in her front yard to fulfill a promise made when petitioning the Virgin for good health and her own home. "I built it because I promised La Caridad del Cobre that in whatever house she would give me I would enshrine her, no matter how old I was. I had been kicked out of several trailer parks that were to be demolished, but I always kept the Virgin wherever I went. I also built it because I was very sick when I was young in Cuba."[22]

Many of these shrines express extra-ecclesiastical devotion. Elsa, for example, told me in her living room one afternoon that she never went to the shrine near downtown Miami and never attended mass at her parish. However, when I asked about her religious beliefs and practices, she quickly and forcefully identified herself as Catholic. Although sometimes yard shrine owners admit to being followers of Santería, more often (like Elsa) they identify themselves as Catholic but have no interaction with ecclesiastical institutions. Sometimes, too, they remain unaware of or untroubled by the "impurities" and "confusions" that preoccupy the priests.[23]

Botánicas, stores that sell plants and artifacts for Santería worship, also dot the urban terrain, and these always include icons of Our Lady of Charity (figure 15). Probably because of the functions they serve for dealing with the daily problems of life—health, money, and sexuality—as well as the role they play in negotiating identity in exile, *botánicas* are a much more prominent feature of the landscape than

Figure 15. Exterior of a *botánica* in Hialeah. These stores, which sell images and artifacts used in Santería rituals, are more common in Miami than they were in the homeland.

they were in the homeland. Old ones close and new ones open all the time, but there are more than seventy stores in the Miami-Hialeah area, with names like Botánica Africana and Botánica Ochún. In those public spaces, Our Lady of Charity's identity is fused inseparably with that of Ochún's even though the image itself is the same one venerated and sold at the shrine. Customers at these *botánicas* include a wide range of Miamians—although most are Cuban—from Santería initiates to Catholic dabblers to curious non-Latino African Americans and Anglos. Worried about the spiritual life of baptized Cuban Americans, the clergy sometimes reluctantly tolerate, and often forcefully condemn, these unsanctioned conceptions and uses of the icon.[24]

Contested Rituals

Tensions between religion as prescribed and religion as practiced also appear in rituals. Of course, Our Lady of Charity's image is present in many ritual contexts condemned by the official Catholic Church, not only parallel rituals at the shrine but also sacrifices and offerings in the homes of Santería practitioners.

Lay-clergy struggles also inform, for example, ritual practices associated with the annual festival on 8 September. Each year the clergy and confraternity from the shrine participate in a ceremony, attended by thousands, in which the image from the shrine is carried by boat (or helicopter) to another site. There a rosary and mass is said, with the Anglo archbishop and the Cuban bishop presiding and many priests and seminarians attending. Yet at the same time that this is going on, many devotees choose to stay at home. One yard shrine owner in Little Havana stands vigil alone in her home on the eve of the feast day, lighting candles and offering flowers to the Virgin just after midnight. Elsewhere in the city, Mauricio, a fifty-nine-year-old exile with obvious leanings toward Santería, organizes a "block party" that draws hundreds of devotees. Each feast day, he revealed in an interview at the Catholic shrine, Mauricio invites a Santería "priest" (*un cura*) to say a "mass" (*una misa*) in front of the eight-foot image of Our Lady of Charity on his lawn. In a similar way, a self-described follower of Santería holds a private ritual in her small backyard on the Virgin's day. "On September 8th I have a big party with drums, music, and a buffet," she confided in an interview. "I invite a lot of my friends. We take the *santo* in my house and place her on a raft and put her in my pool."[25]

The annual festival celebration in 1994 was especially revealing for understanding the competing meanings of the Virgin for Miami's Cubans. The mass was held in Hialeah Racetrack that year because Hurricane Andrew had destroyed the usual site two years earlier and other alternatives were not available. It is interesting that a religious ritual would take place at a racetrack, but more significant is the choice of city and neighborhood. The city of Hialeah, one of two major concentrations of Cubans in the Miami metropolitan area, was home to the Church of Lucumí Babalú Ayé, the so-called Santería Church that won the right to practice sacrifice in a highly publicized Supreme Court battle. Also, within a dozen blocks of the racetrack, down East Fourth Avenue, are several sites that enshrine Our Lady of Charity. Besides the neighborhood yard shrines, three *botánicas* sell statues and holy cards with her image on it, just beside the flora, statues, powders, oils, and beads for Santería rituals. A storefront "chapel" (*capilla*) dedicated to another Virgin, and associated with Santería, on this occasion devoted its window to the patroness. Behind storefront glass, Our Lady of Charity appeared in front of a large Cuban flag, so that drivers and passengers on their way to the official ceremony a few blocks away could see her (figure 16). Farther down the same street, El Rincón, the independent church associated with Santería and dedicated to the "heterodox" Saint Lazarus, held a mass for the Virgin's feast day an hour before the celebration at the racetrack began. In that small building, which resembles a modern suburban American parish, Our Lady of Charity stood on the main altar, surrounded by yellow and white flowers donated by devotees. Still farther down the same street, the other small church which the archdiocese has accused of being affiliated with Santería, but which the followers claim is a "traditionalist" Catholic church, held yet another feast-day mass for the Virgin that night. Unlike the previous year, however, they did not process through the streets of Hialeah afterward. Convinced that the shrine and archdiocese want to "destroy" them, members of the church named after the original shrine in Cuba decided not to openly compete with the ecclesiastical powers. They reluctantly canceled their feast-day procession that year. However, one woman there assured me angrily that none of their members would walk down the street for the "big show" at the racetrack.[26]

Back at the official mass in the racetrack, the presence of Santería was acknowledged. Bishop Román, who spoke at the end of the rite, mentioned his usual topics, including the problem with "confusions." This time, however, he addressed casual and initiated followers of Santería more directly than ever. At one point he asked the 12,000 in the audience, "How many of you worship her as Ochún?" Not sur-

Figure 16. The front window of a chapel in Hialeah decorated for the feast day of Our Lady of Charity in 1994. The Cuban flag forms the background behind the statue of Our Lady of Charity on the right. The Roman Catholic rosary and mass were celebrated only a few blocks away at Hialeah Racetrack that year.

prisingly, only a few hands went up, to a chorus of cackles and whistles. Román assured them that Ochún had no power to grant their petitions, that only Our Lady of Charity did. He then exhorted one female devotee of Ochún who had raised her hand to come to see him at the shrine so that he could correct her views.[27]

These lay-clergy struggles for religious identity at the festival mass, and those at the shrine and around the city, show that however much devotees to Our Lady of Charity might share when they focus on her role as national patroness, the meanings of the symbols at the shrine are contested too. In the next chapter I explore other contested meanings. I focus on the diversity of pilgrims and the variety of practices at Our Lady of Charity's sanctuary in Miami.

3 ✳ Diverse Devotees, Plural Practices, and Multiple Meanings

It was a perfect Monday afternoon in February, the sun gleaming off the shrine's copper roof—one of those days that had lured so many tourists and migrants to this city earlier in the century. But the perfect weather did not draw Manuel and his daughter Yvonne that weekday in 1992. The Virgin did, although it took me some time to discover that since I first encountered the twenty-four-year-old daughter. Dressed in stylish shorts and an elegant blouse, Yvonne was leaning against a white convertible in the parking lot as I approached. We spoke for a little longer than twenty minutes, but still I was puzzled. She confessed to a complete lack of piety, but that made her presence at the shrine inexplicable. Why was she there? It turned out, I soon learned, that she was waiting—not very patiently—for her father, a dark-haired white man of Cuban descent. As he walked down the front steps and toward where I stood at the edge of the parking lot, I noticed his fashionable clothes and expensive shoes. This, I thought to myself, was why some scholars of immigration have celebrated Cubans as the "golden exiles." As he confirmed when we spoke, Manuel had done well since he arrived as a twenty-one-year-old. He had come from Oriente province with the first (and most elite) wave of Cuban migrants in 1961. But that was not all that was on his mind that day. As he fought back tears, he told me that he had flown from Los Angeles to fulfill a vow he made to Our Lady of Charity. His intense devotion to the Virgin had begun as a child, nurtured in a town just three municipalities north of the main shrine in Cobre, one that adjoined the Bay where the three laborers had found the original statue. It was natural, then, that he turned to Our Lady of Charity when family trouble started. "I had some kind of problem with her," Manuel explained as he pointed to his distracted daughter, who by that time had turned on the rental car's radio to pass the time. Before and after I met Manuel, many other visitors cried as we talked at the shrine, but he was as emotional as any. Finally, he began to weep and asked to stop the interview. I never discovered his daughter's "problem." Whatever the problem, the Virgin had resolved it. Manuel, in response, traveled thousands of miles at some cost to express his gratitude and keep his promise. He had visited the

Virgin of Cobre at her Miami shrine. The next day he and Yvonne would fly back to Los Angeles.[1]

In this story of a middle-aged, upper-middle-class white man from Oriente and his secularized, American-born daughter, we can see many of the issues that make the devotees and devotion at the shrine so complex. What are the generational differences among devotees? Do men's and women's devotions differ? What roles do race and class play? Do the practices of those who were born in the eastern provinces of Cuba differ from those born in the western provinces? Manuel came to fulfill a vow, and it was family problems that drew him. What are the varied reasons that pilgrims visit the shrine, and how do they express their devotion?

In this chapter I make four main points. I argue, first, that gender and age divide visitors to the shrine, and they are diverse in other ways too: some venerate other Virgins, some are not Cuban, and some are not devout. Second, despite the diversity, race, class, and region are less important sources of difference among Cuban pilgrims than they were in the homeland: the majority of devotees at the Miami shrine are white and middle-class, and they hail from all parts of the island. Third, those devotees come to the Virgin with a variety of personal concerns, but among the most pressing are health, childbirth, and family. Finally, some Cuban visitors blend piety, leisure, and tourism at the shrine, while others invent new rituals. Most pilgrims, however, offer prayers, gestures, and vows to the Virgin, as the faithful do in nonliturgical devotions at many other Catholic pilgrimage sites.

I explore the diversity of peoples and practices in this chapter in order to avoid oversimplifications, although that is probably impossible. Ethnographies obscure as much as they illumine. Like photographs, they privilege *this* perspective and *this* moment. Despite authors' best efforts, books simplify the complex, still the dynamic, and submerge the ambivalent. To some extent that is inevitable, even helpful. As they should, readers expect guidance in deciding what is important, even if reader and author agree that no representation can exhaustively reveal the subject. Still, I feel obliged to do what I can to convey the complexity of it all. I argue in later chapters that the shrine is a site where many white, middle-class Cuban exiles construct national identity, but—I want to be clear—it is more than that too.

Diverse Devotees

Other Peoples, Other Virgins

A small proportion of visitors to the shrine present themselves as devotees of Mary, not just the Cuban patroness. They emphasize that Our Lady of Charity is but one form of Mary, the Mother of God. For instance, this is true of some Cuban members of the Legion of Mary, the lay Marian association that was founded in Ireland in 1921 and now boasts groups in most parts of the world. Legion members sometimes congregate at the shrine in Miami. One Saturday morning in May—Mary's month—113 Catholics, mostly older Latinas, processed two hundred yards from St. Kieran's Church to the Cuban shrine, singing hymns to the Virgin in Spanish along the way. As the parish priest who led the procession emphasized in his sermon that morning, members petition the same Mary under many different names.[2]

Some pilgrims venerate Virgins associated with the major Marian shrines around the world. From the middle of the nineteenth century to the middle of the twentieth, devotion to Mary intensified among many Catholics in the United States and elsewhere. That veneration has increased again in recent years, with an added apocalyptic tone that seems appropriate for the approaching millennium. The older Marian shrines at Lourdes and Fatima, for instance, continue to attract American pilgrims, including some Cubans from Miami. So too do the newer shrines at Garabandal and Medjugorje, where followers claim that Mary has appeared. One pilgrim to the Miami shrine, Susana, told me that she had encountered Mary at Medjugorje. This Generation X-er who was born in Miami to Cuban parents reported in 1992 that she had recently visited the popular shrine and there she "saw an appearance of the Virgin." That experience shaped her devotion to Our Lady of Charity, Susana indicated, broadening and deepening it. For her, in whatever form she appears, Mary is important for spiritual life: "Without Mary, you find yourself lost in the forest."[3]

Not only do some pilgrims in Miami turn to other Virgins besides Our Lady of Charity to help find their way; a small number are not Marian devotees at all. Like Yvonne from Los Angeles, who waited impatiently for her father outside the shrine, some are invited—they might say dragged—by more pious relatives or friends. Sometimes, though much less often than in prerevolutionary Cuba, that means retired husbands waiting outside for their gray-haired wives. Children and adolescents accompany parents, with more or less glee; and unpious exiles from the urban area escort out-of-town guests from New York, New Jersey, or even Cuba. The shrine does not allow the rites of passage that commonly attract family and friends in large numbers—baptisms, weddings, and funerals—but it does permit prayer requests to be read from the altar during masses. Occasionally the shrine is filled with those attracted by family ties, not devotion, as those gathered memorialize a beloved relative. That was the case, for instance, for Marilyn, a forty-five-year-old woman from New York who had come to obey her recently deceased father's wishes: he had asked that the clergy say a mass for him at the shrine when he died. A dutiful daughter, Marilyn complied. She wanted to make her views very clear, however, when we spoke one Wednesday night in January just outside the central portal: "I grew up in New York with *no* devotion at all."[4]

Visitors who do have devotion to Our Lady of Charity, and they constitute the overwhelming majority, are a diverse group. A small proportion of them are not even Cuban (table 5). Almost no Anglos visit the Cuban shrine in Miami, in part because the priests conduct all of the public rituals in Spanish. Latinos who are not of Cuban heritage visit, however. That makes sense: Latinos make up approximately 80 percent of metropolitan Miami's Catholics, and many of them arrived with Marian devotion of some sort. One Venezuelan-born devotee told me in 1994 that he was worried that I would fail to notice him and others like him: "You should not forget all of the Latinos here who have devotion to Our Lady of Charity." He explained his own practice: for him, Mary is a means to "arrive at Jesus." But he had come to understand and even share the Cubans' attitude toward the Virgin as a national protectress: "I feel sadness for Cuba. . . . I have many Cuban friends and for that rea-

Table 5. Profile of Shrine Visitors Interviewed, 1991–1994: Nativity

Place of Birth	Number	Percent of Total
Cuba	265	87
Other	39	13
Total	304	100

Note: Six percent of the "Other" were born in the United States. Of those born outside the United States (7%), four each were from Haiti, Venezuela, and Colombia. Three visitors were born in Nicaragua and two each in Chile, Puerto Rico, and El Salvador. One was born in Spain, of Cuban parents.

son I ask the Virgin of Charity to liberate Cuba." I spoke with other Latinos at the shrine too: Nicaraguans, Panamanians, Dominicans, Salvadorians, Guatemalans, Chileans, Brazilians, Hondurans, and Colombians. Some of them had a Cuban spouse or relative, but most did not. They came to petition the Virgin, just as they had in their native land, even if her form and name were not, at first, entirely familiar.[5]

Agustín Román and the shrine clergy welcome other Latinos. Even though the site and statue evoke Cuban nationalistic sentiments and the annual calendar is organized by Cuban provincial and municipal affiliation, the shrine staff reserves time for other Spanish-speaking visitors. Each October the clergy formally invite local Latin American migrants; each of the twenty-eight Latino groups has its own day. For example, in 1992 Mexicans visited on 1 October; Colombians on 13 October; and Argentineans on 23 October. Just as the Cubans who hail from the island's eastern provinces return annually for a picnic-pilgrimage on a Sunday afternoon in March, so too Latinos attended the *romería hispanidad* on 25 October to eat, talk, and pray together with other Spanish-speaking Catholics at the Cuban Virgin's shrine.[6]

Haitians have their own official day at the shrine too, and migrants from that Caribbean island have become a small but noticeable presence inside the shrine and, especially, at the annual festivals. That makes sense for at least two reasons: first, there are direct connections between Our Lady of Charity and the creole religion of most Haitians, and second, as one form of Mary, the Cuban Virgin invites all Haitians with Marian devotion to petition her in their need. On the first point, consider what one forty-five-year-old who was born in Haiti told me, which might seem surprising at first glance: "My devotion to Our Lady of Charity began in Haiti." How could that be? It is because in myth and practice Haitians connect Our Lady of Charity, and the African orisha with whom she is associated, with several female spirits who belong to the group called the Ezili. Practitioners of Haitian Vodou, that hybrid tradition that combines African and Catholic forms, associate the Ezili with fertility and love, just as Catholic Cubans view Our Lady of Charity and followers of Santería imagine her African counterpart, Ochún. More specifically still, Haitians on the island and in the diaspora identify the Cuban patroness, Nuestra Señora de la Caridad del Cobre, with Lasyrenn, the black mermaid, one of the most important of the Ezili. For many Haitians, then, the Marian image on the altar at the Miami shrine is a somewhat paler but still familiar female spirit who can help with childbirth, romance, and other concerns.[7]

Our Lady of Charity's links with pregnancy, love, and family (which I explore more fully later) helps to explain the devotional practice of some Haitian visitors I met. Consider the woman I encountered on the eve of the Virgin's feast day in 1994. Meticulously dressed and driving a new Mercedes, that afternoon Marie Claire brought her son, age 16, and her daughter, two years younger, to petition and thank the Virgin. Her devotion to the Virgin of Cobre began in Haiti, she revealed as we spoke by the water's edge, but it had increased in the United States. When I asked why, Marie Claire explained that "my son was born in this city on the Virgin's feast day, September 8." "The Virgin always gives me what I ask," she added. For that reason, and because of the links with her son's successful birth, she visits the shrine regularly and attends the feast-day celebrations each year.[8]

Another Haitian devotee I met on the feast day in 1994 also visited because of her family, but she was more worried about her children. "They are giving me problems," Gloria explained. Immersion in American culture, so much less nurturing and stringent with children, had led her kids to rebel, she reasoned. She came to petition the Virgin, then, "to ask her to change them back to the way they were when they came to the United States." For this forty-two-year-old woman, who had fled Port-au-Prince in 1980, the Cuban national patroness had no special significance, although she did mention that the Virgin of Cobre had traveled on the sea, as she had. More important, Gloria had come to ask Mary, in one of her many forms, for help with her wayward children. She explained: "I pray to all the Virgins. When it is their birthday, I come to pray to them."[9]

Gender: Old Patterns and New Ones

Although shrine visitors include Haitians and Latinos, Marian followers and the irreligious, the vast majority are Cuban devotees of Our Lady of Charity. Further, most of the Cubans who come for private unscheduled devotions are women. That is expected. During most periods and in most places, visitors at shrines and churches in Cuba and the United States have been predominantly female, more than six out of ten, and sometimes an even higher proportion. With some exceptions, women have constituted the majority of religious participants, and Marian devotees, in both nations. That certainly was true of prerevolutionary Cuba. Almost every European and American traveler to that island in the nineteenth century noted the gendered differences in Catholic practice: more women went to church. The churches were filled, one traveler in the 1870s noticed, with "mostly women and children." In the 1850s, one disapproving traveler reported what many devotees at the Miami shrine told me was still true a century later: men would go to church but remain outside. "The young men attend at the doors for the interchange of glances with their fair friends," the traveler observed. Another travel report from later in the nineteenth century made the same point: "The women go to church as worshipers. The males usually attend for the purpose of seeing them worship." One Cuban-born priest in Miami who was fourteen years old when he entered the United States in 1961 recalls similar patterns of religious practice: "In Cuba, men would stay out of the church, in the back. My father, for example, stood in the back of the church during my first communion service."[10]

Table 6. Profile of Shrine Visitors Interviewed, 1991–1994: Gender

Gender	Number	Percent of Total
Female	195	64
Male	109	36
Total	304	100

Women also have been the primary transmitters of piety. As Bishop Michael Pfeifer of San Antonio, Texas, acknowledged at the meeting of the National Conference of Catholic Bishops in 1994, this is true for Catholics in general, not just Latinos. "God has entrusted the future of humanity to women. Women are the primary evangelizers. . . . Our faith comes primarily from our mothers and grandmothers." If my conversations at the shrine are any indication, this is true of Cuban Catholics in Miami. When I asked one thirty-one-year-old visitor how his devotion to Our Lady of Charity began, he offered a common response: "In Cuba my mother and aunt talked with me about her." Most devotees mentioned mothers, but grandmothers, cousins, and aunts also cultivate devotion.[11]

If Cuban Catholic women in Miami nurture Marian devotion and visit the shrine of Our Lady of Charity in greater numbers—they constituted 64 percent of those I interviewed—the patterns have altered somewhat in exile (table 6). When I asked Cuban Catholics about how religion had changed in Miami, I received two answers most frequently. First, as I noted in chapter 1, they reported that all exiles are more religious in Miami. Second, and this is my point here, *men* attend and participate more, especially at the shrine. Remarkably, everyone with whom I discussed the issue agreed that men were much more of a presence in Miami than in the homeland. The priest whose father stood at the entrance during his first communion reported that he found, to his surprise and delight, that in Miami males participate more in religion. "Men come to the shrine," noted this former shrine priest, "and they go in front and kneel at the feet of the Virgin" (figure 17). Another local observer, a Cuban-born scholar who has written about the exile, suggested that male participation was "the main difference between religion in Cuba and Miami." "Men go," she noted, "whereas they did not go very much in Cuba. I cannot remember my father ever going to mass in Cuba."[12]

Men visit and participate more at the shrine in Miami for several reasons. As with Cuban exile religion in general, men go more because they can. It is easier: many live closer than they had in the homeland. The island of Cuba extends approximately 745 miles from east to west, and men from the western provinces had to journey across the island to the mountainous region in El Cobre, where the original shrine sits. In Miami, it is a short drive away. Although we would have to know more to assert this with any certainty, it also might be that this is yet another example of how American gender relations have shaped Cuban American daily life. American men go to church more than men in many Western cultures, although still in smaller numbers than women. In America, families go to church.

Most important, men visit the shrine in greater numbers, and seem to have more intense devotion to the Virgin in exile, because the site and the practices are associ-

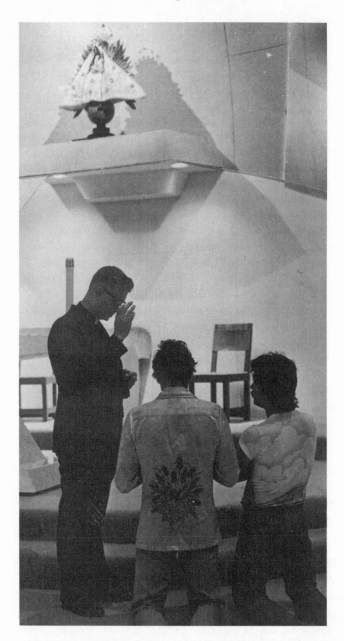

Figure 17. The Reverend Agustín A. Román blesses two
male pilgrims at the Miami shrine in 1975. (Courtesy *La Voz
Católica*; photo by Araceli M. Cantero.)

ated with national identity. The Virgin of Cobre has had nationalistic significance since the end of the nineteenth century, as I argued in chapter 1, but that has intensified in exile. (And one Cuban American scholar reminds us that exile in Spanish is a male noun—*exilio*.) As the male independence fighters wore her image on their uniforms during the battles against Spain, Cuban men in exile are drawn to the national patroness as a unifying and liberating force. The Virgin helped militarily and politically before, many men believe, and she can do it again. One sixty-nine-year-old male devotee, for instance, told me that he came to the shrine primarily to pray for "the salvation and liberation of Cuba, which will not happen without the Virgin's intercession." If the Miami shrine, like many others, rests at the intersection of the private and public spheres, it is the site as public arena that most men visit to construct national identity and petition the national protectress. It is not that women do not approach Our Lady of Charity as the national patroness or that men do not bring other needs to the Virgin. They do. But women are more likely to express other personal concerns and visit when no public ritual is scheduled. As a priest who worked at the shrine noticed, and my own observations have confirmed, women visit more frequently in "ordinary time": on Tuesday mornings or Thursday afternoons. Men join them in greater numbers at the collective rituals on Saturdays, Sundays, and weekday evenings, when the community gathers to make sense of itself as a diasporic people. Although the proportion of men at public rituals never reaches 50 percent by my counting, it approaches that point at times during the municipal masses, provincial romerías, and festival celebrations.[13]

These differences also are reflected in how men and women approach the dominant symbol, which after all is feminine. For example, motherhood is highly valued in Cuban families, and both men and women described the Virgin as "mother." Women, however, were twice as likely to describe her as "my mother," personalizing the Virgin and assigning her a place in the kinship network. Men, on the other hand, were more likely to call Our Lady of Charity "our mother." These subtle differences in language are important. As *my* mother, the Virgin nurtures the individual; as *our* mother, she protects the nation. Of course, it is more complex than this generalization indicates: some men told me that they pray to her as "my mother," and almost all women also emphasize her communal links. Still, I found differences in how women and men encounter the symbol, and these offers hints about why men have been more likely to visit the shrine in Miami than in the homeland.[14]

Age: Generational Differences

If gender distinguishes devotees to some extent, age does so even more. The first pattern that an observer might notice is that the majority of visitors to the shrine seem older, middle-aged to elderly. Among those I interviewed the median age was fifty-two, and even if we consider that I excluded those under eighteen from structured interviews, that still seems revealing. The largest proportion of those I interviewed—more than a third—were between fifty-one and seventy, older than Catholics generally in the Archdiocese of Miami (table 7). A survey of more than 4,000 exile Catholics sponsored by the Cuban-born bishops in Miami and elsewhere discovered a similar pattern. Further, the average age of the Cuban exile community

Table 7. Profile of Shrine Visitors Interviewed, 1991–1994: Age

Age	Number	Percent of Total
16–30	58	19.2
31–50	85	28.1
51–70	113	37.5
71–90	46	15.2
No answer	2	—
Total	304	100

Note: The median age was 52.

as a whole is older than that of both other Latinos and the U.S. population. On the eve of the Mariel boatlift, which made the exile population slightly more youthful, the median age for Cuban Americans was 33.5—because Cubans bear fewer children than other Latinos and the communist government's emigration policy favored the elderly. Cuban exiles' median age was eleven years older than that for other Latinos.[15]

This age structure influences devotion at the shrine. That is not only true on those weekday mornings—as on one spring day in 1994—when the white bus from the Little Havana Activities and Nutrition Center on Calle Ocho pulls into the parking lot and two dozen elderly women and men file out to slowly climb the steep steps to the Virgin's shrine. Surveys show that older Catholics in Miami, and elsewhere, are more likely to attend church. It makes sense, then, that the older Cuban Catholics in Miami—from Little Havana and elsewhere in the region—might visit the shrine more regularly. And middle-aged and elderly migrants at the shrine, those who have some memory of the homeland, have a stronger attachment to the premigratory religious life. That religious life included devotion to Our Lady of Charity. At the same time, the younger generation, those born in the United States or those who came as young children, sometimes do not emphasize her role in constructing national identity. As one first-generation exile who arrived in Miami in 1963 put it: "The young people do not believe as we do because they don't know the Virgin of Charity as the patroness of Cuba."[16]

Some Cuban pilgrims do arrive in multigenerational groups. For instance, one afternoon in September I encountered these three: a grandmother who was born in Havana in 1927, her twenty-seven-year-old American-born daughter, and an impatient toddler in a pink hairbow who was squirming in her mother's arms. When I asked the grandmother and mother separately whether those in the second generation had the same devotion to the national patroness, they both suggested that they did. The adult daughter said that she prayed to the Virgin because she is both "the mother of all children" and "the patroness of Cuba." The grandmother explained the intensity of her daughter's piety: "It is because I have a close relationship with my daughter." If that day was any indication, the granddaughter too someday might return to the shrine, perhaps with her own young daughter squirming in her arms.[17]

As with this family, other devotees told me that the second generation has maintained the same level of devotion to the Virgin, but more of them acknowledged divisions. One twenty-four-year-old Marielita who left Cuba when she was only four felt a bit lonely among those in her generation. "Well, I am one of them [a devotee]. But there are not many young people who attend the church. But if they would, they would definitely love this church and also the peaceful place it is." Echoing the concern of many other immigrant religious leaders in American history, the shrine's director worries that "we are losing the second generation." Clearly there are some in that generation with deep devotion, as I learned in my conversations at the shrine. Still, it seems that the clergy and laity have some reasons for concern. Even those who claim piety, like one twenty-year-old woman I met on a Tuesday afternoon in July, sometimes remain unclear about the full nationalistic significance of the Virgin. Diana confided, "I've always had a strange attraction and devotion to her." Yet when I asked about Our Lady of Charity's connections with Cuba, the young woman confessed to a certain fuzziness: "The only thing I know about the connection is that she helps the Cubans and she's their special Virgin." Note, too, that Diana distanced herself from the others at the shrine in her use of language. She preferred English, as only those under thirty did; and despite her own intense piety, she described Our Lady of Charity as "their" Virgin. Whether or not younger visitors described themselves as only "half Cuban," as another twenty-four-year-old visitor did, clearly the devotion of the second generation does not mirror that of the first, especially that of those who crossed the Straits of Florida during the 1960s.[18]

Most studies of urban immigrants have found intergenerational differences in the practice of religion, so the Cubans seem typical in this regard. In my conversations at the shrine, I found that the intensity of devotion to Our Lady of Charity declines slightly among those who were born in exile or who arrived as young children, those under forty years of age. There is a still more precipitous drop in devotion for those under twenty. So we need to nuance claims about devotion in another way, by noting the generational differences. Although I found a broad range of ages among the visitors, it is the middle-aged and elderly who visit most often.[19]

Minimized Differences in Exile: Race, Class, and Region

Cuban visitors to the shrine are divided to some extent, then, by age and gender; but other social factors—race, class, and region—seem much less important sources of difference among them than the history of devotion to Our Lady of Charity, or Cuban history in general, might lead us to suspect. Despite the political developments in the nineteenth century that linked Our Lady of Charity and national identity, before the revolution of 1959 there still was some truth to the caricature that the devout were disproportionately lower-class blacks living in the eastern provinces near the original shrine. Pilgrims to the Virgin's shrine in Miami, on the other hand, are predominantly white and middle-class, and the majority were not born in the regions of the country that traditionally have had the strongest devotion. This requires some explanation.

First, consider race. Race is a social construction, not an element of human biology; but the invented racial categories—black, mulatto, and white—continue to have social consequences. The harsh effects of racial typing are real enough. The discourse about "race," then, provides clues about how Cubans negotiate identity and relate to one another. Concerning race, I noticed two patterns at the shrine: the devout did not talk about it much, and few Afro-Cubans visited. There might be several explanations for the migrants' relative silence about skin color and ethnic background. Perhaps, like many contemporary scholars in the social sciences and humanities, they too saw the constructed character of racial categories and thus dismissed the topic as irrelevant, though I saw no evidence of this. Many important issues remain unmentioned or underemphasized in interviews and conversations. Perhaps race was very important to them, but they did not feel comfortable discussing it—or at least not with *me*. It also might be that pilgrims talked less about it because I did. None of the questions in my structured interviews concerned race. It was only during the last year and a half of my research that I began to inquire more systematically about racial categories, as I decided that the silence itself needed explanation. It might be, too, that visitors talked little about race because so few devotees of predominantly African descent visited the Virgin at her shrine in Miami. There was no need.[20]

With all these possible explanations, there might be no reason to look for others. Still, there is another compelling interpretation of this tendency to avoid discussion about race—that the Cuban myth of racial harmony has ongoing influence. The island has been home to a significant African population since the origins of slavery there, and as Julia Ward Howe described it in a travel account in the 1850s, using the racial discourse of her day, "The black and white races are, by all accounts, more mingled in Cuba, than in any part of our own country." While there was "mingling" and Cuba did not have segregation laws like the American South, Cubans did classify one another using a system of racial typing based on gradations of skin color—from "pure white" (most desirable) to "pure black" (least desirable). However, white Cubans have tended to overlook or underemphasize this system of racial classification as they assess race relations on the island. The same has been true among white exiles in Miami. As one scholar of Afro-Cuban history has noted, "One of the favorite topics of the white exiled Cubans is the non-existence of racial conflict in Cuba before communism." Another Cuban migrant has named this "the myth of the racial paradise."[21]

This secular myth also has been intertwined with religious legend: as few scholars have noticed, this myth has been encoded in the traditional story of Our Lady of Charity. Cuban society has been diverse since the seventeenth century, especially in the eastern provinces near the Virgin's shrine. Mirroring the diversity of the population, the Virgin herself often has been understood as creole, as ethnically and culturally mixed—Spanish, African, and Indian. In turn, the account of her discovery changed over time as devotees projected their hopes about social harmony onto the sacred narrative. In the original testimony by one of the three laborers who allegedly found her statue floating off the Cuban coast at the start of the seventeenth century, Juan Moreno declared that her rescuers included two Indian brothers and a slave of African descent, Juan himself. As the Cuban historian Olga Portuondo Zúñiga has argued persuasively, however, over time the heritage of the three laborers changed. Altering their names and ethnicity, in a popular version of the tale narrators transformed them into *los tres Juanes*—Juan, the black; Juan, the white; and Juan, the Indian. In some versions the Indian is described as mulatto. As the historian Portuondo argues, in both revised versions of the legend, which Cubans on the island and in exile still tell, the Virgin and her discovery "project a utopia of ethno-cultural unity onto the Cuban people."[22]

Whether or not they are devotees of the creole Virgin and retell the legend of her discovery, some Cuban Americans of African heritage challenge the myth of racial harmony. I attended a workshop on race relations in metropolitan Miami not long after riots had disturbed many in the community. In my small group discussion that morning there was the following exchange: a white Cuban in his fifties explained to our multicultural group that Cuba "had no race problem." As the Anglo and Haitian members of the group nodded and smiled, an older black Cuban stopped him politely. "Well," he countered, "it wasn't all that perfect." He went on to tell stories from the prerevolutionary period about color lines in Cuban society—at work and in neighborhoods. Yes, he admitted, race relations probably were better than in the United States, but they were not utopic.

Although some Cubans contest the myth of racial harmony, many white exiles in Miami continue to retell it, and that myth might help to explain the relative silence about race at that shrine. For example, the bylaws of the Confraternity of Our Lady of Charity in Miami guarantee, in article III, that any person "regardless of sex, status, age, or condition" can venerate the Virgin by joining the lay group. Notice that race is not specifically mentioned. Why? It is not that Bishop Román and other white exiles do not try to cross ethnic boundaries, inside and outside the Cuban community. Sometimes they do. To encourage cooperation among two local Catholic subcultures, for instance, in 1994 Román arranged for a bus filled with white Cubans from the shrine to visit the Haitian Catholic Center, where they would participate in a mass and procession on the feast of Corpus Christi. During the ride to Little Haiti the shrine director tried to prepare the Cubans for what they soon would experience: the only white faces in a crowd of several hundred, all eyes on them. And he tried to promote tolerance. Noting the differences in skin color, he turned to an analogy from Cuban foodways to persuade. He reminded the white Cubans—no one needed reminding—of their traditional love for black beans and white rice. Extending the analogy to Cuban history and identity, the shrine director suggested that "Cuba is beans and rice, black and white." There was in Román's comment some hint of the myth of racial harmony: Cuban history, he implied, has been a blending of black and white. At the same time, however, he called Cubans to greater understanding and cooperation, thereby implicitly recognizing that crossing this ethnic boundary required some effort and reorientation. To return, then, to the confraternity bylaws, I suspect that—despite the clergy's efforts to bridge ethnic barriers—the white Cuban myth of racial harmony is at work in subtle ways. If I am right, the surfaced logic of the bylaws goes something like this: there is no need to mention race, even in that most legal of all documents associated with devotion at the shrine, since Cubans do not have a race problem.[23]

Though this myth, and the other factors I mentioned, may help to explain the relative silence about race at the shrine, it does not explain why so few blacks visit there. The myth did not *create* the white majority at the Miami shrine. That is better explained by two other factors. First, Afro-Cubans always have been more drawn to Santería than to institutional Catholicism. Second, and most important,

they migrated to the United States in much smaller numbers, especially among the
first group of exiles in the 1960s. There is little overt conflict between Cubans of
predominantly African and predominantly European backgrounds because so few
who would identify themselves as black visit the shrine—only 3.2 percent of those
I interviewed formally and a similar proportion of those attending public rituals. The
proportion of Afro-Cubans I spoke with at the shrine, and counted in public rituals,
approximates that in the exile population in Miami. It is that exile population in
Miami, then, that is not representative. The pre-1980 migrants included fewer blacks
than in the homeland. The 1953 Cuban census had counted 27 percent of the island
population as black or mulatto, while their representation in the United States in
1970 was less than 3 percent. In turn, more than 98 percent of the Cuban migrants
during the 1960s classified themselves as white. In the 1990 United States census a
higher proportion (16%) of the Cuban American migrants identified themselves as
black, Chinese, or some other race, after more Afro-Cubans had arrived in 1980
with the Mariel boatlift (estimates ranged from 15% to 40%). However, because the
majority of Afro-Cubans settled in the northeastern states—and for other reasons
too—the Cuban community in metropolitan Miami remained disproportionately
white in the 1990s.[24]

It is important to note that some Afro-Cubans visit the shrine, and those who do
pray for their homeland and identify themselves primarily as Cubans, at least to me.
When I asked Rosa, an elderly black Cuban who works as a maid in Miami Beach,
about the reasons for her devotion to Our Lady of Charity, she answered quickly
and simply, as if it were an odd question and the answer were self-evident: "Because I am Cuban." Rosa makes the pilgrimage every week, she told me, "to pray
for Cuba." She might visit the Virgin there, but some other blacks in exile do not,
eschewing religious practice altogether or preferring the domestic devotions of Santería that mix Catholic and African symbols. Reflecting the composition of the migrant community and the traditional religious divisions on the island, then, Cuban
devotees at the Virgin's Miami shrine are mostly white.[25]

They also are mostly middle-class. As I argued in chapter 1, slaves probably predominated among the earliest seventeenth-century devotees, and some white elites
on the island in later centuries assumed that devotion was defined by class as well
as race. An exiled priest who was trained in the Catholic schools of Havana recalls
that he shared the common belief that devotion to Our Lady of Charity was "only
for the lower classes of society." As Father Sosa observed exiles at the Miami shrine,
however, he discovered that he was wrong. In exile, Sosa noticed, devotion seemed
to cross class boundaries more. We would need more systematic study to be sure,
but my years of conversation and observation at the shrine confirm Father Sosa's
assessment. I talked with maids and nurses, truck drivers and clerical workers, security guards and wealthy bankers. To my surprise, I noticed few differences in what
they said or how they acted.[26]

As with race, to a large extent there is less economic difference and conflict
among devotees at the shrine because there is less diversity in this regard among the
exiles in general, especially among the early migrants. The exiles who arrived
between 1959 and 1970, who form the majority of pilgrims at the shrine, were disproportionately from the middle and upper classes in the homeland. More than 68

Table 8. Native Region of Cuban Migrants Interviewed at Shrine

Province	Number	Percent of Total
Western total	159	60
Havana	123	46
Matanzas	23	9
Pinar del Río	13	5
Eastern total	96	36
Las Villas	44	17
Oriente	33	12
Camagüey	19	7
"Cuba"/no answer	10	4
Total	265	100

percent of the 1959–65 exiles, for instance, were white-collar workers, even though only 23 percent of the workforce on the island enjoyed that status. In their adopted land, many Cubans also have flourished, with median incomes above those of other Latinos, though still lower than those of non-Spanish-speaking Americans. Cubans in Miami, and at the shrine, are diverse; but they are predominantly middle- and-upper class. In exile economic status divides them much less than, say, age.[27]

Those who know the history of Cuba also might expect to find the devout divided along geographical lines, with those from the eastern provinces of Cuba, nearer the shrine in El Cobre, having greater loyalty to the Virgin. Supporting that view, the great Cuban anthropologist Lydia Cabrera suggested that devotion to Our Lady of Charity/Ochún predominated in the eastern half of the island. That certainly was true before the wars for independence from Spain. The pattern continued to some extent in twentieth-century Cuba, even though Catholic parishes dedicated to the Virgin of Cobre can be found in the western provinces as well. In any case, the traditional regional pattern seems to have changed in exile. I was surprised to find that the majority of pilgrims I interviewed were born in the western, not the eastern, provinces; the largest proportion was from Havana (table 8). This is partly because most white migrants who arrived during the 1960s—and those predominate at the shrine—were born in the West. This also suggests that the nationalization of devotion that began in the nineteenth century—together with the crossing of racial and economic boundaries—has intensified even more in exile, as white, middle-class migrants from all regions of the homeland turn to the official patroness in their need. And they turn to her in many ways and for many reasons, as I argue in the remainder of this chapter.[28]

Plural Practices and Multiple Meanings

Emilia, a fifty-year-old white exile who visited the shrine from her home nearby in Miami explained why she had come one June afternoon in 1993: "I have great devotion to La Caridad. I always bring her all of my problems." Emilia also prays privately to the Virgin at home, and as a loyal member of the Confraternity of Our Lady of Charity, she attends every sort of collective ritual. She is a regular. She goes to the masses and rosaries, the romerías and feast-day celebrations. The festival mass on 8 September, which Emilia attends each year, is an official rite of the church, a "liturgy," a term which derives from a Greek word meaning "work of the public." Emilia's nonliturgical practices at the shrine that day when no masses or rosaries were scheduled were individual, not collective: she knelt alone at the altar to pray. But they were not for that reason private as opposed to public. Those bodily practices—kneeling and praying—were, to be more precise, private acts performed in public. Their private character added emotion; their public character increased efficacy. Spontaneous petitions or pious gestures directed at the printed image of Our Lady of Charity on the kitchen wall at home have a certain intimacy and force for devotees, as shrine visitors told me. Yet there is something special about bringing a private prayer to the Virgin at her shrine. It is not that Our Lady of Charity was not listening in the kitchen. She was. However, at the shrine, as on a front porch, the private sphere opens onto the public. In the same way, it is not that the scheduled collective rituals have no meaning for Emilia. Obviously, they do. Still, pilgrims like Emilia also come at all hours to perform a variety of nonliturgical practices there at the shrine, that space that intersects the private and public realms.[29]

Many of those devotional practices in that transitional space concern the homeland, because the patroness's Miami sanctuary is a nationalistic shrine. Interpreters of Christian pilgrimage have identified at least seven types of modern Catholic shrines. Some are founded on a site where a saint performed an important deed, others at the place where she or he appeared. Some are built because a holy relic or image is brought from another place or when an object already at the site proves to have miraculous powers. Some shrines express gratitude for prayers that have been answered. The original shrine to Our Lady of Charity in El Cobre was, in terms of this typology, a "found object shrine," one that developed after an image was found in mysterious circumstances: recall that legend has it that three laborers discovered the dry statue of the Virgin of Charity floating in the waters off Cuba's coast in the early seventeenth century. Our Lady of Charity's sanctuary in Miami is a "devotional shrine," one that is unrelated to miracles or unusual events. Like a relatively small number of devotional shrines in Europe (only 5 percent by one count), the Miami shrine was deliberately created as sacred space by human actions, apart from any religious experiences of the devout. A group of Cubans who were prodded by the Anglo archbishop decided that a sacred site should be established for Miami's migrants. Because Cubans built the shrine to the patroness in order to create a center for a particular national group, I suggest, it is a distinctive kind of devotional shrine, one not mentioned in the scholarly typologies—a national shrine. Further, because exiles built this national shrine outside the geographical boundaries of the homeland and in so doing reclaimed the shared symbol and the original site, it is even more distinctive. It is, in that sense, a diasporic nationalist shrine, as I explore more fully in later chapters.[30]

But pilgrims do not travel to the Miami sanctuary only to express their hopes for the homeland. It has more than nationalistic meanings, as with Emilia, who confided that the Virgin helps her "in *all* things," and a forty-seven-year-old woman from Havana who revealed that she came "for my devotion *and* for Cuba." Devotees make pilgrimages for a variety of reasons, and they engage in a diversity of practices—gestures, prayers, and vows.[31]

Pilgrimage Practices: Gestures

There are no typical pilgrims, but many march up the main steps and kneel at the altar, their eyes (and sometimes their arms) elevated. There, just beneath the statue of the Virgin, they spend ten minutes or so—some much more, some a bit less—communicating with the Virgin. After that devotees might sit in one of the traditional leather chairs inside or stand before St. Lazarus to the right of the altar. They might purchase a souvenir or pick up a pamphlet at the folding table near the front portal. Some pilgrims visit the nuns and lay volunteers at the office in the rear of the shrine, where they buy bottles for holy water and medals for relatives or convey a petition to be remembered at the next mass.[32]

Flickers of light illumine the dark basement altar at the Shrine of the Miraculous Medal in Philadelphia and many other Marian centers in the United States, but no votive candles await visitors to the Cuban shrine in Miami. Sometimes, however, devotees do bring flowers for the Virgin—usually in her colors, yellow or white—even though the clergy encourage contributions for the poor instead. On her feast day, pilgrims carry so many flowers to the Virgin that lay volunteers spend the entire day stopping visitors at the door and encouraging them to leave the bouquets outside in white cardboard vases, sometimes to the devotees' dismay: they had wanted to complete the exchange, to give their gift to the patroness. At less busy times, devotees usually can offer flowers to Our Lady of Charity inside, as did one middle-aged couple who carried a bouquet of yellow asters to the altar and then knelt there together beneath the Virgin's statue for fifteen minutes.[33]

Some pilgrims mark the journey with photographs: posing and photographing also are gestures associated with pilgrimage. One Sunday afternoon in 1992, a young girl smiled artificially as she posed for her mother in front of the circular hedge that surrounds the shrine. That same day an extended family clustered in two arched rows thirty feet in front of the shrine, so that the whole clan, and the building too, might be included in the image. As Hindus in India say that they go on pilgrimage "for *darśan*," to "see" the deity, seeing and being seen is part of religious practice for many Catholic pilgrims. They go to see the Virgin and the shrine—and to see their friends and relatives at that sacred space. It is in this sense that, at the Miami shrine and other modern pilgrimage sites, taking pictures is religious practice. It allows a certain kind of seeing, one that fixes the ritual moment and provides a source of memory. By later viewing the picture framed on the dresser, magneted to the refrigerator, or displayed in the album, the Cuban pilgrim and her extended family can return again and again through the evocative powers of the photographic image.[34]

Photographing might be more often associated with leisure activities than with religious sites, and the boundaries between secular and sacred blur at the Miami shrine, as at many others. That is not only true on the Sundays when pilgrims attend the annual *romerías*, which include food and music as well as rosaries and processions. In some ways, the religious site functions as tourist destination, recreational area, and exercise facility. Consider a few examples. Two families climbed out of a minivan with North Carolina license plates one summer afternoon. One family, it turned out, lived nearby but never had visited—much, I suppose, as locals often fail to visit the sites that attract those from out of town. The other family had driven from Charlotte to vacation in South Florida. The Cuban mother from North Carolina told me that the trip was a journey to her "roots." A short time later she herded six young children back in the van and drove off to visit Metro Zoo, Parrot Jungle, or some other local tourist spot. In a similar way, one couple from New York "came as tourists." The husband, who had arrived in 1962 with the first wave of migrants, had little devotion. He was there "to get acquainted with the Virgin." Clearly, his wife initiated the trip. She has had devotion to Our Lady of Charity since her childhood in Havana during the 1930s and 1940s. She came that day to pray for health and family, she revealed in our long conversation, but mostly she saw the visit as part of their vacation. In the same way that the Washington Monument or the Lincoln Memorial might be the mandatory destination for a family from Iowa, all squeezed in a Ford station wagon, the shrine, as the religious center of Cuban exiles, had become a tourist stop.[35]

In another sense, the shrine resembles a local park or recreational area. The turquoise water of Biscayne Bay surrounds the shrine, and some pilgrims relax at the picturesque pilgrimage grounds by the bay, with its mowed grass, palm trees, and scattered pines (figure 18). On almost any sunny weekday afternoon you will see lawn chairs under the pines by the water's edge. There devotees from the metropolitan region, most of them older women, slouch contentedly in those folding chairs. They usually greet the Virgin at her altar upon their arrival and then set up outside for an hour or two of relaxation. Relaxing is easier there, they told me, because the place is so "peaceful" and "tranquil." I was surprised at first at how many said that. What I originally had failed to understand was that the pilgrim's focus was not exclusively on the altar within. A bit quieter and more accessible than the beaches on Key Biscayne, and near the Virgin too, the shrine grounds provide devotees respite from the obscured vistas and tense exchanges of urban life. As with a young couple who visited on a Saturday afternoon—Robert was Cuban American and Nancy Puerto Rican—others also come for "peace and quiet and to relax." As Nancy explained, the tranquility of the natural site also serves a spiritual purpose: "The shrine is a peaceful place for me to come to and I can think and relax better here. Whenever I come, unlike the beach, there are less people here, therefore, less commotion, which allows me to reach more of my spiritual side and meditate."[36]

Finally, just as joggers and walkers encircle John F. Kennedy Park just down the street in Coconut Grove, some devotees combine exercise and piety. Two young Cubans, a male and his female cousin, biked to the shrine one afternoon. They visited briefly, asked for "protection," and pedaled home. Oscar, an elderly Cuban I met on another day, was especially interesting. Just before dinner on a warm Tuesday afternoon I watched as this older exile circumambulated the shrine. Around and around he walked quickly in the circular parking lot, his arms moving up and down sharply like large gears on a machine. Knowing that circumambulation is part of religious practice at other pilgrimage sites—the Ka'aba in Mecca, for instance—I

Figure 18. The view from behind the shrine, looking out across Biscayne Bay toward the island of Cuba. The sign to the left, in Spanish and English, announces that this is "a place of prayer." It prohibits trespassing, fishing, and swimming and exhorts visitors to "dress properly."

thought that I had discovered a new ritual practice there. In a sense I did. It turns out that Oscar, participating in the fitness craze of his time, each day walks vigorously around the shrine to improve his cardiovascular fitness. Combining leisure and piety, after his workout he visits the Virgin inside before he returns to his nearby home: the shrine as health club and the Virgin as exercise partner.[37]

Words and Music: An Invented Ritual

The practices I have focused on here are mostly nonverbal. They are gestures—kneeling, walking, and photographing. Some devotional practices, of course, also are more verbal. One of the most distinctive and intriguing visitors I encountered combined words and music in an invented ritual. I met Lucía and her husband at the shrine on a spring day in 1994. When I arrived a woman from the confraternity was leading visitors inside in reciting the rosary. Outside on the shrine grounds Lucía was conducting her own ritual. Lucía, a Cuban exile in her sixties, paced deliberately around the grass to the left of the conical shrine. From a distance I noticed that she carried a small rectangular object and her mouth moved as she stepped. As I moved closer I could hear singing. It sounded like more than one voice, although I only could see Lucía. When I found her on the grass, I learned that the object in her hand was a cassette recorder. I greeted her and we spoke for a few minutes before I got to my questions. Would she mind telling me what was she doing?, I asked. Lucía described how she composes and records songs for the Virgin at home, singing unaccompanied into the small tape recorder. I asked how she writes her songs. "I do not write them down," she explained. "They are in my head." And, I thought, they are preserved on tape. On her regular visits to the shrine grounds, Lucía told me, she then plays those tapes as she strolls privately, singing along with the recording as she walks. At my request, she played the tape for me, and as usual she sang along. The first song was a hymn to Our Lady of Charity. The next homaged another Marian figure, Our Lady of Guadalupe, in remarkably similar lyrics and melody. In fact, each of the performances—simultaneously live and taped—were very slight variations on the same melody, with a steady tempo that might suit a processional march. Each of her twelve Spanish-language songs praised the Virgin, in one of her forms or another. They offered thanks and sought aid. Playing and singing these songs with the melodic and lyrical repetition was the central religious practice for Lucía on her visits to the shrine. And, I learned, they were just for Lucía. As we parted, I thanked her for sharing her music. Then I joked that perhaps she would be famous soon. Her husband, who is supportive, even reverential, jumped in: "No," he replied sternly. "She does not want that. They are private." The two then explained that she always goes off by herself on the shrine grounds, as far from other visitors as possible, to play the recording and sing along. For Lucía, this modern invented ritual is too personal, too intimate, to share with other devotees.[38]

Pilgrimage Practices: Instrumental Prayers

Lucía imagined her distinctive nonliturgical practice as a form of prayer, and visitors offered many more conventional prayers at the shrine. I noticed two major kinds. First, the devout present prayers of love or praise, which request no response from the Virgin. In formalized prayers, visitors honor her: "Hail Mary, full of grace, hallowed be thy name." They do the same in less formalized ways too, they told me, at the altar in her Miami shrine. Second, many visitors also offer instrumental prayers, in which the devout petition the Virgin for aid and expect a response. These instrumental prayers, which provide insights about why pilgrims visit, are of different kinds. Some concern the group; others are more individualized. For instance, many pilgrims (male and female) told me that they had prayed to the Virgin "for Cuba" or "for Cubans," as I explore in more detail in part III. A few visitors told me that the Virgin provided material as well as spiritual aid. She helped them with worries about work and money. A retired factory worker from Union City, New Jersey, whom I met as we waited in line to buy a soda on a humid feast-day afternoon told a story about how the Virgin had intervened when he was a bachelor on the island:

> You know that when you are young you spend money as soon as you get it. You like to have fun. Well, when I was a young man, living in Havana, away from my family in Camagüey, one day I looked up to the picture of Cachita [Our Lady of Charity] on the wall above my bed and I said, "Cachita, my father is ill and I do not have enough money to visit him." The next day I picked a number and won. That's the kind of thing she has done for me.

This devotee suggested that he usually asked the Virgin for financial help, and many more of the devout confirmed what Emilia had said—that they bring *all* their concerns to Mary. But visitors told me that three kinds of private instrumental prayers are most important at the Miami shrine. The devout petition the Virgin of Charity about mental and physical health, conception and birth, and marriage and family.[39]

Prayers for healing. Religion and healing combine at many Catholic shrines—at Lourdes and La Salette, in the city of Chicago and the village of Chimayó. Whether it is carrying holy water home from Lourdes, fingering holy dirt at El Santuario de Chimayó, or dabbing holy oil from St. Jude's Chicago shrine, many Catholics have turned to popular devotions for healing. In a similar way, they have turned to Our Lady of Charity. In sixteenth-century Spain she was associated with miraculous cures and enshrined in a hospital named in her honor in Illescas, and she found her first home in El Cobre in the chapel of the hospital adjoining the shrine. Since the Virgin was moved to the main altar of the shrine in the middle of the seventeenth century, Cuban pilgrims, like those elsewhere in the Mediterranean and Latin America, have placed wax limbs and crutches inside the Cobre shrine, which one observer called "the Lourdes of Cuba." They do so to attest to the miraculous intervention of the Virgin in their lives. For those who know that the shrine in El Cobre collects and displays many material expressions of thanks for cures in the "Miracle Room" behind the main altar, the interior of the Miami shrine seems remarkably uncluttered, even sanitized. Inside the Miami shrine, which by an accident of history sits next to a Catholic hospital, no artifacts testify to the Virgin's healing power there, since the clergy and confraternity remove any that are left by pilgrims. That does not mean, however, that Cubans do not turn to Our Lady of Charity when they confront the limits of body and mind. They do.[40]

Some confront psychological problems. Anna, a fifty-two-year-old who dangles a locket of the Virgin around her neck, asked the Virgin for peace of mind, she told me. Anna has prayed to Our Lady of Charity since she was a child in Havana, and she turned to her again for help when clinical depression set in. In turn, the Virgin listened: "She is a miracle worker. I feel that she hears me." The Virgin of Cobre provided "tranquility and peace," she told me in 1992. "When I felt depressed, the Virgin cured my depression."[41]

Many others petition Our Lady of Charity to heal wounds or cure illness, either during the regularly scheduled "healing masses" or at other times, and that function intensifies at the Miami site in some ways because the shrine borders a Catholic hospital. Relatives and friends, and the patients themselves when they are released, visit the shrine next door. For instance, one elderly couple walked slowly to the front portal one day in March, the wife staying nearby as her husband used an aluminum walker to inch toward the altar. Despite his pale complexion and trembling arms, he smiled meekly. I tried to talk with him, but his wife intervened, protecting him from overexertion, I suspect. The wife agreed to talk, but he did not need to do an interview with me too, she proposed, since "they feel exactly the same." I turned to him and asked if that were true: "Exactly?" "Yes, exactly," he confirmed. She then went on to explain that they had prayed that his operation would be successful.

The Virgin complied. So they decided that right after checking out from Mercy Hospital they would visit the adjoining shrine to offer thanks.[42]

I heard similar stories from pilgrims who came to seek release from suffering—from headaches to tumors. Consider two more. Mercedes, a forty-eight-year-old woman from Las Villas, told me a story about her daughter. They had come that day in 1992 to thank the Virgin for answered prayers. "My daughter was mauled by a dog so I asked the Virgin to heal her, and it was done." Two years later, in 1994, I encountered three visitors who came for healing, two of them in wheelchairs. José, a thirty-six-year-old man wearing a Georgia Tech cap, maneuvered his chair with great skill up the winding ramp to the left entrance. He had been in the wheelchair for some time. That was immediately evident. He visits the shrine often, he later revealed: "The only place I can kneel and pray." He did not mean that literally, since he does not get out of his wheelchair at the Virgin's altar; he meant that the sanctuary is spiritually accessible for him. And that day in June he brought two Brazilian friends with him, an eleven-year-old in a wheelchair and her mother. He approached me first—to ask me to bless the girl. After I explained that I was not a priest and directed him to Father Rivas in the shrine office, we spoke again. José explained that the doctors have told the mother that there is no hope for her daughter, but he did not want either of them to accept that. That is why they made the pilgrimage: "To me it is a special place, where miracles happen. I brought this lady with her little girl to ask for a miracle. She needs one. Faith can heal." With the mother fighting back tears and the young girl quiet, even eerily resigned, the three approached the altar to consult the Virgin.[43]

Prayers for conception and childbirth. On another day at the shrine a forty-two-year-old from Oriente also made her way to the altar, but she came to thank the Virgin for a different sort of miracle. Because Our Lady of Charity is closely associated with childbirth, many visitors—women and couples—also come to ask her that they might conceive and deliver a child. As the 3.5" × 4.5" prayer cards at the shrine assure expectant mothers, the Virgin's "maternal heart" (*corazón maternal*) provides her with special insights and special powers. When she helps them conceive and deliver a child, the devotees return to give thanks. That is what brought a woman from Oriente. "The Virgin saved my daughter," she explained, "and allowed her to be born because I almost lost her in the womb." A month later in 1992, a Chilean married to a Cuban, one who has attachment to Our Lady of Charity, also visited to thank the Virgin for her help in conception. "My husband is Cuban and devoted to the Virgin of Charity. I wanted to have a child, and we tried for eight years. I asked the Virgin for a baby, and so I have come to give thanks to the Virgin because she granted my wish."[44]

Prayers for marriage and family. Even more broadly, Our Lady of Charity helps with marriage and family. As at some other shrines, younger men in their twenties will accompany their fiancées to ask the Virgin to bless their coming union. That is what brought Jeannette and John, an engaged couple. John is a Colombian with "not very much" devotion to Our Lady of Charity, he told me that day in January. He never attends the feast-day mass or any other scheduled ritual at the shrine. Jeannette, however, has deep attachment to the Virgin. Born in Havana and brought to the United States as a teenager, she appeals to Our Lady of Charity during public rituals—masses and rosaries. She also visits the shrine at other times. That day she came to pray for her impending marriage because Our Lady of Charity "is very powerful." She has the power to safeguard their marriage, Jeannette believes. Other Cubans agree, and that is why they also return to reaffirm their commitment to their spouses at the shrine. Some couples celebrate their wedding anniversaries by returning to see the Virgin. In an even more formalized way, Ricardo (whom I introduced in chapter 1) and his wife Claudia renewed their marriage vows in 1991 at the shrine, with Bishop Román officiating.[45]

Once the Virgin has guided them in marriage and helped with childbirth, she remains available to the devout to help them with ongoing family problems. Many Cubans told me how important *la familia* was—much more so than with Anglos, they emphasized. The Cuban family in exile has changed in important ways, however. Cuban Americans still might have a widowed or dependent grandparent living with them, but mothers work outside the home more than their parents did on the island. Courtship patterns have changed too, following American custom: parents are less likely to supervise their unmarried daughters' dating. For most middle-class Cubans in the Miami area, their children—half Cuban, half American—follow the social patterns of the wider culture: they play video games, eat hamburgers, and watch MTV. Their parents, to the clergy's dismay, also intermarry and divorce. They disperse geographically. As the major theological document of exiled clergy puts it, they have "different conceptions and customs." The clergy believe that all these social patterns constitute a "crisis of the family." To remedy this, the shrine graphically admonishes the exiles to avoid the corruptions of American popular culture and exhorts them to set aside a "family night." The schedule of annual events for 1992 presented this message vividly. Four boxes divide the space on the page. The upper left corner depicts four disruptions of Cuban American family life—television, sound systems, telephones, and the habit of retreating to bedrooms alone. Large X's through the television and sound system make the point clear. In the other three squares the clergy use images to call Cubans to rebuild the family by eating, playing, and praying together.[46]

This is an issue on which clergy and laity seem to agree. Both worry about the status of the family and the fate of the children. For lay devotees at the shrine, the concern for family often means mothers praying about children. Consider Pilar's story. A mother of three who arrived from Havana in 1981, Pilar has had devotion to Our Lady of Charity since she was ten years old, a little older than the two children she brought with her that day. As her six-year-old son pulled up flowers on the shrine grounds—I felt guilty about distracting her and, so, being indirectly responsible for her son's re-landscaping—Pilar explained why she had visited that day. At first she told me only that she had come for "personal" reasons. After we spoke awhile longer, however, she revealed more. She told me that her sixteen-year-old daughter is "missing." She ran away from home. "And you believe that maybe the Virgin can help?" I asked. "I hope so," she said as she began to cry. Pilar had come to ask the Virgin to find her lost daughter. Other pilgrims, mostly women, petition the Virgin for help with their teenage or adult children who are lost in other ways—unemployed, abused, or addicted.[47]

Pilgrimage Practices: Vows

Many pilgrims who are worried about their family—or other life crises—also make vows. As at many other Catholic shrines, vows (*votos*) or promises (*promesas*) are important to religious practice in Miami. They specify the reciprocal action the pledger will take in the event of a favorable outcome. One young Cuban-born mother visited the shrine in Miami to keep her promise to the Virgin, she told me in 1994. "I made a promise that if my son was healthy, I was going to bring him to the shrine." This twenty-one-year-old Cuban had a difficult pregnancy, she explained. Now the son was two years old, and the mother completed the spiritual exchange with the Virgin. One sixty-three-year-old mother wears a medal with the Virgin's image on it to fulfill a vow she made about her son. Another younger woman, age twenty-one, keeps her promise to the Virgin in gratitude for the "miracle" she performed by visiting the shrine every Saturday at noon.[48]

That miracle was to safeguard that exile's passage to the United States as she made the dangerous journey by raft in 1989, and many other visitors' vows—and instrumental prayers—are linked with the departure from and return to the homeland. Some Cubans vow that they will visit the shrine in Miami if the Virgin, the protectress of the seas, sustains them on their journey. One middle-aged man who arrived in 1994 asserted, as his three friends nodded their agreement, that "all those who come to Miami from Cuba make a promise to the Virgin that they will come to the shrine if they arrive safely." That claim seems somewhat exaggerated, but he is right about the pattern. Because of promises they made to the national patroness, many recent arrivals make the shrine their first stop in the new land. I met one woman on the day after she had arrived from Cuba: the shrine pilgrimage was her first public act in America. Several pilgrims I encountered also were current residents of Cuba (and thus bound to return soon), who had made vows to visit the Miami shrine if the Cuban government ever allowed them to visit relatives in the United States. In turn, some exiles in Miami have made vows to visit Our Lady's shrine in Cobre. One seventy-three-year-old man from Las Villas, not far from the Bay of Pigs on the southern coast, told me in 1994: "I made a promise [*una promesa*] that if it is possible I would visit the Virgin in Cobre, Oriente, when communism falls."[49]

Like this man's, many vows and prayers concern Cubans, on the island and in the diaspora. Mercedes, who thanked the Virgin for healing her daughter who was mauled by a dog, also confided that her devotion was connected with her feelings for Cuba: "For twenty-two years I have prayed for my country and my brothers [on the island]." The young woman who came to fulfil her vow about pregnancy also told me, that same day, that she prayed "that Cuba soon would be free." Manuel, whom I introduced in the opening of this chapter, came not only to thank the Virgin for helping with his daughters' unnamed "problem." Like the overwhelming majority of Cuban pilgrims I met at the shrine, he reported that he prayed for the "liberation" of the homeland from communism. His devotion to Our Lady of Charity is important to him, he explained, because "it is that which maintains my hope to see my country free, and to return to it is very important."[50]

This, I argue in part III of this book, is the shared nationalistic meaning of the artifacts and practices at the shrine. Gender and generation divide the devout to some extent, and they make the pilgrimage for a variety of reasons and engage in a range of nonliturgical practices. However, most of the predominantly white, middle-class Cubans who visit the shrine in Miami share a common purpose. They come as a dispersed nation to construct collective identity before a shared national symbol.

III ✳ *Shared Meanings at the Shrine*

Figure 19. The busts of national heroes Félix Varela (*left*) and José Martí (*right*) behind the shrine building, facing toward Cuba. In this photograph taken in 1995, the busts form the background for a rally attended by exiles who wave Cuban flags. (Photo by John Jessup.)

4 ✳ *Nationalism, Religion, and Diasporic Identity*

An Interpretive Framework

Even if Manuel and Mercedes also petitioned the Virgin about other personal concerns—about health and family—they told me that they came to pray for Cuba and Cubans. Even if Lucía sang her songs alone on the grass, ladies lounged in lawn chairs by the water, and Oscar circumambulated the shrine for exercise, they also visited the national patroness inside to bring her their concerns about the Cuban community. In that way they had a great deal in common with almost all other Cuban pilgrims to Our Lady of Charity's Miami shrine. Despite their differences, they are bound together by their sadness and longing, by the disorientation of exile—and by their common devotion to Our Lady of Charity as national symbol. Men come as well as women. Those who hail from both eastern and western provinces visit. Even the most unpious teenagers, who cannot recall the smells and sights of the island, acknowledge that the shrine is a special place for Cuban exiles. There at the Virgin's shrine the devout reconnect with the homeland. There they re-create the Cuban community—those on the island and in the diaspora—as an imagined nation.

To provide a theoretical framework for interpreting the shared nationalistic meaning of artifacts and rituals at the shrine, as I do in chapters 5 and 6, here I use the Cuban American case to reflect on how displaced peoples construct diasporic identity. In particular, turning more theoretical than I am elsewhere in this book, I explore how nationalism and religion interact in that cultural process.

Diasporic Nationalism

Cubans in Miami use several terms to name their collective identity—*la diáspora*, *el exilio*, *la nación*—and each points to related but distinguishable components of their self-understanding. "Diaspora," the central term in my analysis here, highlights their dispersion from a center. "Exile" signals that the dispersion was not fully voluntary and that return remains a possibility for some of the dispersed. Their use of the term "nation" to describe themselves signals that the displaced resist the usual associations of that term with a state and territory and instead construct an imagined community that includes those in the homeland and the diaspora.

First, Cuban Americans in Miami describe themselves as part of a diaspora. The notion of a diaspora, or a dispersed people, originally was used to label Jews who had been displaced from their homeland and cultic center. Especially recently, the term has been embraced by a number of groups and those who study them. In that extension of the idea, scholars speak of the African diaspora. It also has been applied, for example, to Armenians, Palestinians, Tibetans, Asian Indians, Chinese, Koreans, Poles, Hungarians, Vietnamese, and indigenous peoples who have migrated within or across national borders.[1]

If the term "diaspora," then, seems to have interpretive power when applied to a range of experiences, it remains difficult to identify precisely what these dispersed peoples share. As James Clifford has argued, it is most helpful to avoid defining "diaspora" too narrowly or certainly. At the same time, the concept loses interpretive power if no working definition is offered. Modifying William Safran's somewhat restrictive list of the main features of a diaspora, I suggest that it points most fundamentally to a group with some shared culture which lives outside the territory that it considers its native place, and whose continuing bonds with that land are crucial for its collective identity. Members of the diaspora need not assign themselves to the same racial, ethnic, or religious group, and they need not feel unaccepted in their host country. They also might feel ambivalently about, or even reject, an actual return to the homeland, although in most cases they will be deeply concerned about its current condition and future state. Further, the displaced share a language, even if some members of the group also speak another tongue as well, and they appeal to common symbols (such as flags, heroes, or parades), even if they struggle among themselves over their meaning. Most important, these migrants symbolically construct a common past and future, and their shared symbols bridge the homeland and the new land.[2]

Taken in this way, "diasporic" might apply to a range of migrants—voluntary, impelled, or forced; permanent, temporary, or circulatory. Some Cubans who fled to Miami were ordered to do so after being released from prison. Most, however, were not forced to flee in this way. In that sense, their migration was impelled rather than forced, to use a distinction that some scholars have drawn. Most Cubans had some say in whether they left after the revolution of 1959. It was not always—as with some "removals" of Indian peoples in the Americas—at the point of a gun. At the same time, Cubans in Miami usually portray their migration, whether it followed the revolution by months or decades, as beyond their control to a great extent. Neither entirely forced nor fully voluntary, then, these migrants see themselves as displaced by political forces set in motion by the socialist revolution. It is in this sense that they understand themselves as political exiles.[3]

Not all diasporic groups feel compelled to leave their natal land, nor do they all envision their new life as an exile, but those who do often retain stronger emotional attachments to the homeland and experience even more disorientation in the host country. This makes sense because, as the geographer Yi-Fu Tuan has suggested, "to be forcibly evicted from one's home and neighborhood is to be stripped of a sheathing, which in its familiarity protects the human being from the bewilderments of the outside world." The exiled community's sense of meaning and identity is threatened because it has lost contact with the natal landscape, which is "personal and tribal history made visible." Exile is, as Edward Said has put it, "the unhealable rift forced between a human being and a native place, between the self and its true home." Both Said and Tuan emphasize spatial separation, but exile involves a disruption of time as well as a disorientation in space. "Before" and "after" periodize exilic history, just as "here" and "there" map exilic space. This can be seen, for instance, in the way one Cuban American writer in Miami signed the introduction to a collection of essays in Spanish on "the elements of our national identity." At the bottom of the introduction's last page she wrote "Exilio, 22 de agosto de 1993," marking this moment as a time after disruption and this place as a space apart.[4]

If diasporic time and space are both reoriented, the space of exile is especially odd. As one character in a Cuban American novel opined, "Cuba is a peculiar exile. . . . We can reach it by a thirty-minute charter flight from Miami, yet never reach it at all." This refers not only to the difficulties—some of them very real—involved in visiting the island. Even if they could reach it by air, or boat, they could not arrive.

This is clear if you consider the use of the term "la nación" (nation) by the Cuban American diaspora in South Florida. For example, the Miami writer who marked the date of her book's introduction by noting that it was a time of exile also referred to the Cuban "nation" (*la nación*) and "national identity" (*la identidad nacional*) in that collection of essays. But what can that mean in this context? Whatever it might mean for exiles in general and Cubans in particular, "nation" cannot refer to either a state or a territory. For most exiles in Miami, Castro's socialist government is seen as the main problem, and the displaced live outside their homeland's political boundaries. What the use of the term points to in this context is the constructed character of national identity. Here, however, my interpretation diverges slightly from that of some Cubans in Miami, who would protest that their national identity is not so much imaginatively *constructed* as it is faithfully rediscovered or steadfastly reaffirmed. One Cuban exile and Marian devotee in Miami who read portions of this book in draft politely dissented from my view on this point: "I do not feel that our case is about 'constructing' our identity, which is by far long defined. Instead, I would say that we 'reaffirm' or we 'act to keep alive' our national identity." I see his point, of course. There is a sense in which national identity has a past. When Miami exiles wave the Cuban flag or sing the Cuban anthem (or pray to the national Virgin), they do not create a new emblem or compose a new song. It is precisely *because* others before them have waved that flag and sung that anthem that these practices hold emotional power. Still, and here is where my interpretation begins to diverge, the meanings of those shared symbols and practices have varied over time and among groups on the island, as has the meaning of Cuban identity. Although exiles might project national symbols and practices (and one contemporary meaning of them) into a distant past, they arose at a particular historical period and in a distinctive political context: in the Cuban case it was the nineteenth and early twentieth centuries, during and after the wars for independence. For Cubans and others, nationhood is dynamic, not fixed, and created, not given. That is even more clear when those using the term are exiles, those living outside the political borders. For exiles, *nation* becomes deterritorialized. It is a supralocal or transregional cultural form, an imagined moral community constituted by the diaspora and those who remain in the homeland.[5]

Diasporic nationalism, then, refers to a displaced group's attachment to the traditions and geography of the homeland; but like other forms of nationalism, diasporic images of nationhood are multiple and contested, even within the same migrant community. There is no such thing as diasporic nationalism in general: migrants always construct (and long for) a particular image of the nation's cultural landscape—and its present, past, and future. An antisocialist form of Cuban diasporic nationalism, with its antipathy for Fidel Castro and celebration of democratic capitalism, is advocated by the overwhelming majority of Cuban residents in Miami, and it is the only view I heard expressed at the Virgin's shrine. To understand this popular form of diasporic nationalism, which I focus on in this book, it is important to realize that one's political stance in Cuban Miami is defined to a great extent by one's attitude to Fidel Castro, the contemporary socialist state, and those who remain on the island. As one Cuban exile who has championed a moderating position has suggested, "Within this web of representations born of the Cold War, there is little room for a more nuanced and complex vision of how Cubans on the island and in the diaspora give meaning to their lives, their identity, and their culture in the aftermath of a battle that has split the nation at the root." In terms of the stereotypes, then, for many exiled Cubans the islander is a "brainwashed cog of a Marxist state," and from the perspective of many on the island the exile is "a soulless worm lacking any concern for social justice." In turn, in Cuban Miami's Spanish-language public sphere there is little room for those who profess any sympathy for Castro or socialism, or for those who offer more nuanced judgments of the revolution—for instance, acknowledging that education and health care have been improved while condemning the government's ongoing repression of real and imagined opponents. A small minority in Miami who are more sympathetic to the revolution, or who profess that their primary concern is with the people themselves and not the government, advocate contact, exchange, and dialogue with Cubans on the island. And they sometimes have found themselves the victims of coercion and violence. The most fervent anticommunists in the Miami exile community vigorously reject all contact. Although they welcome temporary visitors and new migrants from Cuba, they do not travel to the island or send packages to relatives there. For this large segment of the local population, even donations of medicine and food are suspect—not, they say, because they wish those on the island ill but because these exchanges extend the rule of a tyrannical dictator. To send a dollar or an antibiotic is to support the communist government another day.[6]

And to end socialist rule in Cuba and replace it with a democratic government and capitalist economy is the aim of the vast majority in the Miami exile community. Some of those who are more sympathetic to the socialist revolution interpret this predominant form of diasporic longing as a morally dangerous nostalgia for the privileges and inequities of the Bastista regime of the 1950s, a reactionary desire for a Cuba with rampant illiteracy, widespread corruption, economic disparity, and poor health care. While many of the first middle- and upper-class exiles in Miami—those who arrived in the early 1960s—supported Batista and enjoyed privilege on the island, they would respond by claiming that it is not the social injustices of Batista's Cuba for which they long. They yearn for the freedoms of democracy and the opportunities of capitalism, which (most admit) were not fully realized in 1950s Cuba.

If nationalism involves attachment to the homeland, in expressing diasporic nationalism these anticommunist exiles attach to the utopia of memory (and desire) and not the dystopia of the contemporary socialist state. They celebrate a Cuba that fades with each year of exile—like the paint on the buildings in contemporary Havana—and imagine a "liberated" nation that never fully existed and, for all of their passion, they cannot will into being. That is why exiles cannot go home, even by the short charter flight from Miami. That is why the space of exile is so odd.

For all exiles, no matter which nation they imagine, diasporic nationalism also entails "geopiety," or an attachment to the natal landscape. This includes feelings for the natural terrain, the built environment, and the mental map of neighborhood, town, province, and country. And it involves affection for the remembered traditions. For Miami exiles, that means passionate concern for Cuban culture—including its music, fashion, architecture, language, and food. Some of these cultural practices remain only slightly altered in contemporary Cuba; others exist now only in the diasporic imagination.[7]

Cubans in Miami express diasporic nationalism in a variety of ways. As most Cuban Americans boast, and some non-Latino blacks and Anglos complain, members of the diaspora tenaciously hold to their understanding of the Cuban past and continually plan its democratic capitalist future. In voting, most ask first about the candidate's stance toward communism and Castro. Musicians and singers who have visited Cuba have been banned from performing in the city. Even those who are less consumed with these issues scan the news for signs of instability in the revolutionary government and for stories about the latest *balsero*, or rafter, found bobbing in the Straits of Florida. Spanish-language radio stations hold contests to guess the date that Castro will fall, and local astrologers search the stars for clues. "This is the end," Mary García assured readers of her astrology column in a Spanish-language magazine in August 1994. "It could be weeks, it could be months, but at this moment Castro's situation is the bleakest I have seen since I have been studying his chart." Equally confident but on different grounds, paramilitary groups, as well as associations of business and education leaders, plan for the future in a free (democratic) and prosperous (capitalist) Cuba. According to surveys, less than one-quarter of Cuban exiles say they definitely would return to live if democracy and capitalism were restored. But even those who might not return still repeat the expression commonly heard at Christmas Eve family gatherings: "¡La próxima Nochebuena nos comeremos el lechoncito en Cuba!" (Next Christmas Eve, we shall eat the traditional roast pork dinner in Cuba).[8]

Cuban Americans express their attachment to the imagined homeland in the arts. Even as Cuban American literature slowly becomes a literature of settlement, to some extent, rather than a literature of exile, memories of a Cuban past and longings for its future have predominated in diasporic poetry and fiction. As one scholar has noted, "The difficulty of returning to Cuba has generated an imaginary island that exists only in an exile's memory and fantasy." Roberto G. Fernández's experi-

mental novel *Raining Backwards* draws heavily on fantasy, as it irreverently documents diasporic memory. One character, a first-generation Cuban in Miami, recalled
a utopic homeland: "In all the beaches in Cuba the sand was made out of grated sil-
ver, though in Varadero it was also mixed with diamond dust." In a similar way,
Cuban American poetry surveys—to use the phrase of one first-generation exile
poet—"the irregular map of [their] nostalgia." Sometimes the map might be a literal
one, as in the poem "The Map" by Ricardo Pau-Llosa, which narrates the tale of a
young Cuban American girl who memorized the locales on the pre-1959 map her
parents had tacked on her bedroom wall. More often it is imagined, as in Pura del
Prado's "Letanía de la patria," a remembrance of the homeland that chants the
phrase "mi patria" (my country) again and again as it charts the sights and smells of
the island.[9]

As part of the imaginative process of creating diasporic identity, migrants often
shape their new environment in the image of the old. Most Cuban exiles, like other
recent American migrants, have lived in cities; so it has been in urban spaces—
alleys, streets, stores, apartments, and parks—that diasporic nationalism has been
expressed most clearly. In Miami, which already has a similar climate and terrain,
exiles have transformed the built environment. Cuban restaurants and businesses
dot the landscape, and streets and parks named after Cuban leaders mark space in
the predominantly Cuban neighborhoods, which spread out in a V-shaped pattern
from the port of Miami.[10]

For example, the diasporic imagination has transformed the cultural landscape of
Little Havana, which is 3.32 square miles of small houses and shops located west of
downtown Miami and adjacent to the Miami River. Ninety-three percent of the district's 70,000 residents are Latino. Others from Latin America, especially Nicaraguans, have moved there since the 1980s, but most of the residents still are Cuban.
And they are transported to their homeland in restaurants like La Carreta and book-
stores like Librería Cervantes that line Calle Ocho, the street that centers the Latin
district and pulses with mambos and salsas each spring as 1 million locals and visitors attend the largest Latino festival in the United States.[11]

Diasporic nationalism is expressed even more clearly in other areas of Little
Havana. One park there is named after José Martí, the leader of Cuba's revolution
against Spain and one of its most beloved political figures (for the left and the right).
Another park that fills with old men playing dominoes, smoking cigars, and dis-
cussing politics is named after Antonio Maceo, a hero of the Cuban war for inde-
pendence. Two blocks east of that park is Cuban Memorial Boulevard. There six
Cuban memorials stand in a row from southwest Eighth Street to southwest Tenth
Street along Thirteenth Avenue: the Bay of Pigs memorial, the memorial for Nestor
A. Izquierdo, a statue of the Virgin Mary, the memorial for José Martí, a large map
of Cuba, and a VFW memorial. For anticommunist Cuban Americans, the Bay of
Pigs memorial has the emotional power of the Vietnam Memorial in Washington,
D.C. The cylindrical stone monument remembers those men of Brigade 2506 who
died during the failed Bay of Pigs invasion in 1961 (figure 20). Atop that civil shrine
a torch burns continuously, symbolizing the enduring commitment of the exiles to
"freedom" for their homeland. If the shrine to Our Lady of Charity in Miami is the
religious center for most in the antisocialist Catholic exile community, this monu-

Figure 20. The Bay of Pigs memorial on Cuban Memorial Boulevard in Little Havana. The inscription reads: "Cuba. To the Martyrs of the Assault Brigade. April 17, 1961." The monument memorializes the failed attempt by United States–trained Cuban exiles to overthrow the government of Cuba.

ment and the other five that share this public space in Little Havana mark its political center. In the Martí memorial, the most recent addition to this space, religious and political sentiments blend. On the rectangular white stone block mounted on the dark concrete monument sits an image of Our Lady of Charity. The Virgin is at the center and top of the plaque, the largest image there. Just below her image is the Spanish inscription dedicating the monument to the leader of the independence movement and the other "martyrs who have spilled their blood for the liberty of Cuba." A large image of the Cuban island, in metal on poured concrete, stands yards

Figure 21. Another of the six nationalist monuments that line Cuban Memorial Boulevard in Little Havana. In this one, exiles map the homeland onto the new urban landscape by affixing an image of Cuba onto a concrete background.

farther down the same street (figure 21). It quite literally maps the terrain of the homeland onto the urban landscape, as its abstract, meditative quality—there are no divisions on the image—encourages viewers to contemplate the imagined nation and project onto it their memories and hopes. Their contemplation might be encouraged further by the inscription. It is a passage from José Martí—"la patria es agonía y deber"—that reminds them that a free homeland emerges through suffering and duty.

Around the corner from that image of the island is the headquarters of one of *los municipios en el exilio*, and those organizations also imaginatively map the history and geography of the homeland onto the new urban landscape. Prerevolutionary Cuba was divided into six provinces and 126 municipalities or townships (map 2). In Miami, those organizations, the "municipalities in exile," preserve and intensify old regional and local affiliations. There are 110 officially recognized *municipios en el exilio*. Twenty of them have permanent buildings, and some of the larger ones, like Havana and Santiago de Cuba, list almost a thousand members and meet a few times each year. In their official headquarters, or in rented halls and restaurants, those who hail from the same Cuban township regularly congregate to sip Cuban coffee and converse about common concerns. Many of these organizations also publish newsletters. A representative issue of a typical bulletin, one distributed to members of the township of Santa Cruz del Sur in 1994, included poems with nationalistic referents, a quotation from José Martí, advertisements from Cuban merchants, and news of births, birthdays, and deaths in the extended families of the exiles from that town. At the bottom of the second page was a simple drawing of the Cuban island, all in black, with three words inscribed below it—"Cuba será libre"—expressing the diaspora's hopes for a liberated homeland.[12]

Diasporic Religion

The editor of that newsletter is an active member of the Confraternity of Our Lady of Charity and a frequent visitor to the shrine in Miami, and that is not surprising because national and religious meanings intertwine as diasporas construct collective identity. That is especially clear when the object of devotion, Our Lady of Charity, is the national patroness. As I have argued, Our Lady of Charity had been associated with Cuban collective identity since the late nineteenth century. Cubans' linking of religion, place, and identity, however, is hardly unique.[13]

Most theorists of religion since the Enlightenment have privileged time over space in their analysis, though some locative referents indirectly informed their thinking. Some classifications of religions had little to do with place, such as those that distinguished traditions according to their views about ultimate reality (monotheistic, polytheistic, and so on) or according to their doctrinal soundness as measured by the standards of the classifiers' traditions (true and false). Yet other classificatory schemes implicitly refer to space as they sort religions according to their degree of diffusion. An evolutionary model that had influence in the late nineteenth and early twentieth centuries distinguished increasingly "developed" forms of religion, those that cross geographical boundaries, from those tied to a particular place. C. P. Tiele, in his influential article on "Religions" for the ninth edition of *Encyclopedia Britannica*, set up a scale of five religious types, from localized "primitive naturalism" to transnational "universal religions." The local is denigrated in this scheme. Devotion to sacred powers connected with a natural space, as in many indigenous traditions, is subordinated to the supposed "placelessness" of Christianity, Buddhism, and Islam. Theorists who have followed this flawed line of thinking—and there have been many—acknowledge that these supralocal religions have their sacred centers—Jerusalem, Bodh Gaya, and Mecca. At the same time, "universal" religions' alleged superiority rests in part in their claims to cross all boundaries—racial, national, linguistic, and geographical.[14]

Although these classification schemes draw on geographical language in a loose way, they offer little aid for those who want to understand how religions might arise from and inform experiences of place or, to put it differently, how religions might be understood as spatial practices. Other theorists—such as Emile Durkheim and Mircea Eliade—have explored the significance of place more fully. Although I might want to modify their views on other grounds, I think that we owe them a debt because they introduced into the study of religion more serious attention to place. Durkheim's understanding of religion as a "system of beliefs and practices relative to sacred things, that is to say, things *set apart*," prepared the way not only to notice the mapping of the world into sacred and profane space but also to consider how, extending the analysis further, religions might be understood as spatialized and spatializing cultural forms.[15]

Without denying their temporal dimensions, it can be useful, especially in the analysis of *displaced* peoples, to highlight the significance of locality for religion. As the historians of religion Jonathan Z. Smith and Charles H. Long have suggested, religions can be understood as ongoing cultural processes whereby individuals and groups map, construct, and inhabit worlds of meaning. This involves affect

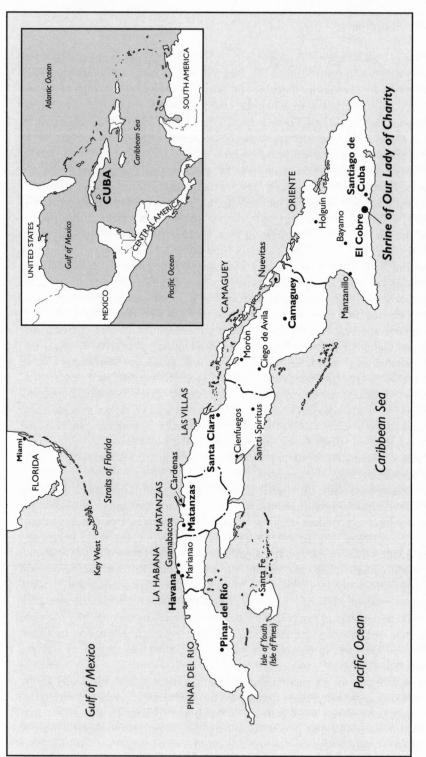

Map 2. The six (prerevolutionary) provinces of Cuba and the shrine in El Cobre. (Adapted from Thomas D. Boswell and James R. Curtis, *The Cuban-American Experience: Culture, Images, and Perspectives* [Totowa, N.J.: Rowman and Allanheld, 1983], 13.)

as well as cognition, as followers form emotional bonds with spaces and places. Religious cartography also is active, not passive; processive, not static; constructed, not given; and contested, not consensual. In this sense religions involve power as well as meaning. In my view, constructing place religiously involves engaging in contests with others within the natural terrain and at social sites. The latter include not only churches, workplaces, and homes but also bodies, laws, and artifacts. With and against others in the community, I suggest, religious men and women are continually in the process of mapping a symbolic landscape and constructing a symbolic dwelling in which they might have their own space and find their own place. They map religious space in a variety of ways—ritually, narratologically, philosophically, legally, materially, and institutionally.[16]

This religious orientation in space also informs collective identity. Where we stand names who we are. As Jonathan Z. Smith noted, "It is through an understanding and symbolization of place that a society or individual creates itself." Religious women and men are most truly themselves when they are *in place*. That place, however, is not "natural" or given; it is contested and constructed. Collective identity, including religious identity as it fuses with national identity, is created over and over again through narrative, artifact, and ritual. In this sense it is precarious.[17]

The significance of religious mapping, as well as the precarious character of both spiritual cartography and identity formation, seems clearest when peoples become *out of place*. How does the disorientation of migration affect displaced people's attempts to map, construct, and inhabit worlds of meaning? In the remainder of this chapter, I sketch the outlines of an answer to this question. Drawing on my study of Cuban American devotion at the Miami shrine, I offer a tentative characterization of "diasporic religion."[18]

In *Map Is Not Territory* Jonathan Z. Smith offers help in this regard. Smith identifies two "coeval existential possibilities" for religious mapping of the world. The "locative" or native worldview emphasizes place. It is associated with the center. The second possible mode of religious cartography, according to Smith, is "utopian" rather than locative. This vision, which he identifies as that of diasporas and exiles, values transcending space or being "no place." It is associated with the periphery. According to Smith, then, the worldview of those in the homeland is locative, while that of the diaspora is, we might say, supralocative.[19]

Smith draws on a variety of sources to illustrate, most often from late antiquity; and his model reveals much about the religious life of displaced peoples, especially Jews who found themselves dispersed without a sacred center after the destruction of the Temple. Smith suggests that "for the native religionist, homeplace, the place to which one belongs, was *the* central religious category." That changed in exile. "There was a lessening of concern on the part of those in the diaspora for the destiny and fortunes of the native land and a relative severing of the archaic ties between religion and the land." Certain cultic centers, he claims, might remain the site of pilgrimage, but the old beliefs in national deities and their sacred places will be "weakened." Smith's analysis illumines the experience of later generations of "exiles," who seem to diminish their bonds with the homeland over time. Those "thoroughly diasporic members" seem, to varying degrees, to disentangle their identity from the natal land.[20]

Yet my study of Cuban exiles in Miami suggests a slightly different model. If the Cuban American case is illustrative, attachment to the homeland is extremely powerful in the first generation religion and persists for a generation or more after that, depending on a variety of factors. As Smith himself noticed but did not emphasize, the new immigrant in a diaspora might express "nostalgia for the homeplace" and find "cultic substitutes for the old sacred center." Indeed, longing for the homeland is a central component of diasporic identity as it is negotiated religiously.[21]

Despite the diverse motives that bring visitors to the shrine to Our Lady of Charity in Miami, the overwhelming majority share a preoccupation with their native land and its people. As pilgrims repeatedly told me, a primary reason they come to the Virgin's shrine is to pray for Cuba. One middle-aged female visitor, who was in Miami only temporarily and had to return to Cuba in a few weeks, explained that "all is connected for me, the homeland [*patria*] and the Virgin." Those who reside more permanently in exile share her views. When I asked pilgrims why they came to the shrine, many told me what one man from South Florida said—"because she is our patroness." They come, then, not only to petition the Virgin for health and wealth, or to ask for aid with other personal crises in their lives. They come to pray for the Cuban "nation," on the island and in the diaspora. Luisa, who had arrived from Havana twenty-five years earlier, told me that she visited the shrine one afternoon, just after thousands of *balseros* had taken to the sea to find American shores, "in order to pray to the most holy Virgin for all the Cuban rafters and that our country will be free one day." Dolores, a middle-aged woman who had arrived six years earlier, revealed that attachment to the homeland was at the root of her passionate devotion to Our Lady of Charity: "The Virgin of Charity is the patroness of our country, and I pray to her often for the freedom of our beloved Cuba." Dolores's devotion to the Virgin began in Cuba when she was five years old, and now that she is in exile, her devotion not only transports her spatially to the homeland but also carries her back in time—to her childhood and her country's past.[22]

For Cubans in Miami and other displaced peoples, diasporic religion, like diasporic nationalism, is transtemporal and translocative. Diasporic peoples' identity formation involves movement across time and space. I use the prefix "trans-" rather than "bi-" to signal that diasporic peoples do not inhabit two times or two places, as is sometimes said. They are not *bi*temporal and *bi*locative. Rather, if Cuban Americans are representative, migrants are constantly moving "across"—the meaning of the prefix "trans-"—history and geography. Diasporic time is fluid, slipping from constructed past to imagined future, and both the past and future inform the experience and symbolization of the present. Diasporic religion, in turn, negotiates diasporic identity as followers remember the homeland's past and imagine its future. Similarly, diasporic space shifts continually between here and there, Miami and Havana, homeland and exile. Diasporic religion is translocative.

In proposing this theory, I modify Smith's typology of religious mapping by adding a third possibility and reformulating the other two. In my view, then, religions can map and inhabit worlds of meaning in at least three ways. These might be described as *locative*, in which religion is associated with a homeland where the group now resides; *supralocative*, which names the inclination in later generations of some diasporic peoples to diminish or deny the significance of both the homeland and the adopted land in their religious life; and *translocative*, my focus here, which refers to the tendency among many first- and second-generation migrants to symbolically move between homeland and new land.

These translocative and transtemporal impulses are expressed religiously in a variety of ways in diasporic religion. In religious *narratives*, diasporas remember and compose tales that express attachment to the natal land, sacralize the new land, or form bridges between the two. The people and the clergy compose stories about the suffering and disorientation of displacement. Cuban priests narrate them in public spaces, like pulpits and magazines. The people, too, tell their stories, and not only in private conversations. For instance, María Elena, a recently arrived lay devotee in Hialeah, wrote a poem in Spanish in 1994 that narrated her own story of displacement; she then mailed it to Bishop Román at the shrine. She closed the twenty-seven-stanza poem with the hyperbole and passion that characterize much exilic narrative, oral and written. Turning to capital letters and exclamation points to make sure the reader would not underestimate the force of her sentiment, María Elena wrote:

> TU ERES LA TIERRA MÁS BELLA
> QUE HAN VISTO LOS OJOS HUMANOS!!!!!!!!!
> [You are the most beautiful land
> That human eyes have ever seen]

What makes this poem—which probably never will be published—significant for understanding diasporic narrative is that it repositions the reader, and the author, in time and space by telling stories and juxtaposing images of the homeland. What makes this diasporic narrative *religious* is that the Virgin of Charity is the leading character in the author's biography and her homeland's history. "Our lives," María Elena explains, "rest in Her." Finally, it is the Virgin who "offers liberty" for Cubans and thus promises to bring the sad tale of displacement to its joyful end.[23]

Even more important than these sorts of personal narratives, however, traditional myths about nationalistic deities and saints—such as the Cuban story of the miraculous discovery of the image of Our Lady of Charity in the Bay of Nipe—become especially important in exile. And those are remembered in domestic spaces and recounted, again and again, in public sites like the shrine. The shrine clergy tell the story often.

Diasporic *theology* also is translocative and transtemporal. It is bound up with the nation's history and territory in important ways. Those who articulate diasporic theology, especially but not exclusively the religious leaders, focus on the community's past and the homeland's fate. They also become more concerned than ever to define the tradition doctrinally as the group struggles to maintain a national identity in the face of a host culture that appears to threaten it. What was taken for granted in the homeland, and perhaps not well defined, seems to need greater delineation in the new cultural landscape. This, I suggest, explains the Cuban clergy's vigorous efforts at the shrine to prevent the "mixture" of Santería and Catholicism. In addition, diasporas highlight dominant symbols with nationalistic significance in their doctrinal articulation of the faith more than they might have done if they had not experienced dislocation. This explains, in part, the Cuban clergy's strategic efforts to refer centrally to the Cuban patroness in their reconstructions of Catholic doctrinal "orthodoxy."

The special attention to collective history, the heightened concern for orthodoxy, and the increased attention to national symbols appear again and again in sermonic theology and published reflections. Cuban clergy regularly set out the doctrines of their diasporic faith in homilies from the shrine pulpit, in pamphlets published by the shrine, and in local religious periodicals like *La Voz Católica, Ideal*, and *Cuba diáspora*. The main features of diasporic theology are also clear in the most systematic theological statement produced so far by the Cuban exile community, the final document of Las Comunidades de Reflexión Eclesial Cubana en la Diáspora (CRECED). CRECED was a two-year project (1990–92) organized by the Cuban clergy outside the island. It aimed to renew the faith of the scattered Cubans, reflect on their obligations at that historical moment, recover "the historical memory and the Cuban and Catholic identity" of exiles, celebrate the fifth centenary of the Evangelization of the Americas, and "renew spiritual ties with our Church in Cuba." The final document, which was compiled and composed by three exiled Cuban bishops (Boza of Venezuela, Enrique San Pedro of Galveston, and Román of Miami), has four main parts. The first and second sections of the document survey the history of Cuban religion, on the island and in exile. There the concern for natal land and national history is emphasized. The third and fourth sections offer theological reflection and pastoral direction. The pastoral section outlines a "nueva evangelización" that aims to purify popular religion and attract exiles to the institutional church. Finally, the document's theological section begins by talking about "la iglesia peregrina" (the pilgrim church) and explores the biblical foundation for a diasporic theology by elevating the Jews of the Babylonian exile as "a model" for Cubans. This theological reflection culminates, in a revealing way, by celebrating the dominant national symbol, Our Lady of Charity. "Mary, invoked under the name of Our Lady of Charity," the widely distributed document declares, "speaks in a special way to the Cuban community on the island and in the diaspora. It is valid to say that Mary of Caridad constitutes a living synthesis [*una síntesis viva*] of all the yearnings, the faith, the hope, and the love of the Cuban people." As the community looks toward the future, this clerical theology suggests, that dominant symbol is important for their continued journey as an exiled people: "With Her as our guide and protectress we continue our pilgrimage, until arriving at the dawn of our final liberation."[24]

Diasporic religion involves more than narrating collective history and theologizing about dominant symbols. Religious *institutions* also emerge in the adopted country in relation to the homeland and its history. These translocative institutions are important for the diaspora, even more important than they were before the displacement. As I have argued, many of those who might have been "unchurched" or at least ambivalent about clergy and churches also identify more closely with diasporic religious institutions. Cubans in Miami, like other exiles, affiliate with parishes more fully and attend services more regularly than they did in the homeland.

Diasporic religious institutions like the Confraternity of Our Lady of Charity at the Miami shrine focus on shared nationalistic symbols with historical importance. That institution also maps the landscape of the homeland onto Miami by organizing the list of 42,000 members according to native regional affiliation. The confraternity, then, is the religious equivalent of the "municipalities in exile." As with those secular organizations, exiles from the same township are brought together. The confraternity at the shrine does this in an ingenious way. Each of the 126 townships is reconstituted and celebrated in one weekday mass during the year. Using the membership list to identify devotees, volunteers from the confraternity spend hours telephoning exiles to invite them to the mass for their township. Alfredo, a member of the confraternity who makes many of these calls, told me that they remind members whom they contact that the mass for their native region is coming soon. They then record information to update their files on the exiles, so that they can be sure to stay in touch. Through this exilic institution, then, the dispersed return to their past and their native region.[25]

As with those weekday masses for the 126 townships, diasporic *rituals* bridge the two worlds and construct an imagined community, the Cuban "nation." In this sense the horizontal rather than the vertical dimension of ritual is emphasized. As I argue more fully in chapter 6, diasporic ritual moves participants outward more than upward, forging bonds with others in the homeland and in exile. Rituals connected with unifying mythic figures, such as Our Lady of Charity, are emphasized. Unifying impulses can arise, often by necessity, as groups who were separated in the homeland join each other to worship in the same place. As in most Hindu temples in the United States, multiple regional or tribal deities might be housed together in the diaspora. In this sense, too, translocative ritual behavior draws the displaced together. In a similar way, those carrying the Cuban patroness through the crowd after the festival mass in Miami and those participating by waving handkerchiefs, singing, and shouting create bonds among exiles—black and white, young and old, rich and poor, male and female. Since the Virgin also remains a dominant symbol associated with Cuban nationality on the island, the Miami diaspora also ritually aligns itself with those who remain there.[26]

Finally, religious *artifacts* also take on great significance in exile because of their ability to transport followers to the homeland—and its remembered past and imagined future. Those diasporic artifacts are of four main kinds—utilitarian objects, art, architecture, and cultural landscape. For instance, some artifacts are self-consciously created as objects of art. One middle-aged devotee carried to the festival mass in 1992 a five-foot canvas on which she had painted in oil an image of the patroness. This self-trained artist exhibited her noncommissioned work in a makeshift gallery by leaning it against a wall to the right of the altar. Elsewhere in Miami, even the children of the exile are encouraged to use and create aesthetic objects with religious meanings. A coloring book, distributed by the most prominent Cuban radio station, printed the contours of the Virgin's image. The Spanish-language message beside it on the page identified her as the patroness of Cuba, narrated her discovery at sea, and instructed the young artists who were about to take up their crayons: "The cape is blue and adorned with gilding; the dress is white, and the aura is golden."[27]

Buildings like the shrine transform the natural terrain they inhabit, and both those buildings and the larger cultural landscapes they create are artifacts. Just as Cubans express diaspora nationalism in Little Havana, they inscribe diasporic religion on Miami's cityscape—in yard shrines, cafeterias, cemeteries, and churches. Of these transtemporal and translocative religious artifacts in the urban landscape, the shrine to Our Lady of Charity is the most important. In the next chapter I consider more fully the significance of that shrine—as well as the objects that fill it and the environment that surrounds it—for exiles' construction of diasporic identity.

5 ✳ *Religious Artifacts and Diasporic Identity*

More than 10,000 Cuban exiles gathered on a chilly Sunday afternoon in 1973 to dedicate the new shrine of Our Lady of Charity in Miami—waving flags, singing songs, and chanting petitions to the national patroness. After six years of work, the committee of laity and clergy that had assumed responsibility for planning and constructing the building had managed to raise $420,000, mostly in small donations from recent exiles who could not afford it. The conical-shaped concrete structure, which they had toiled so hard to build, rose ninety feet above the crowd (see figure 11). Over the portal was a tiled image of Our Lady of Charity; perched on the rear were busts of two influential nineteenth-century Cubans. The focus inside was the pedestaled fifteen-inch statue of the patroness, the one that had been smuggled out of Cuba in 1961. In front of her stood the marble altar and the steps that led down to the circular interior. There only 290 chairs (replicas of *los taburetes*, traditional Cuban stools made of wood and leather) awaited the Virgin's devotees in the small shrine. No one knew then that on many nights 400 or 500 Cubans, with more spilling out down the steps, would crowd into that small space, pressing close to the patroness. Only the throng outside for the dedication that day signaled how important this shrine would become for Cubans in the diaspora.[1]

The building came to be important for a variety of reasons, and observers inscribed onto it a range of meanings. As I noted in part II, for some visitors it is a Santería holy site; for the clergy, by contrast, it is a Catholic missionary outpost. Some laity and clergy compare it to the Statue of Liberty because it serves as "a place of refuge" for migrants. For others the building is a source of miracles, a tourist destination, or a recreation area: visitors journey there to be healed, return to their "ethnic roots," or lounge in a lawn chair by the water's edge.[2]

In the idiom of art history, the shrine is an instance of "sculptural modernism." It is "sculptural" because, like Charles-Edouard Le Corbusier's famous chapel in Ronchamp, France, its design uses "molded concrete forms." As with other "modern" architecture, the shrine's Cuban American designer eschewed ornament, displayed twentieth-century technology, revealed the building's structure, and created free-

flowing spaces in, around, and through it. Few Cuban visitors, however, used this
art-historical language to describe the shrine. One twenty-four-year-old visitor did
tell me in 1994 that the edifice was "moderno"; but she, like the other devotees, was
less concerned with its modern form than with its religious function.[3]

It is, after all, a pilgrimage site. As such it shares many features—formal and
functional—with the more than 360 Catholic shrines in the United States and thousands of pilgrimage centers, Christian and non-Christian, around the world. Like
other shrines, which literally are "receptacles" of sacred meaning and power, the
building dedicated to Our Lady of Charity in Miami memorializes earlier miracles,
enshrines an image, heals infirm pilgrims, transmits religious tradition, and delin-
eates sacred topography by thresholding this world and the other that lies beyond.[4]

But there is more going on. Like other structures consecrated by diasporic peoples, the Miami shrine functions as a transtemporal and translocative religious symbol. It not only transmits lore about the past but also imagines a liberated future. It
not only vertically links the profane and the sacred realms but also propels Cuban
exiles out toward the homeland, uniting those on the island and in the diaspora as
an imagined nation. This, I suggest, is the *shared* meaning of the shrine, the artifacts that fill it, and the landscape that surrounds it. For the overwhelming majority
of the lay visitors with whom I spoke, and for Cuban clergy as well, the building is
a shared national symbol.

This has been evident since its dedication in 1973. At the dedication ceremony,
according to the newspaper's account, one woman who was "overcome by emotion"
bounded through a security line to the elevated platform where the mass was being
performed. There she prayed before the shrine's central portal, with a statue of the
patroness in one hand and the Cuban flag in the other. A man in the crowd, also
overwhelmed with emotion, reported that "today I feel as if I am in Cuba. Even the
sky resembles the Cuban sky." To ask the Virgin to transport all exiles there, those
around him in the crowd chanted, "Virgen de la Caridad, devuélvenos a Cuba" (Virgin of Charity, return us to Cuba). Those sentiments, and the significance of the
building as a diasporic symbol, have intensified as the years of exile have passed.
By the 1990s, the building had become "the other Cuba," in the phrase of Vicente,
an Afro-Cuban devotee. "It is . . . the Cuba which Castro separated from their families, the Cuba which has wept and bled to live in exile." At the same time, the shrine
not only embodied the suffering diaspora; it also reconstituted that diaspora as the
imagined "nation," transporting exiles to the homeland before separation and after
liberation. In this chapter I explore how the shrine functions as a diasporic religious
symbol, highlighting its significance for the construction of collective identity and
considering, in turn, the site, the interior, and the exterior.[5]

The Site: The Sea and the Island

As students of material culture have suggested, artifacts include not only artistic
representations, utilitarian objects, and architectural spaces but also cultural landscapes. More specifically, the terrain as modified by humans can be understood as
an artifact with significance for diasporic identity. This is true not only of patriotic

monuments in Little Havana or yard shrines in Hialeah, however. Even the natural terrain immediately surrounding the shrine to Our Lady of Charity in Miami—the lawn, palms, and bay—can be understood as a diasporic artifact (see figure 18).[6]

Yet it might have been otherwise. When Bishop Coleman F. Carroll first explored the possibility of a Cuban shrine, in a letter to a Cuban American priest in 1964, he had not settled on a site. "The thought occurred to me," Carroll wrote in confidence, "that perhaps somewhere in the Miami Diocese there should be a shrine in honor of Our Lady of Cobre, possibly at St. John Bosco Parish, Flagler Street, the grounds of the Mercy Hospital, St. Peter's and Paul's, or Corpus Christi Parish." If the shrine had been built on that downtown Miami street or at one of those three urban parish churches it would have been a very different place.[7]

Instead, by the time Carroll proposed in 1966 that Cubans build the shrine, he had already decided to position it on the one-acre site beside the Catholic hospital, where his predecessor, Archbishop Joseph P. Hurley of St. Augustine, had planned to construct a monument to the Catholic "martyrs" to communism in eastern Europe. Many Cuban American pilgrims to the Virgin's shrine told me that the selection of that site enhanced its power as a diasporic symbol because it was aligned with the island and juxtaposed to the sea. That accident of history, then, has had enormous influence on how Cuban pilgrims have experienced the place.[8]

Further, local exiles designed it so that by standing in front of the patroness's image inside pilgrims are positioned in a line with Cuba. And the rear of the building faces south toward the island homeland, which is approximately 200 miles away. In both ways, exiles told me, the shrine's alignment with the island was important to them. When I asked visitors about the site in structured interviews, time after time they told me that it had special significance because it was "frente a Cuba" or "cerca de la patria." An elderly exile who arrived just after Castro's revolution, for example, claimed that "being close to [the island] we are united with the Virgin of Charity and with Cuba."[9]

Even more frequently, pilgrims mentioned the importance of the shrine's proximity to the sea, which, in turn, had significance for a variety of reasons. For some it linked the site and the narrative of the Virgin's miraculous discovery: one forty-eight-year-old woman from Havana told me that the site was important because "it is beside the sea, and it was in the sea where the original image was found." For others it recalled the topography of the island nation. Carla, an exile who visits every Sunday, said, "For me it has special significance for being close to the sea, since the island of Cuba is surrounded by water on all parts." Sara, a recent arrival from Havana, connected the site, the homeland, and her family. The place reminded her of the sea, she revealed, which evoked images of her father. Also, most exiles arrived by boat or raft, so it memorializes their journey and those of others. "It is right by the water," one woman from Hialeah told me, "closer to Cuba. And the water is the path that we Cubans used to get to this country, including myself." Some noted that the position by the sea reminded them of the *balseros* who continued to arrive on South Florida's shores. The sea, and thus the building by the sea, also repositioned exiles in the homeland. Many visitors emphasized how close the island was: "A couple of miles and there it is," one female exile calculated. One confraternity member feels the space of exile close at that site: "All that separates us [here] is the precious sea." Ramón, a male devotee who was born on the northern coast of Cuba and spent more than three decades near the water there, claimed that just seeing the sea behind the shrine "unites us with Cuba." The site itself, with tropical palms beside the bay that stretches toward the island, transported exiles in time and space. So did the building's interior.[10]

The Interior

In some ways, the shrine's interior looks like many late-twentieth-century Roman Catholic places of worship. Three doors open onto the circular space, two on either side of the sanctuary and one in the narthex. That portal directs visitors down the central aisle toward the chancel. The main altar there is set apart from the back wall so that the priest can face the congregation during the eucharistic celebration, in accord with the prescriptions of the documents of the Second Vatican Council. Near the left entrance a mahogany tabernacle calls visitors to the sacrament. The confessional by the opposite door is "a reminder of God's merciful love and forgiveness," as the official shrine pamphlet proclaims. Two concrete bands encircle the walls leading to the sanctuary, breaking up the vertical interior space; and on the lower band is a scriptural passage in gold lettering that might be found in any Catholic church (except that it is in Spanish). "My soul magnifies the Lord and my spirit rejoices in God my Savior . . ." Somewhat more unusual, the clergy tries to shape the experience of the architectural space, and take advantage of the evangelical opportunity, by playing Spanish-language tapes over the sound system that catechize and exhort the nominal Catholics who visit the Virgin.[11]

Despite the stylistic parallels with Catholic churches and the clerical attempts at evangelization, it is the expressions of diasporic nationalism in the building's interior that stand out for most pilgrims. The clergy remind pilgrims of these nationalist meanings in free pamphlets and many sermons, but the themes already are quite familiar to most Cuban visitors. Consider the vivid expressions of diasporic nationalism in the cornerstone, the statue, the souvenirs, and the mural.

The Cornerstone: Enshrining Native Soil

Those who recall the design and construction of the building have reported that decisions about its form were made by the Construction Committee of the Monument and Shrine to Our Lady of Charity, which included Archbishop Coleman Carroll, two priests, seventeen laypeople, and the pious Cuban architect José Pérez-Benitoa Jr. As they did with other features of the interior and exterior design, the Cuban American committee (the archbishop was the only Anglo) decided to inscribe diasporic significance onto the cornerstone that lies beneath the altar, at the liturgical focus of the Catholic building (figure 22). That six-sided concrete cornerstone, which rests in a triangulated space created at the altar's base, literally maps the natal terrain onto the Miami shrine. Affixed on each of its six sides are samples of soil and stone from the six Cuban provinces. Those fragments were mixed with water taken from a raft on which fifteen refugees perished at sea. The

Figure 22. Cornerstone of the Miami shrine. Each side of the cornerstone contains stone and sand from one of the six provinces of Cuba, thereby reaffirming the regional divisions of the homeland and transplanting the native soil to the new land.

homeland's regional divisions, recent history, marine environment, and native soil all are represented in that powerful diasporic artifact. Further, its triangular shape recalls the contours of the statue of the national patroness directly above it on the altar.[12]

The Central Image: The Virgin

The statue of Our Lady of Charity is the visual and devotional focus of the interior of the shrine (figure 23). The diminutive Virgin—only fifteen inches tall—holds the infant Jesus in her left arm. She wears a golden crown, symbolizing her authority, and a beaded white mantle that spreads out in a triangular shape. Her hair is dark and straight, and her complexion, which identifies her as Cuban, is a shade between the ebony of Ochún in African shrines and the white of Mary in American parishes.

This, of course, is not the image that the three young men supposedly found floating in Cuban waters in the seventeenth century, although it resembles it closely (see figure 5). The original statue remains pedestaled in front of a large and ornate *reredos* in the main altar at her sanctuary in eastern Cuba. Nonetheless, the exiled Marian image has authenticity and power for devotees. In part that is because the Virgin, like the older migrants, came from Cuban soil. As I noted in chapter 1, the Miami Virgin had been enshrined in the parish of Guanabo in the province of

Figure 23. The statue of Our Lady of Charity inside the Miami shrine.

Havana before her exile in 1961. Both her origin in the homeland and her exile in Florida add to the image's sacred power. Our Lady of Charity, the exiles believe, is one of them.[13]

Her image also is marked as holy by its adornment. Like the original statue in Cobre, and many other pilgrimage sculptures and paintings, the statue in the Miami shrine is unimposing. Yet the women of the confraternity regularly sew elaborate new garments for her. For Hilda, who groomed and clothed the patroness for more than a decade, it is a devotional practice which evokes awe and delight simply because it allows intimacy: "I can have her in my arms," she explained. More important for other visitors, however, the adorning of the image marks it as sacred. This, the Virgin's elaborate cloak indicates, is not just any image.[14]

As the art historian David Freedberg has argued persuasively, the power of sacred images, and sculptures and paintings in general, is that they generate diverse and intense responses—emotional, cognitive, and behavioral. Viewers confer meanings onto artifacts; but those objects, in turn, evoke responses in observers. As Freedberg reminds us, viewers "break pictures and sculptures; they mutilate them, kiss them, cry before them, and go on journeys to them; they are calmed by them, stirred by them, and incited to revolt. They give thanks by means of them, expect to be elevated by them, and are moved to the highest levels of empathy and fear."[15]

In a similar way, the image of Our Lady of Charity in the sanctuary evokes powerful responses. Devotees weep, smile, kneel, sing, wave, hope, complain, thank, and petition. She has the power to elicit such responses among Cuban exiles, I suggest, because they have consecrated her as a translocative and transtemporal symbol. She is linked, first of all, with the natal place. One male devotee echoed many other visitors at the shrine when I asked him about the connection between the Virgin and Cuba. "They are the same thing for me since to say Cuba is to say Virgin of

Charity." Time after time shrine pilgrims explained that to look at the image of the national patroness was to see Cuba. In her they encountered the landscapes of the homeland—the home, neighborhood, region, and island.[16]

A second reason that the image in Miami evokes such powerful responses is that it positions devotees temporally. Our Lady of Charity stirs personal and collective memory. For the older exiles, the image calls up both events in the homeland and the people associated with those events—a child's birth, a neighborhood's festival, a grandparent's death. More important for understanding devotion at the shrine, the Virgin has been identified with Cuban struggles for independence, as I noted in chapter 1. As "la Virgen Mambisa," the protector of the Cuban liberators at the turn of the century, she also has special relevance for those who feel forcibly evicted from the homeland. Exiles carry their petitions to the patroness, and she promises them protection; they bring their sadness to the national liberator, and she gives them hope.

Secondary Images: The Souvenir Table

As at almost every pilgrimage site, varied reproductions of the central image are purchased at the shrine to be worn on pilgrims' bodies, displayed in their cars, or niched in their homes. In that way they not only recall the journey but also embody, display, or privatize the national patroness's power to offer protection or inspire hope. In 1995 the shrine staff launched a fund-raising campaign to expand the facilities, and those plans included a gift shop. In the years I visited, however, pilgrims bought artifacts inside the shrine itself. Just inside the central portal the Sisters of Charity or lay women from the confraternity sell mass-produced souvenirs that are displayed on a simple formica-topped folding table. And most of those artifacts—including photographs, statues, prints, medals, shirts, and prayer cards—are charged with nationalistic significance, whether or not they explicitly allude to natal place or collective history.[17]

Some secondary images are intended for display in the home, and many visitors told me that they placed them there. One photograph of the shrine's statue poses the image against a background of the sea. Beneath her are carved representations of the three men who discovered her in Nipe Bay. In one diasporic artifact sold at the shrine, that photograph is mounted on a plastic background with a circular magnet attached. That refrigerator magnet consecrates devotees' kitchens as it holds in place telephone messages, dentist appointments, and children's drawings. A larger but still inexpensive reproduction of that same photograph of the Virgin is hung on bedroom and living room walls. A narrative and prayer fill the space on the opposite side of that ten-inch color photograph, which was printed by the Miami shrine in 1990. The inscription recounts her miraculous appearance, subsequent enshrinement, and proclamation as patroness, and it closes by petitioning the Virgin for protection.

These photographs consecrate domestic space; other secondary images displayed on the souvenir table sacralize cars. Devotees can buy a four-inch plastic statue of the patroness so that she can vibrate from their dashboard as they drive through the streets of exile. They also might purchase a plastic key chain so that as they negotiate

Figure 24. A vendor sells T-shirts inside the front entrance of the Miami shrine on the Virgin's feast day in 1993. At the center of the T-shirt is Our Lady of Charity, with the Cuban flag in the background and two angels hovering on either side. At the bottom is a representation of the discovery of the statue in the seventeenth century and the familiar petition: "Virgen de la Caridad, Salva a Cuba" (Virgin of Charity, Save Cuba). (Photo by Michael Carlebach.)

those streets—and even the elderly women who never learned to drive spend time in automobiles—they can bring their national symbol with them. As the key chain dangles from the ignition, on one side of it they see the patroness. On the other side they see an illustration of her shrine in Miami, identifying her as an exile like them.

Bodies become icons, and many of the diasporic artifacts sold on the souvenir table are worn or carried by devotees. They buy medals bearing the Virgin's image to encircle their necks and prayer cards to crevice in their pocketbooks. In the week before the annual festival, and at other times too, they also might buy T-shirts, like the one made in 1993 that reproduced a colorful image of the patroness and inscribed an often repeated plea, "Virgen de la Caridad, Salva a Cuba" (figure 24).

These diasporic artifacts sold in the shrine express exiles' hopes for a liberated homeland and inscribe memories of their collective past. The large mural that covers the altar wall does this even more vividly.

The Mural: Narrating National History

Continuing a long tradition in the Americas of painting walls with religious images, a tradition shared by indigenous peoples and European colonists, a large mural dominates the Miami shrine's interior space (figure 25). Like the contours of the Virgin's statue, the 740-square-foot painting is wider at the base and narrower at its zenith, rising thirty-six feet from the sanctuary floor. Assembled in panels, not painted directly on the wall, the painting features sixty-three human images executed in varying shades of brown. It was begun in July 1974, several months after the shrine had been dedicated; finished thirteen months later; and consecrated on the patroness's feast day in 1977.[18]

The self-taught Cuban muralist, Teok Carrasco, donated his services for the project, working on his painting for 364 hours. He had been born not far from the original shrine in Oriente province in 1916, the same year that the pope declared Our Lady of Charity Cuba's national patroness. Other paintings that he finished before and after his exile in Miami in 1969 hang in the White House and the Vatican, and his murals adorn architecture in Cuba, Spain, Mexico, and the United States. He volunteered to design and paint the shrine mural, he revealed to me in an interview shortly before his death in 1993, because he had long-standing devotion to Our Lady of Charity and a great love for his natal land.[19]

Many visitors to the Miami shrine, including one male devotee who was born in Cuba ten years after Carrasco, told me that they liked the mural. Most were not offering an aesthetic judgment, however. The painting evoked strong emotions in viewers because Carrasco had managed to combine religious devotion and national sentiment in a narrative that recounted the Cuban past. Carrasco saw himself as a historian: "It is my job as a painter to bring history to life." And the shrine mural, *The History of Cuba in a Glance*, told a story of the Cuban nation from the voyages of Columbus (in the lower left corner) to the journeys of exiles (in the lower right corner). Like Diego Rivera's mural *The History of Mexico*, which adorns the Mexican national palace, Carrasco's work is national history with a point. Unlike Rivera, however, Carrasco did not aim to show the ill effects of colonization, evangelization, and commercialization. There are no Spanish soldiers slaying natives in Carrasco's mural. Instead, colonization and evangelization intertwine benevolently in the left side of the painting, as Carrasco narrates several centuries of his homeland's history. Similarly, on the mural's right side, which recounts the nineteenth and twentieth centuries, Cuban history marches triumphantly and inevitably toward the successful wars for independence, with religious, cultural, and political leaders all playing their parts.[20]

The largest image on the mural is that of the Virgin, who is cloaked in traditional Spanish costume and carrying the infant Jesus. Her central placement makes sense because, for the muralist and most exiles, she is inexorably linked with Cuba's past and future. At the consecration ceremony in 1977, Carrasco explained her place on the mural and in national history: "The Cuban community [*el pueblo cubano*] encounters its salvation in the arms of the Virgin of Charity." Those arms are covered in the mural's painted image of the patroness, but her face, which was modeled on Carrasco's daughter's, looks out benevolently toward the Cuban visitors in the

Figure 25. The mural at the Miami shrine, which was painted by the Cuban exile artist Teok Carrasco and dedicated in 1977. (Photo by Michael Carlebach.)

shrine, offering them her intervention. Immediately beneath that painted image is a boat with three men in it. Just in front of the boat, the statue of Our Lady of Charity is placed on a pedestal. The effect is striking. From the chairs in the interior, the statue appears to be standing in the painted boat, so that by trompe l'oeil the recovery of the statue at sea is vividly and three-dimensionally recreated (see figure 23).[21]

As the narrative moves from Columbus's encounter with the "New World" to the exiles' landing on American shores, it recounts a variety of events and enshrines forty-four historical figures—including priests, governors, physicians, presidents, philosophers, poets, composers, and generals. For the visitors who cannot identify all the people and events, a pamphlet about the mural explains it all, as the clergy sometimes do in their sermons. Few visitors need to rely on the pamphlet to notice that in the left corner of the mural stands Columbus. He holds a banner with a Christian cross to the wind, symbolizing for Carrasco "the entrance of faith." Above Columbus, Father Bartolomé de Las Casas (1484–1566), the early chronicler of Cuban history and advocate of the natives, contemplates the image of the Virgin enshrined in her first crude home on the island. The natives are scattered in front of that shrine, hard at work on various daily tasks. In the panel above the thatched shrine, the muralist venerates the sixteenth-century Cuban priest and musician Miguel Velázquez and recalls Apolonia, the young girl who had an apparition of the Virgin on Cobre Hill. It is at the site of that miraculous event, Cuban oral tradition suggests, that the present shrine in Cobre stands. In the panels above, a number of influential Cuban clergy look out toward the visitors.[22]

In the center of the mural, just above the Virgin, is the Miami shrine. That, in turn, points toward the large image of Félix Varela y Morales (1788–1853), who stands with his arms outstretched to the exile community. Varela himself was an exile in the United States, as well as an early voice for Cuban independence from Spain. Cuban history peaks for the muralist, then, with that nineteenth-century priest and patriot who blended religion and nationalism, as the artist confirmed in our conversation. Just above the priest, at the apex of the painting, two angels ascend to heaven on a cloud, wrapped in the Cuban flag.

Cuban history moves toward independence from Spain as the narrative descends on the right side of the mural, and religion and nationalism intertwine ever more closely. There religious figures share space with revolutionaries and generals and presidents. The story begins with Narciso López (1798–1851), who led an unsuccessful campaign to loosen Spain's control over the island in 1850–51 and so is venerated by some Cubans as a precursor of Cuba's later independence movement. Beneath López, whose face appears in the upper right corner, is the author of the Cuban national anthem, Pedro Figueredo (1819–70). Farther down on the right is the mustached countenance of Máximo Gómez (1836–1905), a general in Cuba's revolutionary army and one of the most popular heroes in the struggle that ended Spanish colonialization. The largest face on the right side of the mural is that of José Martí y Pérez (1853–95), widely recognized as the leader of the late-nineteenth-century wars for independence. Positioning Martí's image next to the Virgin's highlights the bond between religious and national identity. So does the image immediately below Martí's, Jesús Rabí. Rabí served as a general in the wars for independence, and, just as important for devotees of the Virgin, he was the leader of the veterans' reunion which decided to petition Pope Benedict XV to proclaim her national protector. Carrasco included an image of that pope just below Rabí's, surrounding it with Cuban generals and presidents. Beneath Pope Benedict, a sketch of the shrine in Cobre, which was built in the 1920s, brings Cuban history into its tumultuous period as an independent nation.[23]

The social injustices of the Batista era are not represented; and, as if to banish the painful event from collective memory, the muralist also avoids any explicit reference to Fidel Castro or the successful revolution he led in 1959. Yet Carrasco represents clearly the ill effects of that event—political exile—with two hands bridging the waters that separate the homeland and the new land. A prominent symbol for other immigrants to that new land, the Statue of Liberty, points skyward from the lower right side of the painting. To its left are several Roman Catholic leaders—including Cuban bishops and archbishops and the American cleric who proposed building the shrine in Miami, Coleman Carroll. Bringing the narrative to the present, in the lower right corner a boat filled with exiles, some of whom lie limp over its sides and will not make it to shore alive, floats in the sea between the island and the American coast. It is not surprising that many Cuban pilgrims told me that this painted narrative evokes emotions—sorrow, pride, anger, and longing.

The Exterior

The shrine's exterior shapes collective memory and forms diasporic space in similar ways, and two figures who appeared prominently on the mural inside, Martí and Varela, also adorn the rear exterior wall.

The Sculpture: Claiming Martí and Varela

José Martí and Félix Varela, two of the most influential Cuban writers of the nineteenth century, are contested symbols, social sites at which Cubans on the island and in the diaspora struggle over power and meaning. The committee that planned the shrine placed copper-colored busts of each man on a ledge on the rear of Our Lady of Charity's shrine in Miami (see figure 19). From there the two prominent men watch the sea for signs of rafters and, like other exiles in Miami, scrutinize developments on the island. Cuban communists lift up both Martí and Varela as proto-Marxists who anticipated, and posthumously endorsed, the revolution of 1959. Castro's government, for instance, has named an award in political science after Varela. On the other hand, migrants in South Florida remember these men, who both lived as exiles in the United States, as champions of democracy, advocates of freedom, and defenders of faith.[24]

There is a great deal in their writings—poems, essays, and speeches—to sustain the view of them as allies of the exiles' political cause; and Varela, an ordained priest, clearly defended the Catholic faith, on the island and in exile, against those who challenged it. He had impassioned debates with Anglo-Saxon Protestant nativists in New York in the 1830s and 1840s, for example, vigorously pleading the

Figure 26. The Cuban flag painted on stones in blue, white, and red in the small garden that encircles the shrine.

cause of the Irish immigrants and the reasonableness of the Catholic tradition. Varela might have welcomed his place on the shrine. It is less clear, however, how Martí might have felt about it. In ecclesiastical periodicals and shrine pamphlets, the Cuban exile community has aligned Martí with orthodox Catholicism and, more specifically, Marian devotion. One article from *Cuba diáspora*, the annual magazine published by exiled Cuban clergy, reminded readers that the Cuban patriot had written a poem to the Virgin, which opened by homaging her as "the mother of my life and my soul" and closed with a reference to the homeland, "la Patria." That poem also is reproduced in the shrine pamphlet that identifies the historical figures on the mural. Martí did have some devotion to the Virgin and even approved of worshiping, in his terms, "God-Patria." Yet he was a rationalist and a Mason who, as one biographer has argued, was suspicious of religious institutions and their tendency to assume political control. Martí's writings present a man whose views more closely resembled those of Enlightenment deists like Thomas Jefferson than pious and orthodox Roman Catholics in the United States or Cuba. Yet by installing his image on the shrine's exterior, the exile community has claimed Martí, along with Varela, as a diasporic religious symbol.[25]

The Flag

Haitian, Anglo, or Colombian visitors to the shrine might miss some meanings inscribed in the busts of Martí and Varela, but even cultural outsiders would note the links with nationalism established by the flag (figure 26). Though some of the diasporic artifacts are more subtle, the Cuban flag painted on stones to the left exterior makes its point loudly. Devotees built a wooden border and filled it with stones. Those rocks, in turn, were painted to re-create the national emblem. A single white star rests in a red triangular space, with two white stripes and three blue stripes pointing toward the shrine. By placing an image of the Cuban flag in the circular garden immediately surrounding the building, exiles reclaim that national symbol for their political cause and religious agenda. They identify themselves as the true Cuban nation and mark the site as Cuban territory.

The Supporting Buttresses and the Natal Landscape

Architecture, as one political anthropologist has suggested, is a "symbolic structuring of territory" through which a group constructs its collective identity. That is especially significant for displaced peoples. As with the cornerstone, Cuban natal territory is mapped onto the shrine by the six exterior columns that support the structure (see figure 1). As Bishop Agustín Román explained, "The six columns are the symbol of the six provinces." These buttresses thereby re-create the regional divisions of the homeland and reconstitute the citizenry of the provinces.[26]

Not all Cuban visitors recognize the diasporic significance of these buttresses, but some do—either because they decode it themselves or because they hear the clergy explain it. Gladys, who was born in the year of the revolution and exiled three years later, told me that "the provinces of Cuba are united on the six sides." A middle-aged female visitor, Angela, referred explicitly to the symbolic functions of the six buttresses but added her own interpretive twist: the six columns represent not only the regions of the homeland but also "the pain of exile."[27]

The Building's Form as Historical and Natural Symbol

Even the form of the building's exterior, which alludes to historical and natural symbols and shapes the visitors' experience of the interior space, holds significance.

Unlike the modern conical shrine in Miami, the style of the building in Cobre, which was dedicated in 1927, self-consciously memorializes the Spanish colonial past (see figure 6). That neocolonial architectural idiom links the Cuban structure with the time of the Virgin's discovery in the seventeenth century as well as the geographical origins of the Europeans who colonized the island. It establishes the cult of Our Lady of Charity as long-standing tradition and intertwines the Virgin's biography with Spanish history. According to participants in the planning for the Miami shrine, cost prevented this newly arrived exile community from producing grand architecture or mirroring Cobre's design. That is not surprising: first-generation migrants, whether they see themselves as exiles or not, rarely build large and expensive religious structures. Still, the Miami Cuban community might have slapped an inexpensive neocolonial facade on a small cinder-block structure if the construction committee had believed that style would have stirred communal memory most effectively. Instead, they chose a modern exterior design, but its form still transported viewers to a collective past, as one pilgrim reminded me.[28]

In an interview at the shrine, Juan, a recently arrived exile, said that he thought the contours of the building itself—not just the mural or sculpture—was "like the

Figure 27. Taíno Indian dwelling in Cuba. Note the parallels with the shrine in Miami, including the conical shape and the six exterior columns. (From Irving Rouse, *The Taínos: Rise and Decline of the People Who Greeted Columbus* [New Haven: Yale University Press, 1992], 10.)

history of Cuba." No other visitor said exactly the same thing, but the more I pondered his interpretation the more it illumined for me. The building's exterior form inscribed multiple meanings, intended and unintended. It recalled architectural traditions in their collective history—not Spanish but Native, African, and Cuban.[29]

To my surprise, a few devotees suggested that the shrine was "typically" Cuban because its form resembled the "huts of the Cuban Indians." Cuban natives did appear on Carrasco's narrative in the mural, and most Cuban exiles know something about the indigenous peoples who inhabited the island when the Spanish arrived. Yet from the surviving records it seems that neither the architect nor any other member of the building committee wanted to elicit those memories in the shrine's design. Nonetheless, there are striking structural parallels with Taíno Indian dwellings called *caney* (figure 27). Notice that these Taíno structures, like the shrine, were conically shaped and had six exposed columns for support on the exterior. Of course, they had a different size and function. *Caney* were small thatched dwellings, not large concrete shrines. Yet those huts, too, had their religious functions: the natives kept sacred images not only in cave temples but also in niches or on tables in domestic interiors. These natives who greeted Columbus had two main *zemis*, or deities—the supreme god Yúcahu and his mother, Atabey, the goddess of fertility to whom women prayed for success in childbirth. As a leading scholar of the Taínos has suggested, both were represented in domestic images. It is intriguing to contemplate the formal, unintended parallels, then: both six-sided conical structures, the Virgin's home in southern Florida and the Taíno dwellings in eastern Cuba, enshrined female sacred figures associated with childbirth.[30]

The Catholic Virgin was more directly identified with the *orisha* of Santería, especially the African goddess of the river, Ochún; and in another unintended architectural allusion, the exterior form of the Miami pilgrimage site also hints at the contours of African shrines and, concomitantly, the ritual practices of slaves in Cuba. For example, the Ohori-Yoruba rondavel shrine in Benin is a cylindrical altar to

Legba, the African orisha. The thatched structure is topped by a conical clay mound with a protruding phallus. The formal parallels are less striking than with the Taíno dwellings. There are not six exterior columns, for instance. Nonetheless, the designs have certain resonances. Those are ironic, of course, since they link the Catholic shrine with African religion, and distinguishing the two is a preoccupation of local Cuban clergy. In this sense, these meanings are not simply unintentional. They are oppositional, because the clergy envision the site as a place for evangelizing nominal Catholics, especially those influenced by Santería. I should be clear, then: all the clergy and most lay devotees of Our Lady of Charity would vigorously reject this excavation of African historical referents, although it is interesting to note that Juan, the visitor who saw "the history of Cuba" in the shrine's exterior form, was of African heritage.[31]

Clergy and laity alike would agree, however, that the shape of the Miami shrine inscribes other, intended historical significations: it re-creates the contours of the statue of the national patroness. The Cuban architect told a reporter at the dedication ceremony in 1973 that he had designed the building "through the inspiration of the Virgin of Charity." Other surviving documents reveal more about the effects of Marian inspiration on his design. In 1969 one printed appeal for donations circulated by the construction committee, which included the architect, announced José Pérez-Benitoa's aim: "The primary intention of the architect was to create a distinct design that would immediately be recognized by the exiled Cubans at the shrine and monument of the Patroness. By establishing a strong and direct relationship between the architectural design and the familiar image of Our Lady, the Monument will impart emotional appeal to the hearts of the Cuban people." That seems to work, and shrine clergy have drawn on its emotional appeal as they have repeated this interpretation in sermons and documents since the building's dedication in 1973. For instance, in a pamphlet published by the shrine, Bishop Agustín Román explained to devotees who might have missed the intended meanings, "The shrine is the symbolic expression of the short prayer that the Cuban people say in moments of difficulty: 'Most Holy Virgin, cover us with your mantle.'" Not all shrine visitors have heard this interpretation, but many have adopted it from the clergy or found it on their own. One twenty-seven-year-old exile who had only recently begun to pray to the patroness told me that the edifice was "historic, protective, in the shape of our Mother's garment, covering her children from all kinds of danger." An elderly devotee who arrived in 1966 put it similarly: "It is the mantle of the Virgin, which protects her children." Many other visitors who spoke to me repeated this view, with only slight variations.[32]

The shrine exterior is simultaneously a historical and natural symbol. On the one hand, it represents the patroness who has been linked with national history. But it also hints at several natural forms. Its exterior approximates a mountain and its interior a cave. As Isabel, a fifty-one-year-old devotee, proposed, "It is something symbolic. Since we are not able to have the true temple, it is a mountain like in Cobre. The architecture of the shrine is like a symbol of elevation." But it most directly recalls the human body. More specifically, as with classical Greek temples, Byzantine Christian churches, and traditional Hindu sanctuaries, it is associated with the sacred body, in this case the Virgin's. The body of the Virgin, in turn, is associated with a mother's body. As I noted in chapter 3, the devout in Miami, like Marian followers in many other places and periods, regularly use maternal language to describe her. Many devotees, especially but not exclusively women, identified Our Lady of Charity as "my mother" (*mi madrecita*). Hundreds of visitors talked about her in intimate terms, describing how they confided in the Virgin, just as they did with their own mothers. As many other studies of Catholic devotion have suggested, devotees envision interactions with the saints in familial terms, with Mary as mother and the others as extended family. Male and female devotees in Miami also often described Our Lady of Charity as "*our* mother," emphasizing her role as national patroness as well as personal protector. For example, one twenty-four-year-old woman, like many other visitors, described her as the "mother of the Cubans."[33]

It is possible to extend this interpretation in ways that visitors did not, then, while building on what they did say about her role as mother and the shrine as her mantle. Nationalism, like Catholic popular piety, establishes metaphoric kinship networks; and consecrating the Virgin (and her shrine) as a maternal image has significance (mostly unacknowledged) for the exiles' construction of collective identity. Since the exterior form re-creates the contours of the Virgin's cloak, to seek refuge there is to cling to the mother's body. Many devotees I spoke with used language that approximated this. No one mentioned, however, that the small and dark interior space which the conical exterior created also alludes to the womb, as do many other religious structures. In this sense, to enter the shrine is to return to the womb; to exit it is to be reborn. Further, since the shrine is the body of Cuba's mother, devotees enter as strangers and emerge as kin. They go in as exiles, alienated from their homeland and its people, and they come out bonded with all on the island and in the diaspora as citizens of the true Cuban nation.[34]

Conclusion

In this way too, then, the shrine of Our Lady of Charity is a transtemporal and translocative symbol, a social site at which the diaspora constructs collective identity. Cubans make sense of themselves as exiles, I have argued, through artifacts at the shrine. The site of the Miami sanctuary, with its proximity to the sea and the island, repositions the diaspora in the Cuban landscape, just as the cornerstone enshrines native soil and the buttresses map natal regions. The diasporic artifacts at the shrine not only reposition devotees in space, acting as a crossing point with the homeland; they also stir memory and hope. In the mural, souvenirs, busts, flag, and exterior design the diaspora constructs its collective past and imagines its liberated future.[35]

But the meanings of artifacts also arise, in part, from the practices associated with them, and Cuban exiles also negotiate identity ritually. In the next chapter I consider how Cuban exiles at the shrine in Miami also construct collective identity through transtemporal and translocative ritual practices.[36]

6 ※ *Religious Rituals and Diasporic Identity*

At 8:30 on a Wednesday night in 1993 several Cuban-born men from the confraternity, dressed in traditional white *guayabera* shirts, carried the statue of Our Lady of Charity into an auditorium in Miami for her annual feast-day mass. Recently arrived by boat from her short journey from the shrine, the Virgin was welcomed by thousands of devotees. She made her way through a sea of fluttering white, red, and blue as followers waved white handkerchiefs and Cuban flags. Fathers lifted children onto their shoulders for a better view. Flashbulbs ignited. Some in the crowd pushed toward her. From my vantage point a few rows from the altar I noticed that some elderly women and men nearby were weeping. One woman sobbed aloud, "May she save Cuba. We need her to save Cuba." Many others smiled widely as they waved to their national patroness. As the Virgin weaved her way down the aisles of folding chairs toward the temporary altar, a local Cuban priest led the crowd in a series of chants. "¡Viva la Virgen de Caridad!" he boomed into a microphone to be heard above the shouting and singing. "Salva a Cuba" (Save Cuba), the crowd responded again and again. The men from the confraternity lifted her onto the left side of the stage, where she stood in front of a twelve-foot triangular background. Arched across the top a prediction was inscribed in yellow flowers: "Libre '94," signaling the people's hopes that the homeland would be "liberated" from communism during the coming year (figure 28). Finally, Our Lady of Charity rested triumphantly on the altar, where she would preside over the rest of the ceremony, as the clergy positioned themselves on the altar to begin the mass and the crowd boisterously sang the Cuban national anthem.[1]

To interpret the opening scene of this important Cuban American ritual is to make sense of the bodily practices that constitute it—waving, lifting, standing, reading, weeping, photographing, chanting, and singing (figure 29). The meanings of those practices were multiple. Some in the crowd that night participated as followers of Ochún, and some clergy who were present worried about that. Some more "orthodox" devotees traveled there burdened by personal concerns about health, money, or family in order to petition the Virgin for aid. They also came as male and female,

Figure 28. The plea and prediction "Libre '94" (Free 1994) is inscribed in flowers above the Virgin's image at the feast-day mass in 1993. Male members of the confraternity, who carried the Virgin in from the boat and will carry her out again, stand beside Our Lady of Charity on the altar of the auditorium. (Courtesy *La Voz Católica*; photo by Araceli M. Cantero.)

black and white, poor and rich, young and old, and the ritual moment did not dissolve all differences. The child on his father's shoulders, for instance, did not experience the Cuban national anthem as his grandfather beside him did, who, after all, had sung it as a boy in the homeland, in the homeland before exile.[2]

Yet almost everyone at that feast-day mass shared something, as did almost all those who have attended these rituals since the first one in 1960. They came as exiled Cubans to negotiate diasporic identity at the annual celebration of their national patroness. That is the shared meaning of this diasporic ritual. If all religious rituals place participants temporally and spatially, *diasporic* rites like the feast-day mass do so in particular ways. They position Miami's exiles in a time before displacement and after "liberation." In this sense, the diasporic practices of Cubans are transtemporal—retrospective and prospective, moving followers back in forth in time. They also are translocative. They transport exiles to the homeland. As they

Figure 29. Devotees wave white handkerchiefs as the Virgin enters the feast-day celebration in 1993. Others hold banners representing some of the lay groups that have been important among Latino Catholics in Miami (and elsewhere), including Cursillos de Cristianidad, which was founded in Spain in 1947 and emerged in Cuba and the United States in 1957. (Photo by Michael Carlebach.)

move across space to the island and forward in time to an imagined future, Cubans ritually construct their precarious identity as an exiled "nation." As one man who was in the crowd that evening told me, the ritual practices are "intimately connected with Cuban nationality."[3]

In this final chapter I explore how those connections are worked out in several collective rituals at the shrine. I consider, in turn, initiation and memorialization rites, Saturday masses broadcast to Cuba, weekday masses for Cuban municipalities, and yearly *romerías* for Cuban provinces. In the final section I return to the annual festival, the most important diasporic ritual of all.[4]

Living and Dying Cuban

Most Catholic rituals connected with transitions in the life cycle are not permitted at the shrine: there are no baptisms, weddings, or funerals. Still, devotees are initiated as Cubans and memorialized as Cubans at the shrine. On the one hand, followers link the Virgin with newborns. Printed prayer cards distributed at the shrine petition her for a successful delivery, and as I noted in chapter 3, pregnant women and new mothers travel to the shrine to make vows and keep them, to seek help and give thanks. At the same time, families bring newborns there to transform American-born exiles into citizens of the imagined Cuban "nation," much as parish baptisms wash inherited "original sin" from infants' souls and welcome them into the Christian community. The shrine clergy conduct rites of initiation for exile children on the first Sunday of each month. Some visitors told me that the "consecration to the Virgin of children born in exile," as they call it, was the central scheduled ritual. Even if few said that, many agreed that it was important for making sense of life in the diaspora.[5]

Many young Cuban couples bring their newborns to meet the Virgin at other times—often in crisp white dresses or pressed blue jumpsuits. Sometimes they come directly from the maternity ward at nearby Mercy Hospital. More often, they visit a few weeks or months later. José and Rita, a couple from Miami, brought their two-month-old son one weekday afternoon. After they visited the Virgin inside, they carried the boy to the shrine office. There they asked a priest to bless the child. That blessing, and the visit to the altar, formally incorporated their son into the exile community. For similar purposes, a Cuban family from New Jersey visits the shrine each time they return to see relatives. Roberto, the father, arrived from Cuba in 1964 at two years of age, and he brought his own two-year-old one Thursday afternoon in June. As they had done when their son was a newborn, the young couple again carried the child to the altar. Their eyes on the Virgin above and the toddler's searching the interior for interesting sights, they knelt together to pray. After a few minutes, the family left the dark shrine for the sunny parking lot. When I asked them why they had come that day, Roberto explained that it was "to introduce him to the shrine." Our Lady of Charity is "the guardian of all Cubans," as the father put it, so to bring their son there was to initiate him into the Cuban community.[6]

To be brought to the shrine as a child is to become Cuban; to be remembered there in the prayers from the sanctuary is to die Cuban. As in all Catholic masses, at the shrine's eucharistic rites laity and clergy offer petitions for various purposes. Many of those memorialize the dead. For instance, the stack of prayer requests to be read at the mass was thick on a Wednesday night in January 1992. Even though the mass was not formally a funeral, most of those in the shrine that evening were there to remember a Cuban man who had died recently at the hospital next door. As I noted in chapter 3, his daughter Marilyn, who had little devotion herself, told me that her father had visited the shrine "all the time." That was why the relatives, several of whom even had traveled from Cuba for the service, had decided to remember him at a mass at the shrine. For the deceased exile, it was the only way to be buried in his homeland. To be with the national patroness, to hear his name spoken aloud at her shrine, transported him to the island he remembered so fondly.[7]

Crossing the Sea on Radio Waves

Cubans in Miami, living and dead, cross the sea another way. Each Saturday night, exiles assemble at the shrine for a mass. All rites held at that site carry significance for the construction of diasporic identity. The Virgin, after all, is the national patroness. However, these Saturday evening masses are especially important because they are broadcast to Cuba the following day by federally funded Radio Martí to several million listeners. Because of communication technology—and the U.S. political climate, which supports broadcasting into communist Cuba—new ways of crossing the boundaries of exile emerge. Those affect life in the homeland, as one of the many letters written to the shrine in Miami from Cuba illustrates. In June 1994 a thirty-year-old Cuban wrote to the director of shrine, Bishop Agustín Román, to express unity with "your religious community there in Miami." In that note, which itself is a spatial practice and pilgrimage rite, Alejandro revealed that he, like many others in the homeland, "every Sunday sit[s] beside the radio to listen to your mass at five in the afternoon on Radio Martí." The broadcast of a diasporic ritual connected with the national patroness creates bonds with the community still on the island.[8]

It also affects exiles in Miami, most of whom have not returned to the island since they emigrated. Those attending the Saturday mass at the shrine tell me that the mass can be a powerful experience. Even though I am not Cuban, it was powerful for me too, especially since I had read letters written by those on the island and spoken with exiles who had described the significance of these masses for them. To remind devotees at the shrine of its importance, before each Saturday mass Miguel, a leading male member of the confraternity (who has not missed a mass in years), announces that the ceremony is heard in Cuba. Knowing that those on the island, some of them relatives, will hear the petitions, the sermon, and the hymns adds emotional power to the ritual for those who long to return temporally and spatially. It is their way of traveling to the island, the best that they can manage from exile. As that confraternity leader told me one Saturday before the rite: "It is the most important mass of the week because it is broadcast by Radio Martí to Cuba." It is important because it closes the space of exile and reunites the Cuban nation.[9]

Mapping the Natal Landscape

Two other collective rites at the shrine do the same by ritually mapping native municipal and provincial affiliation onto the urban landscape in Miami. If we are shaped by where we live, migrants are defined, to some extent, by where they used to live. American Catholics and their leaders have known this and have used this insight to organize religious life. German immigrants in the nineteenth century clustered in "national parishes" that attracted others from the homeland. Attending even more specifically to the geographical point of origin, Catholic immigrants also have organized along local and regional lines. Nineteenth-century Italians in East Harlem, for example, formed mutual aid societies this way, with those from the same town and province gathering to assist and socialize. Bishop Román's decision to shape devotion at the Virgin's shrine according to natal geographical affiliation, then, is noteworthy not for its originality but for its effectiveness. To a large extent, most observers agree, it has attracted exiles to the shrine.[10]

Román settled on that strategy only after a good deal of prayer, thought, and observation, he told me in one of our many interviews at the shrine. He considered other plans, including focusing devotion there on the patron saint of each Cuban parish. He rejected that idea, however, when he noticed that Miami's Cubans visited the provisional chapel that housed the Virgin's image according to native township. He discovered what he already knew, he explained. "The Cuban people are naturally organized by the towns they lived in the past." So in December 1967, six years before the permanent shrine would be built, Román began to put into effect his plan to organize devotion geographically. He started by making phone calls to Cuban immigrants at night. Lots of phone calls. A self-deprecating man who is not given to overstatement, even Román admitted that "it was difficult work." Each time Román contacted a potential devotee he would record information—their name, address, phone number, and hometown. He then would ask if they knew anyone else from that municipality. Then he would contact that person. Slowly the list grew. By the mid-1990s it contained information on more than 42,000 Cuban exiles, about half of whom are active members of the confraternity. Lay volunteers from the confraternity do most of the work now to preserve and update that list, which is organized by municipality and province. The confraternity consults it to remind those from the same Cuban municipality to attend *las peregrinaciones*, the weekday masses for each of the 126 municipalities. Also, just before each of the two *romerías* each year they refer to it as they call those who hail from the same Cuban provinces.[11]

Las Peregrinaciones: *Masses for Municipalities*

As they have been doing since the late 1960s, Cubans meet at the shrine each Monday, Wednesday, and Friday evening for the masses for the municipalities. On each of these days those from one Cuban township are invited to reunite in exile, much as the secular "municipalities in exile" regularly congregate at other sites in the urban landscape.

The attendance at these masses varies. Some of the smaller townships manage to lure only a dozen or so former residents for their mass. Others have large turnouts, complete with greeters and refreshments. For example, the mass for Fomento, a town in the eastern province of Las Villas, attracted almost 300 pilgrims on a Monday night in May. The mass for Havana, the largest Cuban city, usually attracts large crowds as well. One woman from that city, whose former residents gather in large numbers each year in August, regularly attends the celebration. This seventy-year-old who arrived just after Castro took power in 1959, comes to the shrine and attends the municipal masses because the Virgin is "the patroness of my country." Her ritual practice is linked, she said, "in all things" with her feelings for Cuba and Cubans.[12]

The same is true of most attendees at the other municipal masses. One celebration for exiles from Holguín, the second largest Cuban city, was typical, except that the shrine's director had gone into Mercy Hospital for heart surgery that same day. By eight o'clock, when the mass was scheduled to begin, the shrine's 290 seats were filled. As happens with other weekday masses, some devotees came to reunite with their natal town. Others brought more personal petitions to Our Lady of Charity. This night there were several main concerns expressed—Bishop Román's health, Félix Varela's sainthood, and Cuba's future. Before the mass, confraternity members distributed holy cards with Father Varela's image and biography on them. Varela, the Cuban priest who is memorialized on the bust and in the mural, lived as an exile in New York in the nineteenth century and worked from there for the independence of his homeland. Lay volunteers distributed information about him before this mass, a member of the confraternity explained, because "we are trying to get him canonized." It is no accident that Cuban exiles would take up his canonization as their cause, because he, more than any other Cuban, has come to embody Catholic faith and exilic nationalism. The only other priest who holds as much power in the diasporic imagination is Bishop Román, and some visitors that evening were there to petition the Virgin for his recovery. That, one lay volunteer announced before the mass, was one reason they had gathered.[13]

The other reason, of course, was to remember Holguín and reconstitute its citizenry. The links with diasporic nationalism were clear that night, even from the first petition from the altar. That prayer was for members of that town, on the island and in exile. After the mass, as often happens at the larger municipal masses, pilgrims of all ages gathered on the front steps of the shrine—embracing, laughing, talking. On the top step, a middle-aged man distributed petite plastic cups and poured strong *café cubano*, which women from the township had brewed. I took a cup when it was offered, and as I braced myself for the jolt that surely would follow, I noticed that most visitors had started to pile into their cars for the ride home. By 9:30, headlights from Fords and Volvos and Toyotas followed the contours of the shrine's circular parking lot and flowed down the palm-lined drive that leads back to the main street. Next year many of them would return again on this same night.

Las Romerías: *"Picnics" for the Provinces*

At another diasporic ritual on a warm Sunday afternoon, a woman from one of the three occidental provinces, Matanzas, told me in Spanish that she had come that day because she likes "el picnic." There is no exact translation in English for "la romería," the event she attended. One meaning of the term is "pilgrimage," but these rituals involve more than that English word suggests, including food, secular entertainment, sacred theater, poetry, sermons, speeches, a raffle, a rosary, and a procession. *Romerías*, then, are a kind of picnic for pilgrims. They are annual collective pilgrimages that reunite those from the same Cuban provinces and include a variety of practices—eating and singing as well as praying and processing.[14]

These *romerías* are important diasporic rituals because they, like the municipal masses, map the natal landscape onto Miami's cityscape and provide a social space where exiles can negotiate collective identity. Sonia, who has been coming to the shrine for these events for more than twenty years, suggested that "*las romerías* are the point which maintains the unity among Cubans." Eliana, a fifty-one-year-old woman I met at a *romería* for the eastern provinces, revealed that she came to these rituals "to be near my country." "It is like a connection with my roots, and *la Virgencita* is part of those roots." Eliana's use of the term "roots" (*raíces*) is illuminating. It offers some hints about why the varied practices associated with the event, secular and sacred, are important for creating diasporic identity. As the multiple roots of a tree stretch in varied directions, so too national identity includes diverse cultural practices—foodways, narrative conventions, and musical traditions as well as stylized petitions to shared religious symbols like Our Lady of Charity.[15]

Each *romería* differs in important ways, but there is a pattern. They are always held on Sundays, with the 100 to 200 pilgrims starting to arrive just after noon. Many male members of the confraternity stand out because they wear their white shirts with yellow and blue lettering, with "Cofradía" inscribed above the pocket and "Nuestra Señora de la Caridad" below it. Groups of pilgrims sit in folding chairs and along the stone wall that borders the lawn, balancing paper plates in their laps. Women sell traditional Cuban foods—*frituras de bacalao* (cod fritters) and *buñuelos* (fried dough)—at modest prices. As many of the adults eat, drink, and gossip, clusters of children dressed in traditional costume giggle in the grassy patch beside the wooden stage, nervously awaiting their chance to perform.

Around one o'clock, taped secular music in Spanish begins to play from the speakers on the small wooden stage to the left of the shrine. Often the speakers pulse with the rhythms of mambos, salsas, and rumbas. One Sunday it was Gloria Estefan's Spanish-language recording "Mi Tierra," celebrating the homeland and its customs, and it is difficult to attend one of these provincial reunions and not hear the classic Cuban song "Guantanamera."[16]

At two o'clock or so, the live entertainment begins. Usually at the start the leaders of the provinces-in-exile take the microphone to say a word or two, often remembering the land and expressing their hope that someday it will be free. A member of the confraternity or a priest then introduces a series of performers, many of them children or adolescents, who sing or play traditional and contemporary Latin music. Some dance. Some recite poetry. Many mouth the words to popular musical recordings. For example, at one *romería* in March a group of children from José Martí Elementary School, who earlier had been giggling on the grass, filed onto the stage to mouth the words and gesture theatrically as the loudspeakers played a song praising the Virgin (figure 30). Next, a young girl dressed in a long, sequinned, traditional gown mouthed the words to a popular secular song with a Latin beat, to the delight of the crowd. Turning the mood more reflective, a middle-aged man then rose to recite a long Cuban American poem, "Mi Tierra," which celebrates the homeland's landscape and customs and ends rather ominously with a warning that Cuba will be liberated or destroyed.[17]

Even—or perhaps especially—in the entertainment, then, national identity is negotiated and exilic themes emphasized. This can happen in indirect ways too. To offer one example, in 1994, a year in which the number of *balseros* from Cuba had increased significantly, a young man who had arrived two years earlier on a makeshift raft took the stage. There Ernesto played songs from rural Cuba on his guitar, to vigorous applause. The confraternity member who had introduced him emphasized that the performer was a recently arrived *balsero*. That explained, in part, the especially warm reception the crowd gave him. As that *balsero* told me earlier that day, "our Patroness" had helped him make the dangerous journey. "It was all blue sea and sky, and I prayed to Our Lady of Charity." She provided the "miracle" he needed, guiding him to the South Florida shore. Those in front of the stage that

Figure 30. The children of Cuban exiles perform on the outdoor stage at a *romería*. Boys lift a statue of the Virgin in the background as the girls press their palms together in a gesture of prayer. The older girl at the front mouths the words to a Spanish-language hymn playing over the loudspeakers.

day did not know the whole story of his crossing, of course, but they did not need to. They had heard other stories. They had their own. For them, Ernesto was a shared symbol, like the Virgin herself. To know that he had arrived recently by raft was enough. He symbolized all those who had fled their homeland in rafts and boats and planes. To applaud him was to celebrate their own journeys, mourn those whose rafts washed ashore without them, and encourage those on the island who still might muster the courage, or foolishness, to venture across.[18]

Initiating the more explicitly catechetical portion of the program, Bishop Román usually takes the stage after the entertainment ends, mixing religious and nationalistic themes in his remarks. At a *romería* in March 1992, he began by praying for the well-being of exiles from the three eastern provinces and for the fate of their country. At another one the following year he used the occasion to advertise the festival mass on 8 September, exhorting everyone to attend. He added, with a wry smile, that this year the annual celebration would be held in Cuba. Of course, that did not happen; but the delighted crowd greeted his suggestion with laughter and applause. He had said aloud what many of them had hoped—that their land would be "free" soon.[19]

After Román's remarks the sacred theater begins. In this part of the *romería* male devotees dressed in costume gesture dramatically as they mouth passages from a recorded religious dialogue. The scene usually is taken from the Bible or the biography of a revered Cuban religious figure. At one *romería*, for example, it was the Sermon on the Mount; at another it was the Last Supper, with two recently arrived *balseros* playing apostles and a member of the confraternity in the main role as Jesus.

This part of the festivities is hardly the favorite for most attendees, as the squirming and whispering indicates, and it has little direct significance for national identity. It is important to the clergy, however, who often hush the audience during the long performances. Some scholars have argued that all ritual is theatrical, and sacred theater certainly has been a part of many religious traditions. In Roman Catholicism it has been important in religious life since the Middle Ages. For Cuban clergy at the shrine, and some lay members of the "liturgical community," these "living pictures" (*tableaux vivants*) are tools of evangelization. As Bishop Román explained in one interview, clergy use them because they are "tangible" and thus "more effective than sermons." Missionaries have long used images and theater to communicate religious doctrine. (Remember that Román had been trained at a missionary seminary and had worked among the natives of Chile.) So, too, clergy at the shrine use religious drama at the *romerías*, which draw crowds because of their connections with national identity, to catechize the nominal Catholics in the Cuban community.[20]

Shortly after the polite applause ends for the men playing Jesus and his disciples, or whoever the religious characters are that day, the main religious event of the afternoon starts. That is the rosary and procession. Several men from the confraternity remove a replica of the Virgin from the storage room in the convent and administration building to the left of the shrine, the image that is used for most processions. They reverently carry her across the parking lot and into the side entrance of the shrine. A handful of pilgrims remain outside and ignore the scheduled ritual; for example, one Sunday a group of four teenagers stayed outside and confided to me in a whisper that the rosary was "boring." Most, however, go inside to join the collective prayers. In the middle of that rite, everyone processes outside. Led by the Virgin and a Cuban priest, the crowd walks deliberately down the drive in front of the shrine and then circumambulates the building, repeating "Hail Marys" and "Our Fathers" as they march (figure 31). They reenter to conclude the rosary. After that, some stay to offer private petitions at the altar; others gather less pious relatives from the lawn. Most begin their journey home by six o'clock.[21]

Moving in Time and Space: The Annual Festival

I opened this chapter with an account of the entrance of the Virgin at one feast-day mass because that ceremony is the most significant diasporic religious ritual for most Cubans in Miami. Again and again devotees told me that. When I asked why, they said, in various ways, that it brought together dispersed Cubans and allowed them to express their hopes for their homeland. Before the feast-day mass in 1991

Figure 31. The procession at a *romería* begins. During the middle of the rosary, which ends the day of socializing and praying, the devotees exit the building to circumambulate the shrine, with the Virgin leading the way.

one woman explained, "The Virgin is the patroness of Cuba, and above all we want to petition her to make Cuba free." A fifty-seven-year-old woman who arrived in 1966 gave a similar explanation of why the festival was so important to her: "For me it is a way of celebrating the Virgin's day united with all to ask for the liberty of Cuba."[22]

The feast-day celebrations in Miami began just a year after Castro marched into Havana, and they have been held each year since. As I noted in chapter 1, in 1960, Cuban clergy celebrated a feast-day mass in a local parish in Miami, Saints Peter and Paul Church. Eight hundred exiles attended. The first rite held at an arena that allowed a large crowd, however, occurred the following year, just after the failed Bay of Pigs invasion. Most local Cubans remember that festival mass in 1961 as the first in exile.[23]

That event was noteworthy for Anglos as well as Cubans in Miami. The *Miami Herald* put the story on its first page the following day, with the headline "Exiles Pray for End of Tyranny." The *Herald* reporter, an Anglo, noted that 25,000 Cubans—the clergy estimated 30,000—had "inundated" Miami Stadium, which then was used mostly for baseball. He went on to describe the scene and assess its significance for local readers, who recently had watched the first wave of Cuban refugees wash ashore: "Clutching their rosary beads, they spilled down from the stands and ringed the outfield grass, five and six deep. Some wept openly. Many had to be turned away, confined to the corridors beneath the hot dog and popcorn signs. It was, doubtlessly, the first time exiled Cubans of all political leanings were thus united." Flora was one of the Cubans "united" in the stadium that evening, and she remembered the event twenty-five years later: "It was a most beautiful fiesta. There was enormous enthusiasm among Cubans because we had hope of an imminent return."[24]

Of course, they did not return immediately to their homeland as they expected, but many exiled Cubans have returned to the annual mass each year to carry their hopes to the patroness. From 1961 until 1971 they did so at masses in Miami Stadium. In 1972 the Archdiocese moved the event to Miami Marine Stadium, only a few miles from the site where the shrine would be dedicated the following year. The mass was celebrated at the Marine Stadium until it was damaged by Hurricane Andrew in 1992. Since then the feast-day mass has moved to alternate sites in the Miami area—Bayfront Park (1992), Dinner Key Auditorium (1993), and Hialeah Racetrack (1994–96). Attendance at these feast-day masses has varied from 6,000 to 25,000, according to the size of the arena and the situation in Miami and on the island. In the mid-1990s, after more than three decades of exile, the ritual still regularly attracted 10,000 to 12,000 devotees.[25]

Some of those who attend the feast-day mass on 8 September have visited the shrine during the preceding week. Father Juan Sosa, liturgical coordinator of the festival and former priest at the shrine, explained that there is "a week-long buildup" to the feast day. Anticipation is an important part of life for those who see themselves as temporary exiles, and hundreds of Cubans gather at the shrine for a "vigil" (*una velada*) the evening of 7 September to await the Virgin's day. Sosa, however, has no hand in coordinating that diasporic ritual. In fact, I sensed in conversations with some clergy that it might be a bit too "secular" for their tastes, even though the entertainment follows a mass and includes prayers and hymns and much of the poetry and music praises or petitions the national patroness. In any case, all of the singing, reciting, applauding, and weeping—yes, there is weeping here too—negotiates diasporic identity.[26]

The evening's events are framed by Bishop Román's remarks, some of which concern national identity. One 7 September Román bridged the mass and the entertainment by suggesting that "we came here with the hope that Cuba will be free." That closed the mass, which was broadcast to Cuba by Radio Martí, and after a few minutes to prepare the altar for the entertainment, the celebration of Cuban nationalism began. That vigil opened with a reading of a poem, "Mi Tierra," the same one that locals recite at *romerías* and other Cuban American gatherings. Before the three-hour vigil ended just after midnight, with a Mexican mariachi band serenading the Virgin and the bishop offering closing remarks, the standing-room-only crowd of almost 500 heard a number of exiled singers and poets. Two well-known local performers, for instance, offered their interpretation of a "song of return," which included familiar petitions: "Virgencita del Cobre, give Cuba liberty." As one poet did, many of the performers signaled their devotion to their patroness and homeland by facing the statue of the Virgin, their arms and eyes elevated. The crowd, meanwhile, recited some of the familiar poems along with those on the altar. They also enthusiastically sang the rousing tunes—including the Cuban national anthem—or respectfully listened to the quieter ones. Like one elderly man down the aisle from me, some wept. After each number, everyone applauded wildly. Perhaps because these vigils take place inside the small shrine instead of near the outdoor stage, or perhaps because they usher in the Virgin's day, they are even livelier than the *romerías*. And they are at least as important for the construction of diasporic identity, whether or not the clergy fully endorses them.[27]

The festival celebrations continue the following day, on 8 September, with a

Figure 32. The Reverend Pedro Luís Pérez, a Cuban-born parish priest, waves to the crowd during the feast-day celebration as he leads the chants that petition Our Lady of Charity to "save" Cuba. (Photo by Michael Carlebach.)

morning mass at six o'clock and another for the sick at noon; but the main event begins at seven o'clock that evening, with the rosary and mass. Except that it was held in a smaller indoor arena, the 1993 event, which I began to describe at the opening of this chapter, was typical.[28]

The program I was handed as I entered the auditorium immediately signaled the significance of the ritual for diasporic identity. It read, in Spanish, "Virgin of Charity, Reunite Your Native Sons in Your Love." Whatever other motives brought them that evening, the thousands of Cuban native sons—and daughters—came to ritually reconstitute the imagined community. That was clear in the rosary. As he has done since the first large feast-day mass in 1961, Father Pedro Luís Pérez, the pastor at San Lázaro Catholic Church, led the recital of the rosary from the altar (figure 32). But this is no ordinary rosary. It is Pérez who interrupts the stylized prayers to incite the crowd to chant "Save Cuba!" each time he shouts "Virgin of Charity!" If someone were to wander into the rite as these chants were going on—as two floral-shirted German tourists did in 1992, when the event was held near a downtown tourist attraction—they might think it was an athletic contest or political convention. Like a college cheerleader or keynote speaker, Pérez stirred the crowd with these repeated chants. An Anglo seminarian sitting behind me mockingly retorted, "Amen, Hallelu-

Figure 33. The Virgin arrives by boat for the feast-day rosary and mass in 1993. (Photo by Michael Carlebach.)

jah," to the priest's nationalistic shouts. Some ordained Cuban clergy, who asked not to be named, also expressed displeasure at the overt nationalism. "Some people think that Father Pérez could evangelize more and do less political screaming," one Cuban priest confided. Pérez is aware that not all agree with his approach, but he defends it. "The Virgin of Cobre is the only symbol of unity, of patriotism, for the exile community," he told me. When I asked about the chants, he explained, "They need it." It offers the people comfort and hope. If the overwhelming response from the crowd in 1993, and other years, is any indication, Pérez is right.[29]

Just after the rosary, the Virgin arrived. Her arrival and departure are probably the two most important moments in the several-hour rite. In 1994 and 1995 she was helicoptered in by Brothers to the Rescue, the organization of pilots who rescue Cuban rafters off the Florida coast. However, in all other years since the 1970s the Virgin traveled from her shrine by boat. That was true in 1993 as well (figure 33). That journey is significant because it recalls the geography of the island nation, her discovery in the Bay of Nipe, and, just as important, the almost daily attempts since 1959 by Cuban *balseros* to reach American shores. As Pérez noted in his remarks during the rosary in 1993 and Román mentioned again the following year, Our Lady of Charity was "la primera balsera." Rescued from the waters off the Cuban coast in the seventeenth century, she was the first Cuban rafter. To make the point more explicitly, the floral background for the Virgin at the 1994 feast-day celebration included representations of four small rafts, and just after the homily that year a large inner tube with a burlap covering was carried down the center aisle and placed at the Virgin's feet, as Father Sosa explained to the crowd, "She is a symbol of liberty." That was an especially poignant moment in 1994, because thousands of Cubans had taken to the sea that year in similar vessels. Many had died. Thousands were still detained in "camps" operated by the United States government. The aquatic symbolism, and references to rafters, was powerful in 1993 too, as in other years. How she arrives at these celebrations, then, has been as important for the crowd as when she arrives.[30]

After Our Lady of Charity arrives, she processes to the altar as the people sing. As in other years in 1993 she began her entrance while the crowd sang "La Virgen Mambisa," linking her with those who fought for Cuban independence in the nineteenth century: "All your native sons shout to you, *Virgen Mambisa*, that we may be brothers." Of the twenty-nine songs that evening, many of them highlighted her identity as patroness and her link with nationalism—for instance, "Ave María, Caridad del Cobre" and "Plegaria a la Virgen de la Caridad." These links were even clearer when the crowd broke into the Cuban national anthem as Our Lady of Charity settled on stage.

The archbishop of Miami, who every year since the creation of the diocese in 1958 has been an Anglo, leads the procession onto the altar. There he celebrates the low pontifical mass in Spanish. From 1961 to 1976 the archdiocesan leader and co-celebrant was Coleman F. Carroll. From 1977 until 1994, the Most Reverend Edward A. McCarthy officiated. In 1995, John Clement Favalora took over the role. A host of local clergy assist the archbishop, and many local priests and seminarians attend. Most important for the people, Bishop Agustín Román has been on the altar for these feast-day celebrations since the late 1960s.

The mass in 1993 proceeded as most of them have. There is little change in the structure of the rite, since that is fixed by the church. What changes slightly from year to year are the setting, the crowd, and the clergy's message. What endures is the emphasis on diasporic nationalism. A woman in the row behind me sobbed loudly as the mass began. As I found out soon afterward, she was distraught because the Virgin's feast-day celebration reminded her of the homeland, where her two sons remained imprisoned for "political" crimes. The sermon that evening, by a local priest, focused on the notion of exile. He suggested that exile, and all of life, is a pilgrimage. Mentioning those two most famous Cuban exiles, José Martí and Félix Varela, the homilist defined exilic nationhood: "The Cuban nation is not just a geographical or physical idea. It is a people." He made clear at the end of the sermon that the Cuban "people" included those on the island and those in the diaspora. He ended, to loud applause, by petitioning the Virgin: "Mother of Charity, save your native sons. Mother of Charity, save Cuba." The crowd participated in the celebration of diasporic nationalism not only by applauding and chanting. Two women and a man in their thirties waved a very large Cuban flag in front of the altar just after communion. At the same time, approximately 100 men and women surrounded the image of the Virgin, despite the continued efforts of the confraternity members to keep them at a distance.[31]

As at each mass, the archbishop and bishop had the last word. Archbishop

McCarthy, speaking in halting Spanish from a prepared text, used the opportunity in 1993 to evangelize, to bring those nominal Catholics who attend the feast-day celebration to the parishes on Sunday. Román did the same. The people, however, seemed more interested in the patroness and the homeland.

Just before eleven o'clock, they got their chance to express diasporic nationalism again as the clergy stopped speaking and the Virgin began her departure. To protect the diminutive Virgin from the devotees who pressed in for a closer look, the confraternity joined hands to form a protective barrier as they carried her back through the crowd and toward the truck that waited to transport her to the shrine. As they had at her arrival, the croud erupted in loud song. Again they waved handkerchiefs and flags as she processed out. Again Father Pérez took the microphone to lead the chants: "Virgen de la Caridad," he screamed. "Salva a Cuba," came the loud reply. Several hundred devotees followed the Virgin out to the Ford Ranger, a small white pickup truck owned by a confraternity member. As they lifted her reverently onto the back, several men gathered the yellow and white flowers that surrounded the image. They tossed them to those who encircled the truck. Devotees, in turn, pushed and leaped and shouted to get a relic to carry home. Some in the parking lot spontaneously began to sing the Cuban national anthem as the patroness drove off, secured in the rear of the truck by the men from the confraternity.

While the mass was taking place at the arena, hundreds of followers had spent the evening back at the shrine singing and praying. For them, her departure and return were especially important, perhaps because waiting had taken on new significance in exile or because the Virgin's return foreshadowed the day they would go back to the island. In any case, at 11:20 P.M. she finally appeared, riding in the back of the pickup truck. Those who had waited more than four hours at the shrine applauded and sang "Ave Maria" as the statue was unloaded. Some approached the truck, taking the remaining flowers that lay scattered there. A devout male member of the confraternity, whom I had come to know well over the years, carried Our Lady of Charity down the shrine's main aisle, climbed a ladder with the image in hand and returned her to the pedestal on the altar wall. At that the devotees broke into the Cuban national anthem, and a lay follower shouted from the seats, "Virgen de la Caridad." The others answered, as at the mass, "Salva a Cuba."[32]

Conclusion

As at other diasporic rituals, at these festival celebrations devotees ritually negotiate collective identity. They continually re-create an imagined Cuban nation by ritually positioning themselves in time and space. That is the shared meaning of these practices.

First, the translocative diasporic rituals move participants spatially. They ritually remap Miami and reclaim Havana. To sing songs to the patroness is to travel to the land she protects. To wave a Cuban flag at her as she passes is to position yourself in the natal landscape. The broadcast of the mass to Cuba by Radio Martí only intensifies the translocative function of the symbolic actions. To participate in a mass that is broadcast to Cuba is to return. That, for example, was why Eduardo, a recently arrived *balsero*, attended the 1993 festival mass. "We came from a fishing town where everyone is devoted to the Virgin," he revealed. "I came here because I know my mother in Cuba is listening to a radio broadcast of the mass. She'd never forgive me if I didn't come." The feast-day mass transports the displaced community to the homeland.[33]

Concomitantly, it unites the exiles themselves, if only partially and temporarily. Despite the portraits painted in English-language periodicals and books, Cubans in Miami are diverse. Almost all participants agree, however, that the shared symbolic actions of the feast-day mass bring many of them together. In part this is because ritual requires only a minimal level of consent about beliefs and values. To put it differently, it allows, even invites, diversity. And, in fact, the collective diasporic rituals, especially the feast-day mass, attract the widest range of participants —"orthodox" and "heterodox," male and female, young and old. Even black and white: although no exact counts are available, the black Cuban attendance at the feast day mass seems to approximate closely their proportion in the exile population. White, middle-class, middle-aged women might come to the shrine for private devotions in disproportionate numbers, but many of Miami's Cuban Catholics feel at home at the collective feast-day rites.[34]

To offer just one example, in 1993, a fifteen-year-old named Martha wore a T-shirt to the mass which affirmed her devotion to two animated characters on a television show, one that some adults condemned as offensive. The lettering on Martha's shirt read, "Beavis and Butthead." Below that, there was a message: "I don't like stuff that sucks." This Cuban American girl, who never saw the homeland her parents mourn and celebrate, vigorously waved her handkerchief at the patroness as she passed, singing loudly in Spanish all the while. In the idiom of her T-shirt, apparently this ritual didn't "suck." She might not visit the shrine regularly or fully share her parents' religious view, but Martha could participate in the festival celebration of diaspora nationalism.

The feast-day ritual is also transtemporal, moving participants back and forth in time. It positions participants, first, in the personal and collective past. As one scholar has noted, "All beginnings contain an element of recollection." From the first feast-day mass in Miami in 1960, when exiles gathered to petition their patroness, this has been true. The festival, in a sense, is an act of collective remembering. For those old enough to recollect life on the island, it means recalling family and home and neighborhood—the feel of the cool, smooth statue in their living room, the sight of their mother kneeling before it, the sounds of the processions through their streets. For their children and grandchildren, who are too young to remember the island, it means positioning oneself in a time that was important to those whom you love. For almost all, participating in the feast day mass returns them to a collective past. To sing "La Virgen Mambisa" as the statue enters is to align oneself ritually with *los mambises*, those who fought for Cuban independence in the late nineteenth century.[35]

As was obvious at the 1993 mass and at all the festivals I attended, transtemporal diasporic rituals are also prospective. They position devotees in an imagined future. This was perhaps most intensely expressed in 1991, when the decline of communism in Europe stirred exiles' hopes for an imminent return. "Next Christmas in Havana!"

several priests predicted from the altar during that feast-day mass. The next year, however, they once again ate the traditional Christmas Eve dinner in exile. That did not silence their expressions of hope for the homeland's future, however, even if there was more sadness and less confidence in their voices in subsequent years. The message arched above the Virgin's image at the 1993 mass, then, petitioned more than predicted: "Libre '94" expressed a shared desire lifted to the national protectress. By the mid-1990s, few Cubans in Miami would predict confidently when democracy and capitalism would be restored in the homeland. However, thousands have returned year after year to the feast-day mass and the other diasporic rituals to reconstitute their precarious identity as an exiled "nation"; and whenever Cuba finally was liberated, her devotees told me, they would have Our Lady of Charity to thank.

Postscript

Religion, Place, and Displacement

In this book I have analyzed how Cuban devotees of the national patroness—especially but not exclusively mature, middle-class whites—have appealed to the Virgin at her shrine in Miami to make sense of themselves as an exiled nation. They have done so by, in the words of the shrine's director, painting the image of Our Lady of Charity "in the colors of the Cuban flag." Despite important differences among them, most visitors to the Virgin's Miami shrine turn to that shared national symbol to create collective identity, return to a time before displacement, and transport themselves to the homeland. And many of them, especially those born in Cuba, are preoccupied with that homeland. The experience of exile dominates their lives. However hospitable the United States has been in some ways, it never can be their native land, no matter how much they have managed to transform the urban landscape of Miami into the image of their island home.[1]

At the same time, Cubans are not the only displaced group in Miami, and the exiled devotees of the Virgin know that. Other Roman Catholics in Miami's parishes have suffered similar fates—Haitians, Nicaraguans, and Vietnamese. Some African Americans in the city, Cuban and non-Cuban, have claimed diasporic status and emphasized their brutal separation from their homeland generations ago. The concept of exile and the notion of diaspora, of course, also have religious significance for Jews in the city. In their sermons and writings, Cuban clergy sometimes foregrounded these parallels with Jews and other diasporic groups, usually to make a moral point as they exhorted followers to empathize and cooperate in a city known for its intergroup tensions. The Cuban-born bishop, Agustín Román, had stressed the parallels with Haitians as the busload of Cuban Catholics traveled to participate in a Corpus Christi celebration in the Little Haiti section of Miami. Further, the most comprehensive theological statement produced by the exiled Cuban clergy elevated the experience of the Jews in Babylonian captivity as a "model of our experience"—just as many African American Christians within (and beyond) the city's boundaries had done. The Cuban laity also sometimes acknowledged their common bonds with other diasporic groups like Haitians and Jews. For instance, Ricardo, the prominent devotee of the Virgin who helped to finance and build the temporary shrine in 1967, sounded the simultaneously hopeful and doleful note of all exiles as he compared Cubans and Jews one day in 1994. "They were saying for thousands of years that they would go back to Jerusalem. . . .Where are they now?" he asked with a prescient smile. His point was that as the Jews had returned to their homeland after generations and generations of predicting (and pleading) "Next year in Jerusalem!" so too exiled Cubans soon—very soon—would spend next year in Havana.[2]

Just as a brief comparison of these diasporic groups in Miami identifies parallels that we otherwise might have missed, this study of Miami's Cuban Catholics provides new angles of vision on other groups in other locales. This case study has wider implications for how we narrate the religious past and present of the Americas and, more broadly, how we understand the religion of displaced peoples across the globe. In this regard, I conclude by offering two suggestions. First, the theme of *place*—and the related subthemes of mapping, meeting, and migration—is especially illuminating for narrating religion in the United States and the Western Hemisphere. Second, the theory of *diasporic religion* that emerged from my case study of Cuban Catholics in Miami, a theory which I outlined in chapter 4 and expand here, might prove useful to interpreters as they try to understand the experiences of displaced peoples in other parts of the world.

Religion and Place in the Americas: Toward Other Narratives

Historians and ethnographers tell stories. That is not all they do, of course, but at the heart of most historical and ethnographic interpretations of religion are narratives. Whether or not they acknowledge it, narrators draw on one or more foundational motifs or themes to tell their tales about the religious past or present. In recent decades many readers have challenged the traditional motifs that earlier scholars used to order their narratives of religion in the United States. The liberation movements of the 1960s and 1970s and the concomitant concern in the humanities and social sciences to attend more closely to diverse groups and ordinary people has led many interpreters and readers to look for organizing themes that might allow a wider range of characters to come into view. The most influential earlier motifs— such as Puritanism and secularization—did not seem especially useful for that purpose. Many characters were overlooked. The challenge that scholars face as we try to move toward new accounts is to compose accounts of religion in the United States so that the groups that we now are beginning to know so much more about—from Victorian Protestant housewives and Irish Catholic immigrants to African slaves and American Indians—might also find their place in our stories.[3]

Cuban American Catholics—along with other post-1965 Latino and Asian immigrants—are among the characters who ought to find their place. It makes sense, then, to ask what we can learn from this case study of Cuban Catholics in Miami that might prove useful as we think about how to narrate the U.S. religious past and present. In this study I have foregrounded place—and displacement—for obvious reasons. The Cubans whom I wanted to understand suggested to me again and again, in what they said and did, that exile preoccupied them. In short, they were concerned about *place*. That theme has been important for other Americans as well. As I have argued elsewhere, spatial themes also emerge as crucial when we put Asian Americans at the center of the story. Asian immigrant Buddhists, Muslims, Christians, and Hindus, in different ways, also map the homeland and the new land. Vietnamese American Buddhists have understood themselves as political exiles, but even those Asian migrants who have not done so have still concerned themselves with *place*, especially on arrival. Although my research on Latino and Asian migrants prompted my thinking about place, the more I reflected on that theme, the more it seemed to illumine the experiences of other groups in the United States—African, Native American, and European. It even seemed to include those Puritans, who had been so disproportionately prominent in the earlier scholarly accounts of American religion. The Puritans, too, were migrants. They, too, imaginatively mapped the new land in relation to the old as they set out to build their "city on a hill."

To nominate place as one illuminating theme for scholarly narratives is to high-light three related subthemes—mapping, meeting, and migration—because all three are involved as groups draw on religion to make their own space and find their own place. By *mapping* I refer to the ways that individuals and groups orient themselves in a natural landscape and social terrain, transforming both in the process. Stories of religion in the United States might consider, then, how peoples have viewed their natural and cultural environment—from neighborhood to nation. Narrators should chronicle how religious actors have transformed the built environment—from domestic interiors and cemetery plots to sacred buildings and city-scapes. Taken metaphorically, mapping also refers to the ways that groups have oriented themselves in relation to others in the social terrain, both those who have wielded the most public power and those who have had little clout.

Those sorts of encounters point to a second theme that might prove useful for nar-rating U.S. religion—*meeting*. By this I refer to interactions among groups at "con-tact zones." At various sites in the social and geographical landscape, peoples have met to negotiate power and meaning. Those include not only traditional sites, like church buildings and revival tents, but also classrooms and courtrooms. In Miami, the shrine to Our Lady of Charity is such a site to some extent, but since most Ang-los, Africans, and Asians do not know about that sacred center, it is not an impor-tant zone of contact. In that city, as elsewhere in the United States, schools, busi-nesses, newspapers, and legislative halls have been much more significant sites for intergroup encounters. Those contacts have not only involved newly arrived mi-grants and natives—whether that meant Spanish colonists encountering Tequesta Indians in sixteenth-century Florida or Haitian migrants washing onto Miami beaches in the 1980s. The contacts have included meetings *among* the varied migrant groups, too.[4]

And *migration*, taken most broadly, is a third spatial theme that promises to allow a diversity of peoples to enter our narratives about the religious past and the pre-sent. I have focused on this theme in this case study, but movements across and within national boundaries have been a persistent pattern in U.S. history. It did not start with the so-called new immigrants of the 1960s. It did not even start with the "old" immigrants of the nineteenth century. "The American," as one travel writer argued in an article for *Harper's Monthly Magazine* in 1865, "is a migratory animal." From the first migrations of the American Indians into and throughout the Western Hemisphere to the western movements of wagon trains across the plains to the most recent circular migrations of Mexican farmworkers, the lands now called the United States have been the site where peoples have moved. As long as narrators do not overlook the settled peoples in their attempts to tell the story of the settlers, the motif of migration can be helpful in finding a place in scholarly narratives for a wide range of characters.[5]

As students with only a rudimentary knowledge of U.S. history already know, religion has played an important role in how and why groups have migrated within and across the national borders. That is not only true in the obvious cases—such as foreign missionaries and religious refugees—or with those who have imagined America (or some region of it) as a "promised land" of one sort or another. As with Cuban Catholics in Miami, many migrants have oriented themselves in the new land by appealing to religion. My main point here is that this case study, and other studies too, suggest that place—and, more specifically, mapping, meeting, and migration—might be useful ordering themes for narratives of United States religion.[6]

So far I have highlighted the United States, the area of my own special competence; but there is reason to believe that spatial themes also might illumine the religious past and present of other nations in the hemisphere as well. As early as 1932, the historian Herbert E. Bolton argued that we need "a broader treatment of American history." He meant that U.S. history can be understood best when it is positioned in a wider geographical context. In his extremely suggestive but overlooked essay "The Epic of Greater America," Bolton argued that many of the themes that have been taken as uniquely "American" have hemispheric significance. He mentioned the transnational importance of the frontier, migration, slavery, missions, and Native-European contact. (To this list we might add other transregional motifs—colonialism, civil religion, and nationalism.) Bolton argued that "each local story will have clearer meaning when studied in the light of the others." I think he was right.[7]

Bolton had no special interest in religion, but local stories—taken together—might move us toward a comparative study of religion in the hemisphere. And, I propose, transnational religious narratives might be ordered by appealing to the subthemes of mapping, meeting, and migration. For example, both Europeans at home and colonists abroad imagined the territories of the Americas as a "New World," usually framed in religious terms. In a similar way, Canadians and Argentineans, like European settlers in the United States, turned to religious symbols as they imaginatively mapped "frontiers." As vividly as Puritans in colonial Massachusetts did, Nicaraguan Catholics in the twentieth century have consecrated their territory as a "promised land" and a "city on a hill." Meeting, or contact, is also a transregional religious theme: African and European religions combined to form hybrid traditions in Haiti and Brazil as well as Virginia and Louisiana. Christian missionaries confronted native peoples in Mexico and Guatemala as well as British Massachusetts and Spanish California. In the same way, migrations of all sorts—voluntary and forced, temporary and permanent, inmigrations and outmigrations—have shaped the hemisphere's religious history.[8]

I came to see that most clearly as I positioned myself at Our Lady of Charity's shrine and at other locales in Miami's cityscape because, as the local promotional literature has reminded readers, the city is situated near the geographical center of the Americas. And, as I have argued, that urban area has become a city of exiles. In late-twentieth-century Miami, where migrants have transformed the cultural land-scape, the importance of migration (and mapping and meeting too) seems undeni-able. But that city is not unique. Turning a gaze on Miami, and the experiences of Cuban exiles at the shrine to their national patroness, only helps to bring into focus patterns that have been discernible elsewhere in the United States and the Western Hemisphere.[9]

Religion and Displacement: Toward a Theory of Diasporic Religion

If this case study has implications for how we think about the historical and ethno-graphic narratives of religion in the Americas—and I think it does—it also might provide interpretive tools that could be used to study other groups in other regions. In this book I have focused on one kind of migrant group, one that experienced their movement to a new land as an exile and understood themselves as a diaspora. There has been a good deal of discussion of diasporic peoples recently among anthropol-ogists, sociologists, and historians, although we are still at the start of a long-term project to understand displaced peoples of various kinds. As that conversation con-tinues, scholars will add more groups to the list. Interpreters will note exceptions and offer qualifications. We need not define "diaspora" too narrowly and thereby cut off the conversation before it has proceeded very far. Still, a working definition of the term is useful. In chapter 4, where I took up the issue in some detail, I suggested that diasporas are groups with shared cultures who live outside the territory which they take as their "native" place, and for whom continuing bonds with that land are decisive for their collective identity. They might feel ambivalently about, or even reject, an actual return to the homeland, although in most cases they will be deeply concerned about its current condition and future state. Further, diasporic peoples share a language, even if some in the group also speak another tongue as well, and they appeal to common symbols, even if they struggle among themselves over their meaning. Most important, diasporic groups symbolically construct a common past and future, and their shared symbols bridge the homeland and the new land. This understanding of diasporas draws some boundaries—which include and exclude groups. By this definition, for instance, economic migrants from Germany and Italy in the nineteenth century were not part of a diaspora. Still, the term seems broad enough—we might say, less charitably, vague enough—to allow many groups to be considered "diasporic" at some point in their history—including Armenians, Tibet-ans, Turks, Greeks, Africans, Palestinians, Koreans, Poles, Hungarians, Vietnamese, and displaced "indigenous" peoples in various places. Jews, of course, remain the paradigmatic diasporic group for many interpreters, although as scholars of Judaism have pointed out, the establishment of the state of Israel has complicated Jewish thinking about exile (*galut*).[10]

If scholars have focused on diasporic groups more in recent years—however the term "diaspora" might be defined—they still have said less about religion than we might expect. Or, in some cases, they have noted religious motives and practices in passing but subordinated them to economic and political ones. There have been exceptions, of course. In a case study of twentieth-century Armenians in the United States, Anny Bakalian has described how religious institutions "provided links, both metaphorically and pragmatically, between men and women of Armenian descent in the United States and other Armenians around the world, weaving them into a diaspora." As I noted in chapter 4, Jonathan Z. Smith has theorized about diasporic religion, using the experience of Jews as the model for his analysis. Still, there is a good deal left to do. We need both more case studies and more cross-cultural theorizing.[11]

For now, the outlines of a theory will have to be enough. In chapter 4 I proposed a tentative theory of diasporic religion that emerged from my study of Cuban Catholics in Miami. I emphasized the ways in which religions are spatial practices, and I identified three types of religious mapping. Religions, I suggested, might be *locative* (associated with a homeland where the group resides), *supralocative* (with diminished ties to both the homeland and the adopted land), or *translocative* (moving symbolically between the homeland and the new land). The religions of diasporic groups are, I have proposed, translocative; and in a similar way they are transtemporal. Diasporic religion moves practitioners between a constructed past and an imagined future. As I illustrated by appealing to Cuban piety at the shrine in Miami, diasporic religion's translocative and transtemporal impulses are expressed in a variety of ways. Among Cubans and other displaced groups, then, there are diasporic religious narratives, theology, institutions, artifacts, and rituals.

To put this differently and extend my interpretation a bit, religions can have a vertical and a horizontal dimension, and it is the horizontal that is most important for diasporic groups. To return to the Cuban case to make the point, the artifacts and rituals at the shrine in Miami create a *vertical* opposition between superior and inferior and lift the community of devotees to another, transcendent dimension. The Virgin, for all of her accessibility to devotees, still resides in a realm beyond this world. She can approach us, and we can approach her. Some movement, however, is needed to establish contact. The shrine and the devotions there provide that, as they also elicit the accompanying emotions of vertical religious movement—humility, gratitude, and reverence.[12]

Even more important for the exiled visitors to the Miami shrine, however, the symbolic spaces and practices have a *horizontal* dimension. They highlight, and finally overcome, opposition between here and there, us and them. In this sense, members of the diaspora are propelled horizontally, not vertically. They move out, not up. The shrine's architecture and rituals, as I argued in chapters 5 and 6, unite the Virgin's devotees in Miami with other Cubans in exile and on the island, creating an imagined moral community and generating feelings of nostalgia, hopefulness, and commonality. The symbols and practices bridge the water that separates exiles from their homeland and transport the diaspora to the Cuba of the exilic imagination.

In other words, diasporic religion functions as a *tirtha*, or crossing place, to use (and modify) a term from northern India. In that land, which is dotted with streams, the image of crossing has religious significance. There, many Hindus imagine Indian shrines, and even the holy city of Banaras itself, as a crossing place between this world of repeated births and deaths and the far shore of liberation. Yet that view of religious crossing emphasizes the vertical. If we instead highlight the horizontal impulse, and use the term for different purposes, we might conceive of diasporic religion as a crossing of a different kind. Diasporic religion, as *tirtha*, fords the collective past and future. It bridges the homeland and the new land.[13]

If the religious life of exiled Cubans parallels that of other diasporic groups in many ways, then this case study offers hints about what diasporic religion might look like in other periods and areas. But exactly how diasporic religion varies over time and across cultures remains unclear. Groups that we might classify as diasporic differ in important ways because of the cause, length, density, and environment of the displacement—and because of the character of their religion before they left home.

First, the *causes* of the displacement matter greatly. Consider African slaves and Cherokee Indians. Both were forcibly displaced from their homeland—West and Central Africans transported across the Atlantic Ocean against their will and Cherokees "removed" to reservations in Oklahoma. As much as Cubans and Hungarians might have felt that they had no choice but to flee their communist countries in the mid–twentieth century, most were not forcibly removed. In this sense their exile was, to use distinctions other scholars have drawn, "impelled" but not "forced." All diasporic peoples share a sense that their migration was not entirely voluntary, but they differ in the extent to which they were coerced to leave and remain unwelcome at home.[14]

The *length* of displacement also affects the character of their religion. Now that modern communication and travel technology brings dispersed peoples together more than ever, the usual assumption that attachment to the homeland will decline significantly after the first generation, and even more after the second, seems less self-evident. Now that migrants can telephone, fax, and e-mail their relatives and friends at home, and send things and people more easily and inexpensively from one country to the other, the distance narrows. Still, we can expect some diminution of geopiety as the generations pass. Nineteenth-century German Jews, for instance, had a different symbolic relation to the homeland than those in the first generation of exile. African Americans in the twentieth century, for all the efforts by some to recover African ancestors and cultures, have imagined the natal land quite differently than slaves did as they were marched off ships in colonial Virginia.

The *environment* in the adopted land—both the number of exiles there and the attitudes of local residents toward them—also shapes the character of diasporic religion. Exiles who live with many others from their own country face less pressure to accommodate—and forget. To put it positively, it is easier for these exiles to sustain a sense of identity and maintain connections to the homeland, real and imagined. That has been true of Cubans in Miami, for example, where they number more than half a million and constitute one-third of the local population. In a similar way, the reaction of the host country can affect the character of diasporas' experiences and religions. Landing in a nation with legally sanctioned religious diversity and—maybe as important sometimes—an abundance of work for native and migrant alike allows groups to turn inward and avoid constantly hurdling legal barriers and parrying hostile attacks. Even in such places, like the United States, some local environments still can be hostile for migrants. All of this can shape diasporic religion. For instance, where the cultural environment is more open, they might be able to speak their native language more freely (in religious rituals too) and transform the public landscape more readily (by building according to the architectural styles of the homeland).

More important, the features of diasporic religion vary according to the character of the *tradition* before displacement. Despite the obvious parallels among diasporic groups—for instance, varied diasporic rituals focus on national symbols and carry followers homeward—there are important differences among them too. The more case studies we have, the clearer this will become. Even now it seems that, for example, Creek Indians in Oklahoma, Vietnamese Buddhists in San Jose, and Armenian Christians in Boston *began* their migrations with distinctive symbols and practices. Because their religions each have been in some way transtemporal and translocative does not mean that the common experience of impelled or forced migration smooths out all differences among diasporic peoples. It matters whether the object of the diaspora's devotion is the Corn Mother, Kuan Yin, or Jesus and whether they are participating in the Green Corn Ceremony, chanting the Lotus Sutra, or receiving Eucharist at a Catholic church under the auspices of the Holy See of Echmiadzin in the Republic of Armenia.[15]

Any theory of diasporic religion must be complicated in another way as well. Not only do diasporic groups differ from each other in important ways, but a group might also be diasporic at one point in its history and not at another. Consider Polish Catholics. They once were a diaspora, but it is not clear that they are now. In many ways, there are striking parallels between Cubans and Poles during some points of their respective national histories. Both have suffered through wars and struggled for independence. Both turned to Marian devotion to express their nationalist sentiments and revolutionary impulses. All this remains evident, for instance, in the artifacts and rituals at the National Shrine of Our Lady of Czestochowa in Doylestown, Pennsylvania, where many Polish Americans have pilgrimaged since it was dedicated in 1966. But how has that devotion changed since the fall of communism in Eastern Europe? In what sense, if any, is that piety diasporic today? Or to note other examples, in what sense are Jews in Europe still part of a diaspora now that a state has been founded on ancestral lands? In a similar way, if the Dalai Lama, the leader of Tibetan Buddhists, triumphantly returned to Llasa from his exile in India because Chinese communists had left the region, the diasporic character of Tibetan Buddhism surely would change.[16]

Finally, if Cuban exiles in Miami return to a democratic and capitalist homeland—and, for many of them, it's only a matter of *when* that will happen—that will alter Catholic religious life. I suspect that the diasporic narratives, artifacts, and rituals will not be forgotten, however, but instead will be transformed. Then, for example, the stories that devotees tell will have an ending, the one they had imagined when they were estranged from their island. They will tell how the Virgin, their Virgin, nurtured them in exile and brought them home. Like the biblical story of Jewish exile and return, it will be a narrative of triumph.

For now, however, Cubans at the Miami shrine still ask, "¿Hasta cuándo?" How long must we wait? If the future mirrors the past, when the national patroness does guide Cuban migrants home, another group elsewhere will be displaced and count themselves among diasporic peoples. That new diaspora, then, will join others in offering the familiar plea and prediction of the displaced: Next year in Jerusalem! Next year in Havana! Next year in Saigon, Palestine, and Llasa!

Appendix A

Chronology

1492	Columbus lands on the island of Cuba.
1562	The first miracle is reported at the chapel of Our Lady of Charity in a hospital in Illescas, Spain.
1611–12	The miraculous discovery of Our Lady of Charity off the Cuban coast by an African boy, Juan Moreno, and two Indian brothers, Rodrigo de Hoyos and Juan de Hoyos. Statue taken to Barajagua.
1613	Image of Our Lady of Charity moved to El Cobre, probably first in the chapel of the hospital adjoining the shrine.
1648	By this time, Our Lady of Charity is venerated on the main altar in the reconstructed shrine in El Cobre.
1670s	Toward the end of this decade a new shrine to Our Lady of Charity is erected in El Cobre.
1683	Father Onofre de Fonseca begins his duties as the first director of the shrine of Our Lady of Charity in El Cobre.
1687	In sworn testimony, Juan Moreno describes his discovery of Our Lady of Charity seventy-five years earlier.
1703	Father Onofre de Fonseca writes "The History of the Miraculous Apparition of Our Lady of Charity of Cobre." (It will be published much later, in 1830.)
1788	Félix Varela, influential Catholic priest and precursor of the independence movement, is born in Havana.
1868	The Ten Years War (1868–78), the start of the armed struggle for independence from Spain, begins in Cuba.
1886	Spain abolishes slavery.
1895	War of Independence (1895–98) begins in Cuba, and many appeal to Our Lady of Charity for protection.
1896	The city of Miami is incorporated.
1898	The Cuban-Spanish-American War leads to U.S. occupation.
1902	The Cuban Republic is established and U.S. occupation ends.
1915	Veterans of the War for Independence hold a reunion in El Cobre and decide to petition the pope to name Our Lady of Charity the patroness of the new Cuban Republic.

1916	On 16 May Pope Benedict XV grants the veterans' petition, establishing Our Lady of Charity as Cuba's patroness.
1927	The most recent shrine to Our Lady of Charity in Cobre is consecrated on her feast day, 8 September.
1951-52	Leaving Cobre on 20 May, the Virgin starts a fifteen-month national pilgrimage around the island to celebrate the fiftieth anniversary of the Cuban Republic.
1954	A survey finds that Cuba has the lowest proportion of nominal and practicing Catholics in Latin America.
1958	The Diocese of Miami is established, with Coleman Francis Carroll appointed as bishop.
1959	In January, Fidel Castro and his revolutionary army enter Havana.
	Cuban exiles begin arriving in large numbers in the United States.
1960	The first feast-day mass is celebrated in Miami, as 800 Cuban exiles fill the Church of Saints Peter and Paul.
	The first Cuban children arrive in Miami under the auspices of Operation Peter Pan.
	Cubans constitute 3 percent of the population of metropolitan Miami.
1961	On 17 April a CIA-sponsored exile assault brigade launches a failed attack at the Bay of Pigs.
	A statue of Our Lady of Charity is smuggled out of Havana on 8 September, and it arrives the same day at Miami Stadium, where 25,000 Cuban exiles are gathered for a feast-day mass.
	On 10 September an unsanctioned feast-day procession for the patroness in Havana turns into a political protest, leading a week later to the expulsion of 131 priests.
1964	Bishop Carroll writes to a Cuban priest in Miami about the idea of building a shrine to Our Lady of Charity.
1966	At the annual feast-day mass Bishop Carroll proposes that the Cuban community construct a shrine to the Cuban patroness, on lands donated by the diocese.
1967	A "provisional chapel" is built on the grounds donated by the diocese for the shrine to Our Lady of Charity.
	Bishop Carroll appoints Father Agustín A. Román as director of the Shrine of Our Lady of Charity.
1968	Father Román establishes the Confraternity of Our Lady of Charity of Cobre.
1973	The permanent shrine of Our Lady of Charity in Miami is consecrated on 2 December.
1977	Edward A. McCarthy becomes Archbishop of Miami, and he assumes the duties of presiding at the feast-day masses for the Virgin.
	Teok Carrasco's mural for the shrine is consecrated on 8 September.
1979	Agustín A. Román is consecrated as auxiliary bishop of the Archdiocese of Miami.
1980	122,061 Cubans emigrate to the United States, most of them from the port of Mariel.
1982	A national poll indicates that Cubans rank last in the public's view of contributions made by different ethnic groups (*Roper Reports*).
1985	Federally funded Radio Martí begins broadcasting to Cuba on 20 May.
1990	Almost 1,000,000 Cubans live in the United States, and Cubans constitute 29 percent of the population of metropolitan Miami.

1994   On 20 December John Clement Favalora is installed as the third archbishop of the Archdiocese of Miami.

1995   Agustín A. Román and Manuel Pérez, clergy connected with the shrine in Miami, begin a campaign to raise $800,000 to enlarge the offices, confessionals, and convent and add a reception area and gift shop.

Appendix B

English-Language Version of the
Structured Interview Questions

Study of Devotion to Our Lady of Charity

Today's Date:

1. Male_____ Female_____
2. Where do you now live? City_____ Country_____
3. Age: In what year were you born?
4. In which country were you born?
5. If you were born in Cuba, in which municipality were you born?
6. If you were not born in the United States, in which year did you arrive in this country?
7. Why have you come to the shrine today?
8. How long have you had devotion to Our Lady of Charity?
9. Where did your devotion to Our Lady of Charity begin? Circle one:
    a. Cuba
    b. United States
    c. Another country. Specify:
10. In the United States, has your devotion
    a. increased
    b. decreased
    c. remained the same
If it has increased, in what way?
11. What is the most important reason you are devoted to Our Lady of Charity?
12. In what ways, if any, does Our Lady of Charity help you?
13. How important is this devotion to you?
    a. not important at all
    b. not very important
    c. somewhat important
    d. very important
14. What is your attitude about contemporary Cuba?
15. In what way and to what extent is devotion to Our Lady of Charity connected with your beliefs and feelings about Cuba?

16. In your opinion, does the second generation of Cuban Americans (those who were not born in the United States or who arrived when very young) have the same degree of devotion to Our Lady of Charity? Why or why not?

17. Does the place itself where the shrine was built, the surrounding landscape, have any significance for you?

18. What is your impression of the shrine building?

19. Which aspects of devotion are most important to you personally? (Circle as many as you think are appropriate.)
   a. daily masses
   b. masses for the municipalities (on Monday, Wednesday, and Friday)
   c. rosaries
   d. blessing of the children born in exile (first Sunday of the month)
   e. blessing of the sick (fourth Sunday of each month)
   f. pilgrimage and mass on the feast day (8 September)
   g. pilgrimages of the provinces (once a year)
   h. offerings of flowers after the daily masses during May
   i. personal devotions
   j. other. Specify:

20. How often do you attend the annual rosary and mass on the feast day?
   a. never
   b. occasionally
   c. almost every year
   d. every year

PLEASE NOTE: These questions are part of a research project conducted by Professor Thomas A. Tweed. The study aims to understand devotion to Our Lady of Charity at the shrine in Miami. Your answers will remain confidential. No one will be able to read your answers except Professor Tweed, and he will use them only to understand devotion to Our Lady of Charity in Miami. If Professor Tweed quotes from your answers in any articles or books that issue from this research, he will not identify you by name. (That would be impossible anyway since you have *not* been asked to give your name.) If you have any questions, please contact Professor Tweed at the address above. Or, if you have concerns, you can contact those who oversee research at the University of North Carolina. [At the end of the interview, I gave them a piece of paper with this note on it. The note also included my address and telephone number, as well as that of officials who oversee research at my university.]

Notes

INTRODUCTION

1. A note on terminology is in order. Except when I am quoting or citing another source, throughout I generally use the term "Latino" rather than "Hispanic." As Anthony M. Stevens-Arroyo points out, "Latino" is gradually replacing "Hispanic" as the preferred term among academics. This is not based on ordinary language use; however, it should be noted. I never heard a Cuban at the shrine describe himself or herself as Hispanic *or* Latino. In fact, to make that point some Cubans in South Florida affixed bumper stickers to their cars that read (in Spanish, of course) "I am not Hispanic, I am Cuban." This discomfort with these sorts of generic terms for ethnic identity is shared by other Spanish speakers in the United States. For example, most respondents to the 1990 Latino National Political Survey indicated that they preferred "Hispanic" to "Latino," although the vast majority would rather use terms of national origin—"Cuban," "Mexican," and so on. Whenever possible I use terms of national origin, but when it is necessary to refer to a broader segment of the Spanish-speaking population I use "Latino." It is more inclusive than "Hispanic." The latter identifies peoples with Spain and, thereby, overlooks the Amerindian and African peoples and cultures in the Western Hemisphere. "Latino," for all of its other disadvantages, includes a wider range of people. Anthony M. Stevens-Arroyo, introduction to *Old Masks, New Faces: Religion and Latino Identities*, ed. Anthony M. Stevens-Arroyo and Gilbert R. Cadena, Program for the Analysis of Religion among Latinos, no. 2 (New York: Bildner Center for Western Hemisphere Studies, 1995), 10–11.

2. As I note in the postscript, an important, but neglected, call for hemispheric studies is Herbert E. Bolton's *The Wider Horizons of American History* (1939; reprint, Notre Dame: University of Notre Dame Press, 1967). Jon Butler encourages scholars to compare developments in Europe in "The Future of American Religious History: Prospectus, Agenda, and Transatlantic Problematique," *William and Mary Quarterly* 42 (1985): 167–83. The wider Atlantic world, stretching back to the coast of Africa, is considered in the project described in David W. Wills and Albert J. Raboteau, "Rethinking American Religious History: A Progress Report on 'Afro-American Religious History: A Documentary Project,'" *Council of Societies for the Study of Religion Bulletin* 20 (September 1991): 57–61. Laurie Maffly-Kipp makes a start on considering the Pacific world in "Eastward Ho!: American Religious His-

tory from the Pacific Rim," in *Retelling U.S. Religious History*, ed. Thomas A. Tweed (Berkeley: University of California Press, 1997). Mark A. Noll, like Robert T. Handy before him, considers Canadian and U.S. developments. See Mark A. Noll, *A History of Christianity in the United States and Canada* (Grand Rapids, Mich.: Eerdmans, 1992), and Robert T. Handy, *A History of the Churches in the United States and Canada* (New York: Oxford University Press, 1976). A voluminous literature on collective identity and nationalism has emerged, and for references to key works see note 3 in chapter 2 and notes 2 and 5 in chapter 4. Helpful studies of Catholic immigrants include Jay P. Dolan, *The Immigrant Church: New York's Irish and German Catholics, 1815–1865* (Baltimore: Johns Hopkins University Press, 1975); Paula M. Kane, *Separatism and Subculture: Boston Catholicism, 1900–1920* (Chapel Hill: University of North Carolina Press, 1994); James S. Olson, *Catholic Immigrants in America* (Chicago: Nelson-Hall, 1987); and Robert A. Orsi, *The Madonna of 115th Street: Faith and Community in Italian Harlem, 1880–1950* (New Haven: Yale University Press, 1985). Other scholars also authored important studies of American Catholicism, including Colleen McDannell, *The Christian Home in Victorian America, 1840–1900* (Bloomington: Indiana University Press, 1986), and Ann Taves, *The Household of Faith: Roman Catholic Devotions in Mid-Nineteenth-Century America* (Notre Dame: University of Notre Dame Press, 1986). One study quantified the neglect of religion among Cuban specialists and found that only 2.3 percent of the publications in 1989, down from 3.5 percent in 1971, dealt with religion. See Carmelo Mesa-Lago, "Three Decades of Studies on the Cuban Revolution," in *Cuban Studies since the Revolution*, ed. Damián J. Fernández (Gainesville: University Press of Florida, 1992), 15. Of the nine dissertations written between 1902 and 1991 that deal directly with Cuban or Cuban American religion, only one highlights Catholicism. See Jesse J. Dossick, *Cuba, Cubans, and Cuban-Americans, 1902–1991: A Bibliography* (Coral Gables, Fla: North-South Center, University of Miami, 1992), 80–81. The two book series on Latino religion are The Notre Dame History of Hispanic Catholics in the U.S. Series, which is associated with the University of Notre Dame Press, and the Program for the Analysis of Religion among Latinos (PARAL) Studies Series, which is sponsored by the Bildner Center for Western Hemispheric Studies at the Graduate School and University Center of the City University of New York. The former has published three books, and the latter, four. Two edited volumes in these series offer useful perspectives on the larger issues that arise in the study of Latino religion: see Stevens-Arroyo and Cadena, *Old Masks, New Faces;* and Jay P. Dolan and Allan Figueroa Deck, S.J., eds., *Hispanic Catholic Culture in the U.S.: Issues and Concerns*, Notre Dame History of Hispanic Catholics in the U.S. Series, no. 3 (Notre Dame: University of Notre Dame Press, 1994). The contribution on Cubans in the Notre Dame series was written by a Cubanist who was trained in sociology, Lisandro Pérez, not a specialist in Roman Catholicism or U.S. religion. Lisandro Pérez, "Cuban Catholics in the United States," in *Puerto Rican and Cuban Catholics in the U.S., 1900–1965*, ed. Jay P. Dolan and Jaime R. Vidal, Notre Dame History of Hispanic Catholics in the U.S. Series, no. 2 (Notre Dame: University of Notre Dame Press, 1994), 147–207. Since they have become most visible only since 1959, it is not surprising that scholars of Catholicism, and Latino Catholicism too, have said relatively little about Cuban Americans. Jay P. Dolan's fine social history of American Catholics, which focuses on immigration, mentions Mexicans but not Cubans. Jay P. Dolan, *The American Catholic Experience* (1985; reprint, Notre Dame: University of Notre Dame Press, 1992). The only book-length study of Latino Catholics devotes less than three pages to Cubans: Moises Sandoval, *On the Move: A History of the Hispanic Church in the United States* (Maryknoll, N.Y.: Orbis, 1990), 87, 106–8. Some useful information on Cuban Catholics appears in works by clergy, Michael J. McNally, *Catholicism in South Florida, 1868–1968* (Gainesville: University Press of Florida, 1982), 127–66, and Agustín A. Román and Marcos Antonio Ramos, "The Cubans, Religion, and South Florida," in *Cuban Exiles in*

Florida, ed. Antonio Jorge, Jaime Suchliki, and Adolfo Leyva de Varona (Miami: North-South Center, University of Miami, 1991), 111–43. For scattered but insightful suggestions about religion and displacement see Yi-Fu Tuan, *Space and Place: The Perspective of Experience* (Minneapolis: University of Minnesota Press, 1977), and Jonathan Z. Smith, *Map Is Not Territory: Studies in the History of Religions* (Chicago: University of Chicago Press, 1978). On religion and the post-1965 immigrants see Peter Kivisto, "Religion and the New Immigrants," in *A Future for Religion?: New Paradigms for Social Analysis*, ed. William H. Swatos Jr. (Newbury Park, Calif.: Sage Publications, 1993), 92–108. A number of studies of specific ethnic groups contain insights about transnational religion, though no one yet has attempted to synthesize the results of this research. For example, see Raymond Brady Williams, ed., *A Sacred Thread: Modern Transmission of Hindu Traditions in India and Abroad* (Chambersburg, Pa.: Anima Publications, 1992). Robert A. Orsi's fine historical study of Italian Catholics in New York deals with the issue too, but he focuses on it much less than I do here. Orsi, *Madonna of 115th Street*.

3. My thinking about ethnography has been shaped by a number of theorists and ethnographers, too many to name. On ethnographic writing several books have been important: James Clifford and George E. Marcus, eds., *Writing Culture: The Poetics and Politics of Ethnography* (Berkeley: University of California Press, 1986); Paul Atkinson, *The Ethnographic Imagination: Textual Constructions of Reality* (New York: Routledge, 1990); and John Van Maanen, *Tales of the Field: On Writing Ethnography* (Chicago: University of Chicago Press, 1988). See also Harry F. Wolcott, *Writing Up Qualitative Research* (Newbury Park, Calif.: Sage Publications, 1990). On the practical matters of fieldwork and interviewing, several works are especially useful, including David M. Fetterman, *Ethnography: Step by Step* (Newbury Park, Calif.: Sage Publications, 1989); Raoul Naroll and Ronald Cohen, eds., *A Handbook of Method in Cultural Anthropology* (New York: Columbia University Press, 1973); R. F. Ellen, ed., *Ethnographic Research: A Guide to General Conduct* (London: Academic Press, 1984); and H. Russell Bernard, *Research Methods in Cultural Anthropology* (Newbury Park, Calif.: Sage Publications, 1988). On ethical issues in fieldwork, see the American Anthropological Association's "Revised Principles of Professional Responsibility, 1990," which is reprinted as an appendix in another useful book, Carolyn Fluehr-Lobban, *Ethics and the Profession of Anthropology* (Philadelphia: University of Pennsylvania Press, 1991), 274–79. On fieldnotes see Roger Sanjek, ed., *Fieldnotes: The Makings of Anthropology* (Ithaca: Cornell University Press, 1990), and Robert M. Emerson, Rachel I. Fretz, and Linda L. Shaw, *Writing Ethnographic Fieldnotes* (Chicago: University of Chicago Press, 1995). Following Bernard (204–5), I distinguish four types of interviewing—informal, in which the researcher recalls conversations heard; unstructured, in which the researcher arranges to meet with an informant but exercises minimum control on her/his responses; semi-structured, in which the researcher guides the conversation with a preset list of questions; and structured, in which informants respond to as near identical questions as possible.

4. Ruth Behar, ed., *Bridges to Cuba/Puentes a Cuba* (Ann Arbor: University of Michigan Press, 1995). All translations from Spanish-language published material and the 304 structured interviews conducted at the Miami shrine, most of which were in Spanish, are mine. When citing structured interviews in the notes, I provide the same information in the same order each time: interview number, interview date, gender, age, birthplace, year of arrival in the United States. Interview #1, 26 January 1992, female, age 63, born Guanajay, arrived 1949, Shrine of Our Lady of Charity. This woman, who warmed considerably after we spoke for a while, warned me that most Cubans in Miami do not favor either Fidel Castro or dialogue with his government, so some visitors "might question your motives."

5. Bernard notes that refusal rates are linked with, among other things, educational level. Bernard, *Research Methods*, 242.

6. Social scientists use the term "response effects" to describe the measurable differences in interview data that derive from characteristics of informants, interviewers, and environments. All treatments of ethnographic method deal with this. See, for instance, Bernard, *Research Methods*, 220–24. There Bernard cites a number of studies that show the effects of the interviewer characteristics—race, gender, class, ethnicity, and political views—on the informants' responses.

7. The prayer, in English, is "Most Holy Virgin, save Cuba." Basilica of the National Shrine of the Immaculate Conception, Washington, D.C., 23 November 1993. Our Lady of Charity sits in the Great Upper Church in a niche on the right side of the chancel and just in front of the sanctuary. For another scholar's struggles with related issues, see Robert A. Orsi, "'Have You Ever Prayed to Saint Jude?': Reflections on Fieldwork in Catholic Chicago," in *Reimagining Denominationalism: Interpretive Essays*, ed. Robert Bruce Mullin and Russell E. Richey (New York: Oxford University Press, 1994), 134–61.

8. Donna Haraway, *Simians, Cyborgs, and Women: The Reinvention of Nature* (New York: Routledge, 1991), 183–201. I discuss these epistemological issues more fully, especially with regard to historical representation, in the introduction to Tweed, *Retelling U.S. Religious History*. My views, here and elsewhere, try to steer between various understandings of the nature of ethnographic and historical knowledge—between positivistic and constructivist, scientistic and aesthetic, modernist and postmodernist. I suggest, with Michael Jackson, that we neither discover the world "out there" nor just "make it up." Michael Jackson, *Paths toward a Clearing: Radical Empiricism and Ethnographic Inquiry* (Bloomington: Indiana University Press, 1989), 184. Ethnographic knowledges are always situated and imaginative constructions, but they are warranted knowledges insofar as they self-consciously report authors' sightings from particular sites. My view is close to the "neomodern historical anthropology" outlined by John and Jean Comaroff, *Ethnography and the Historical Imagination* (Boulder, Colo.: Westview, 1992), 3–48. I also find parallels in the position of other anthropologists besides Jackson and the Comaroffs. Michael Burawoy makes a compelling case that we ought to avoid both positivist reductions that falsely claim "scientific" status and postmodernist literary positions that disallow all claims to knowledge: introduction to *Ethnography Unbound: Power and Resistance in the Modern Metropolis* (Berkeley: University of California Press, 1991), 3.

9. *The Oxford English Dictionary*, s.v. "reflexive." Reflexivity has been an important value in cultural anthropology, and it is written into the American Anthropological Association's "Principles of Professional Responsibility, 1990": "Anthropologists must take into account and, where relevant, make explicit the extent to which their own cultural values affect their professional activities." Reprinted in Fluehr-Lobban, *Ethics and the Profession of Anthropology*, 275. Personal narrative and the autobiographical voice have been important in cultural anthropology since the work of the early leaders of the field. Recently, a number of ethnographers have highlighted this idea and raised important questions about how the author, and her/his emotions and beliefs, ought to be present in the text. For example, see Marjorie Shostak, *Nisa: The Life and Words of a !Kung Woman* (Cambridge: Harvard University Press, 1981); Karen McCarthy Brown, *Mama Lola: A Vodou Priestess in Brooklyn* (Berkeley: University of California Press, 1991); and Ruth Behar, *Translated Woman: Crossing the Border with Esperanza's Story* (Boston: Beacon, 1993). Richard Price, in his ethnohistorical work on Surinam, also identifies his own voice as one of four interwoven in the narrative of *Alabi's World* (Baltimore: Johns Hopkins University Press, 1990).

10. Robert J. Smith, "Hearing Voices, Joining the Chorus: Appropriating Someone Else's Fieldnotes," in Sanjek, *Fieldnotes*, 369.

11. A reviewer for Oxford University Press insightfully noted that the organization of the book mirrors the triangular shape of the shrine's exterior. As the shrine widens in a triangu-

lar form as it descends from its peak, this book's three parts expand in size as they move along—with the first part containing one chapter, the second two, and the third three. I am sorry to say that was not intended. Had I spent so much time in that building that the form of my thinking, the architecture of my argument, reflected that? Probably not. But it is interesting to ponder.

CHAPTER ONE

1. The story of the exile of the Virgin that I tell here is constructed from several eyewitness accounts. Three published documents are especially useful. The Panamanian diplomat recorded the events in a letter that was later reprinted by the shrine in Miami: "Carta de Elvira Jované de Zayas" (Elvira Jované de Zayas to Rev. Agustín Román, 29 August 1968), in *Ermita de la Caridad* (Miami: Ermita de la Caridad, 1986), 21–23. Father Jiménez's recollections are recorded in a story about the twenty-fifth anniversary of the Virgin's exile: Ligia Guillén, "Jubileo de la Virgen en el exilio," *La Voz Católica*, 29 August 1986, 1, 5. See also one official account published on shrine stationery: "Historic Data Regarding the Festival of the Lady of Charity," n.d., "Ermita de la Caridad," File, Cuban Archives, Richter Library, University of Miami, Coral Gables. On the festival mass itself, see the front-page story in the local newspaper: John Underwood, "Exiles Pray for End of Tyranny," *Miami Herald*, 9 September 1961, 1A, 2A. I received other valuable information on this ceremony from personal interviews that I conducted with participants. For instance: Interview, Father Pedro Luís Pérez, 9 March 1994, San Lázaro Roman Catholic Church, Hialeah, Florida.

2. The Virgin had several homes in Miami before the shrine was dedicated in 1973—including Casa San Rafael, where the exiled children of the Peter Pan program stayed; local parish churches with Cuban pastors; and finally the temporary shrine on the grounds on Biscayne Bay, which now serves as the convent and administration building for the shrine. I learned this information from several sources, including Father Bryan Walsh, who lived at Casa San Rafael with the Virgin. Interview, Monsignor Bryan Walsh, 17 June 1993, Miami. See also "Historic Data."

3. The quotations, in order, are from: Richard Robert Madden, *The Island of Cuba* (London: C. Gilpin, 1849), 108; Richard Burleigh Kimball, *Cuba and the Cubans* (New York: Samuel Hueston, 1850), 152–55; and James Edward C. B. Alexander, *Transatlantic Sketches*, 2 vols. (London: Richard Bentley, 1833), 1:338–41. All these passages are reprinted in Louis A. Pérez Jr., ed., *Slaves, Sugar, and Colonial Society: Travel Accounts of Cuba, 1801–1899* (Wilmington, Del.: Scholarly Resources Books, 1992), 147–78. A number of books and articles have traced Cuban Catholic history. Two Cubans have written accounts that are rather sympathetic to the Church: Juan Martín Leiseca, *Apuntes para la historia eclesiástica de Cuba* (Havana: Carasa y Cía, 1938), and Ismael Testé, *Historia eclesiástica de Cuba*, 3 vols. (Burgos: Editorial El Monte Carmelo, 1969). Cuban American periodicals also have published some treatments of Cuban religious history. See the brief summary by a Cuban American religious leader: Monsignor Enrique San Pedro, S.J., "La Iglesia en Cuba," *Ideal* 18, no. 256 (1989): 57–60. If these highlight the positive and lean toward the right, the best overview in English is more critical of the Church somewhat sympathetic to the socialist revolution: John Kirk, *Between God and the Party: Religion and Politics in Revolutionary Cuba* (Tampa: University Press of South Florida, 1989). Some valuable documents are reprinted in Leví Marrero's multivolume history: for example, Leví Marrero, *Cuba: Economía y sociedad: El Siglo XVII (III)*, vol. 5 (Madrid: Editorial Playor, 1976), 55–119. See also Hortensia Pichardo, ed., *Documentos para la historia de Cuba* (Havana: Instituto Cubano de Libro, 1973). For accounts that emphasize the twentieth century but contain some historical

information, see the following: Margaret E. Crahan, "Cuba: Religion and Revolutionary Institutionalization," *Journal of Latin American Studies* 17 (November 1985): 319–40; Margaret E. Crahan, *Religion and Revolution: Cuba and Nicaragua*, Working Paper No. 174, Latin American Program, Wilson Center (Washington, D.C.: Smithsonian Institution, 1987); Alice L. Hageman and Philip E. Wheaton, eds., *Religion in Cuba Today* (New York: Association Press, 1971); Manuel Fernández, *Religión y revolución en Cuba: Veinticinco años de lucha ateísta* (Miami: Saeta Ediciones, 1984). For an interesting account of the contemporary scene see the collection by ten Cuban social scientists: Jorge Ramírez Calzadilla, et al., *La religión en la cultura: Estudios realizados por científicos cubanos*, Departament of Socioreligious Studies, Psycological and Sociological Studies Center (Havana: Editorial Academia, 1990). A few studies have focused on Church-state relations since the revolution of 1959. Most of these have been critical of the socialist government, including Margaret I. Short, *Law and Religion in Marxist Cuba: A Human Rights Inquiry* (New Brunswick, N.J.: Transaction Publishers, 1993), and Juan Clark, *Religious Repression in Cuba* (Coral Gables, Fla.: North-South Center, University of Miami, 1985). For Castro's views, see the book that was a best-seller in Cuba: Fidel Castro Ruz, *Fidel y la religión: Conversaciones con Frei Betto* (Havana: Oficina de Publicaciones del Consejo de Estado, 1985).

4. A helpful account of this period can be found in Kirk, *Between God and the Party*, 32–62.

5. For the surveys of Cuban agricultural workers in 1956 and 1957 see the tables reproduced in Kirk, *Between God and the Party*, 46–47.

6. Interview #140, 15 July 1991, male, age 64, born San Antonio de los Baños, arrived 1966; Demoticus Philalethes, *Yankee Travels through the Island of Cuba* (New York: Appleton, 1856), 52, quoted in George Brandon, *Santería from Africa to the New World: The Dead Sell Memories* (Bloomington: Indiana University Press, 1993), 63. On the importance of patronal festivals and regional pilgrimages in Latin America, see Manuel María Marzal, S.J., "Daily Life in the Indies (Seventeenth and Early Eighteenth Centuries)," in *The Church in Latin America, 1492–1992*, ed. Enrique Dussel (Maryknoll, N.Y.: Orbis Books; Kent: Burns and Oats, 1992), 69–80. James Williams Steele, *Cuban Sketches* (New York: G. P. Putnam's Sons, 1881), 174–81. This passage also is reprinted in Pérez, *Slaves*, 174–78.

7. Sydney A. Clark, *Cuban Tapestry* (New York: Robert M. McBride and Company, 1936), 285. For the first time, a professional historian has written a comprehensive and reliable scholarly history of the devotion to Our Lady of Charity in Cuba: Olga Portuondo Zúñiga, *La Virgen de la Caridad del Cobre: Símbolo de cubanía* (Santiago de Cuba: Editorial Oriente, 1995). However, accounts of devotion to Our Lady of Charity in Cuba have been written since the early years of the eighteenth century. The earliest, by a director of the Cobre shrine, was not published until 1830: Onofre de Fonseca, *Historia de la aparición milagrosa de Nuestra Señora de la Caridad del Cobre* (Santiago de Cuba: Impr. del Real Consulado de Santiago de Cuba por Loreto Espinel, 1830). Among the most useful modern accounts is by the North American historian Irene A. Wright: "Our Lady of Charity: Nuestra Señora de la Caridad de Cobre (Santiago de Cuba), Nuestra Señora de la Caridad de Illescas (Castilla, Spain)," *Hispanic American Historical Review* 5 (1922): 709–17. As I suggest in a later note, Wright's thesis was debated by Cuban folklorists, art historians, and clergy in *Archivos del Folklore Cubano* between 1928 and 1930. Most writers who have considered the Virgin's history have been Cubans and/or devotees, and often their tone has been sympathetic, even apologetic. Testé rejects Wright's thesis, which emphasizes natural causes of the events, and he takes on other interpreters too in *Historia eclesiástica*, 3:346–412. But Testé includes a great deal of useful information. Some details omitted in Testé's volumes are included in the brief pamphlet by José Tremols: *Historia de la devoción de la Virgen de la Caridad* (Miami: Album de América, [1962?]). An eighty-eight-page booklet by a Cuban Jesuit is sympathetic to devo-

tees but more judicious: Alberto Villaverde, S.J., *Santa María, Virgen de la Caridad del Cobre*, 2nd ed. (San Juan, Puerto Rico: Publi-RIN, 1994). Leví Marrero's *Los esclavos y la Virgen del Cobre: Dos siglos de lucha por la libertad de Cuba* (Miami: Ediciones Universal, 1980) is a thirty-two-page pamphlet that focuses on African devotion to the Virgin and carries the story through the eighteenth century. It is based on careful mining of the Spanish archives. As I note elsewhere, Marrero also published some key documents in his multivolume work *Cuba*, 5:55–111. Some of those documents, along with testimony and analysis by exiled Cuban clergy, are included in Mario Vizcaíno, ed., *La Virgen de la Caridad: Patrona de Cuba* (Colección: Cultura Cubana; Miami: Instituto pastoral del sureste, 1981). The history endorsed by the Miami shrine was written by Delia Díaz de Villar and included in the forty-seven-page pamphlet it published: "Historia de la devoción a la Virgen de la Caridad," in *Ermita de la Caridad*, 12–20. See also her "Historia de la Virgen de la Caridad," in *La enciclopedia de Cuba*, vol. 6 (San Juan, Puerto Rico: Enciclopedia y Clásicos Cubanos, 1973–74), 259–67. A similar version also was included in public letters and appeals printed by the Miami shrine over the years. For example, "History of the Devotion to Our Lady of Charity of El Cobre," Ermita de la Caridad, Miami, n.d. [after September 1987], in "Virgen del Cobre," Vertical File, Library, St. Vincent dePaul Regional Seminary, Boynton Beach, Florida. The official history also is narrated in an intriguing audiotape sold at the shrine in Miami: Ermita de la Caridad, *La Virgen de la Caridad: Historia y presencia en el pueblo Cubano*, sound recording (Miami: Ermita de la Caridad, 1993). Periodicals sponsored by the Archdiocese of Miami or the Cuban exile community also regularly renarrate this tale, with only slight variations. For instance, see Florinda Alzaga Loret de Mola, "La Virgen de la Caridad en la historia de Cuba," *Ideal* (1992): 5–6.

8. Archivo General de Indias, Sevilla, Audiencia de Santo Domingo, legajo 363. This document was rediscovered by Marrero, who continued Irene Wright's research in the archives by going beyond the date she had left off, 1660. Wright had not found it. It was published in Marrero, *Cuba*, 5:92–93. The document also has been reprinted several times in Cuban Catholic periodicals and pamphlets since Marrero published it in 1976. See, for instance, Vizcaíno, *Virgen de la Caridad*, 11–27, and "Sensacional hallazgo prueba la aparición de la Virgen de la Caridad," *Ideal* (1992): 9–12. Most recently, it has been reprinted in Portuondo, *Virgen de la Caridad*, 298–302. Portuondo also discusses the document: *Virgen de la Caridad*, 128–30. Father Fonseca drew on Moreno's testimony in his *Historia de la aparición*.

9. Marrero, *Cuba*, 5:92–93. Calculating the date of the apparition of the Virgin by using the narrative in Juan Moreno's testimony, Marrero suggested that the event happened in 1611 or 1612. I follow that here. So do most, though not all accounts, published after the document was found. Mario Vizcaíno and Alberto Villaverde have agreed with this date: Vizcaíno, *Virgen de la Caridad*, 3; Villaverde, *Santa María*, 33. Testé and Tremols estimated "between 1604 and 1605": Testé, *Historia eclesiástica*, 3:396; Tremols, *Historia*, 7. As Irene Wright noted in her 1922 article on the subject, the common view had been that the apparition occurred in 1627 or 1628. Wright, "Our Lady of Charity," 709. Most of the official histories in handouts or public letters from the Miami shrine have been more vague on this point, suggesting that it occurred "at the beginning of the seventeenth century." See "Historic Data Regarding the Lady of Charity." The account by Delia Díaz de Villar that is published in the Miami shrine's official pamphlet does not offer a precise date for the apparition: "Historia de la devoción," 12–20.

10. Wright, "Our Lady of Charity." Some accounts say that it was a painting executed in Flanders. If that was a painting, then it could not have been the statue found floating in Nipe Bay by the three Juans in 1612. For one reason or another—oral tradition says he had made a vow to the Virgin—Ojeda seems to have given that image to the local Indians. When the famous missionary and historian Father Las Casas encountered the natives he found them—much to his surprise—worshiping Ojeda's Marian image in a shrine they had constructed.

Testé quotes the passage from Las Casas's "Historia de las Indias" at some length. See Testé, *Historia eclesiástica*, 395.

11. The document which alludes to the Cuban chapel to the Virgin of Illescas is from an enclosure of 150 pages which was sent by Rodrigo de Belasco, the governor of eastern Cuba, with his letter of 18 February 1620. It is in El Archivo de Indias, Sevilla (legajo 16), and it was reprinted by Wright, "Our Lady of Charity" (document 4), 716–17. Wright did the definitive early research on the connections between Our Lady of Charity in Cobre and Illescas, including the work to establish Ojeda's and Sánchez de Moya's links to the Spanish region. The most recent scholarly treatment of the Spanish roots of Our Lady of Charity is in Portuondo, *Virgen de la Caridad*, 43–47. The passage about the popularity of the Spanish shrine appears in Carmelo Viñas and Ramón Paz, eds., *Relaciones histórico-geográfico-estadísticas de los pueblos de España: Hechas por iniciativa de Felipe II, Reino de Toledo*, vol. 2, part 1 (Madrid: Consejo superior de investigaciones científicas, 1951), 497. William A. Christian Jr. deals briefly with Our Lady of Charity in Illescas and quotes the same assessment of the popularity of the hospital shrine in *Local Religion in Sixteenth-Century Spain* (Princeton: Princeton University Press, 1981), 84–87.

12. Irene A. Wright, "Nuestra Señora de la Caridad del Cobre (Santiago de Cuba), Nuestra Señora de la Caridad de Illescas (Castilla, España)," *Archivos del Folklore Cubano* 3, no. 1 (January–March 1928): 5–15; Guillermo González y Arocha, "La piadosa tradición de la Virgen de la Caridad del Cobre," *Archivos del Folklore Cubano* 3, no. 2 (April–June 1928): 97–114; Fernando Ortiz, "La semi luna de la Virgen de la Caridad del Cobre," *Archivos del Folklore Cubano* 4, no. 2 (April–June 1929): 161–63; Ezequiel García Enseñat, "La media luna de la imagen de la Virgen del Cobre," *Archivos del Folklore Cubano* 5, no. 1 (1930): 30–33. Page 33 of the last item contains a note of appreciation for the author's contributions from the journal's prominent editor, Fernando Ortiz ("Nota"). Portuondo's description of Ortiz's unpublished position is found in *Virgen de la Caridad*, 43–47. Ortiz's notes and the outline of his unfinished and unpublished manuscript on the Virgin of Charity have survived: Fernando Ortiz, "Virgen de la Caridad," Archivo Literario de la Biblioteca del Instituto de Literatura y Linguística, Havana, Cuba. Portuondo includes Ortiz's book outline as an appendix in *Virgen de la Caridad* (288–92). Ortiz was so interested in the problem of the origin of Our Lady of Charity, and Wright's thesis, that he visited Illescas, Spain, on 14 November 1928, eleven months after he published Wright's article in his journal. In Illescas he tried to research the continuities and discontinuities between the Cuban and Spanish Virgin. On this see Portuondo, *Virgen de la Caridad*, 44. A U.S. scholar of Latino religion, Anthony M. Stevens-Arroyo, does not refer to the 1920s debate in Cuba, but he argues for parallels between the Virgin of Cobre and Taíno Indian religion. He suggests that the half circle at the feet of the Virgin, interpreted as a half moon by others, evokes the rainbow, a symbol that for the Taínos was associated with the female spirit, Guabonito. On this see two works by Stevens-Arroyo: *Cave of the Jagua: The Mythological World of the Taínos* (Albuquerque: University of New Mexico Press, 1988), 191–94, 216–19; and "The Persistence of Religious Cosmovision in an Alien World," in *Enigmatic Powers: Syncretism with African and Indigenous People's Religions among Latinos*, ed. Anthony M. Stevens-Arroyo and Andrés I. Pérez y Mena, Program for the Analysis of Religion among Latinos Studies Series, no. 2 (New York: Bildner Center for Western Hemisphere Studies, 1995), 113–35.

13. For the official Catholic version of Apolonia's vision of the Virgin, see Díaz de Villar, "Historia de la devoción," 17–18. That account suggests that in the seventeenth century the young mestiza was playing on a hill in Cobre one morning, near the copper mines where her mother worked. There she saw the Virgin of Charity. On that hill, the later shrines were built. It is interesting to note, also, that this Marian vision story repeats patterns in many others. For instance, the person who has the vision is usually an innocent, in this case a young girl.

As the shrine pamphlet explains, "Only children and the pure of heart have enjoyed such a privilege." On Apolonia see also Portuondo, *Virgen de la Caridad*, 145–47.

14. Portuondo, *Virgen de la Caridad*, 90–104.

15. Marrero, *Los esclavos y la Virgen del Cobre*; Marrero, *Cuba*, 5:92. Lydia Cabrera, the great student of Santería, emphasized the traditional loyalty to Our Lady of Charity, and her African counterpart, Ochún, in the eastern half of the island and the significance of Our Lady of Regla, and her African counterpart, Yemayá, for residents of the western half. Lydia Cabrera, *Yemayá y Ochún*, 2nd ed. (New York: C.R., 1980), 56.

16. As Luis E. Aguilar has put it, "The Ten Years War contributed to the growth and maturity of a national conscience. The vague feeling of collective identity which had emerged in the early nineteenth century became a deep, ardent sentiment." Aguilar, in *Cuba: A Short History*, ed. Leslie Bethell (Cambridge: Cambridge University Press, 1993), 26. There is an enormous literature on the three phases of the struggle for independence—the Ten Years War (1868–78), "La Guerra Chiquita" (1879–80), and the War for Independence (1895–98). Of the many works on these subjects, each of them with different perspectives and emphases, see Francisco Ponte Domínguez, *Historia de la Guerra de los Diez Años* (Havana: El Siglo XX, 1972); Asela Artes de Lagueruela, *La Guerra Chiquita* (1953; reprint, Havana: Editorial Letras Cubanas; New York: Distribuído por Ediciones Vitral, 1982); and Miguel Ángel Varona Guerrero, *La guerra de independencia de Cuba*, 3 vols. (Havana: Editorial Lex, 1946). On the period between the end of the Ten Years War and the establishment of a Cuban republic, see Louis A. Pérez, *Cuba between Empires, 1878–1902* (Pittsburgh: University of Pittsburgh Press, 1983). For a helpful list of works by and about Félix Varela, see the Select Bibliography in *Félix Varela: Letters to Elpidio*, ed. Felipe J. Estévez (New York: Paulist Press, 1989), 306–28. Among the many works that note the role of devotion to the Virgin during the wars for independence are Portuondo, *Virgen de la Caridad*, 226–32, and Kirk, *Between God and the Party*, 30. Another work, with original documents as well as analysis, offers a sympathetic treatment of the clergy and the independence movement: Manuel Maza Miguel, S.J., *El clero cubano y la independencia: Las investigaciones de Francisco González del Valle (1881–1942)* (Santo Domingo: Republica Dominicana for the Centro de Estudios Sociales Padre Juan Montalvo, S.J., y Centro Pedro Francisco Bonó, 1993)

17. Testé, *Historia eclesiástica*, 3:404–9. Almost all accounts of the Virgen of Cobre written after 1902 mention her role in the wars for independence. On the Marian devotion of military leaders, see Manuel Rodríguez Adet, "Cuba y la Virgen de la Caridad," in Vizcaíno, *Virgen de la Caridad*, 30–37. See also Loret de Mola, "Virgen de la Caridad." One revealing sign of the increased nationalistic significance of the Virgin of Cobre after the war for independence (1895–98) comes from a comparison of two novenas to Our Lady of Charity published in Havana in 1880 and 1950. The second novena, which appeared after she had been named national patroness, reprinted exactly the novena of 1880, except that the editors affixed a thirty-one-page historical overview that emphasized the Virgin's ties with the veterans and the nation. Compare the two: *Novena a la Virgen santísima de la Caridad del Cobre* (Havana: Pedro Martínez, 1880) and *Nuestra Señora de la Caridad del Cobre, patrona de Cuba: Historia, devoción, novena* (Havana: Liga de Damas de Acción Católica Cubana Consejo Nacional, 1950). For readers who are unfamiliar with Catholic popular devotons, a scapular is a small cloth worn around the neck. It usually contains images on both sides, and most often it has been associated with Marian devotion. The use of scapulars began with religious orders, and lay Catholics wore them as signs of devotion at least as early as the fifteenth century.

18. The "national hymn" to the Virgin of Caridad appeared in the magazine *Bohemia* in 1912, and it was reprinted in Testé, *Historia eclesiástica*, 3:407–8. Some sources have estimated the number of veterans at the reunion as 2,000. See Testé, *Historia eclesiástica*, 3:406.

The veterans' petition and the pope's response have been reprinted in several works, including Vizcaíno, *Virgen de la Caridad*, 28–29. That third president of the republic of Cuba was Mario García Menocal (1866–1941). He was a major general of the army, fighting under Máximo Gómez, Antonio Maceo, and Calixto García. See s.v. "Mario García Menocal" in Jaime Suchlicki, *Historical Dictionary of Cuba* (Metuchen, N.J.: Scarecrow Press, 1988). On the naming of Our Lady of Charity as national patroness and the building of the 1927 shrine, see Portuondo, *Virgen de la Caridad*, 244–55.

19. Clark, *Cuban Tapestry*, 287. Travelers' accounts and tour books published since then continue to mention these artifacts left at the shrine. For example, see Lyman Judson and Ellen Judson, *Your Holiday in Cuba* (New York: Harper and Brothers, 1952), 262. Even tour books published with the endorsement of the socialist government have mentioned them: A. G. Gravette, *Cuba: Official Guide*, National Institute of Tourism, Cuba (London and Basingstoke: Macmillan, 1988), 139.

20. On the national tour of 1951–52, see "Capellán de una peregrinación nacional," *Cuba diáspora* (1981): 92; Tremols, *Historia*, 14; Kirk, *Between God and the Party*, 44; Michael J. McNally, *Catholicism in South Florida, 1868–1968* (Gainesville: University Press of Florida, 1982), 128; and Portuondo, *Virgen de la Caridad*, 267. On the tour of 1959 see Tremols, *Historia*, 14, and "Nuestra Señora de la Caridad del Cobre," in *Ermita de la Caridad*, 32. Another scholar mentions the chants of "Caridad" at the 1959 meeting: Hugh Thomas, *The Cuban Revolution* (1971; London: George Weidenfeld and Nicolson Limited, 1986), 480.

21. Guillermo Villaronda, "Plegaria por Cuba," *Bohemia*, Edición de la libertad, part 3, vol. 51, no. 5 (1 February 1959): 4–5. Castro's famous denial of communist affiliation appeared in the same issue of that Cuban magazine: "Fidel Castro y la revolución: Frases para la historia," *Bohemia*, Edición de la libertad, part 3, vol. 51, no. 5 (1 February 1959): 50–51.

22. The manifesto that would have been read if the Bay of Pigs invasion had been victorious was written by Father Ismael de Lugo, and it was reprinted in Thomas, *Cuban Revolution*, 583. For accounts of the 1961 procession and the subsequent expulsion of clergy, see Fernández, *Religión y revolución*, 112–15; Kirk, *Between God and the Party*, 102–3; and Juan Clark, *Religious Repression*, 10–11. Clark, whose sympathies clearly rest with the Catholic protesters, interviewed two eyewitnesses—José Gancedo and Inocente Santamaría—both of whom were imprisoned for their participation in the procession. He also cited an interview with Boza Masvidal. See Juan Clark, *Religious Repression*, page 102–3, note 13. For the official government version of these events in 1961, which Kirk presents, see "El alto clero no descansa en su actividad por difundir y confundir al pueblo cubano," *Bohemia* 53, no. 38 (17 September 1961): 68. In an interesting development, the young Catholic was elevated as a martyr by both Catholic protesters and government officials. He was buried by government officials with honors as "a martyr of the revolution." On the other hand, many Cuban Catholics, especially those in exile, remember him as a martyr for the Virgin and the nation. For that view, see Julio Estorino, "Arnaldo Socorro: El mártir de la Virgen Mambisa," *Ideal* 9, no. 107 (1 October 1979): 39–40.

23. For useful introductions to Cuban Americans see Thomas D. Boswell and James R. Curtis, *The Cuban American Experience: Culture, Images, and Perspectives* (Totowa, N.J.: Rowman and Allanheld, 1983), and James S. Olson and Judith E. Olson, *Cuban Americans: From Trauma to Triumph* (New York: Twayne, 1995). For an account of Cuban migrants in the United States before 1959 see Lisandro Pérez, "Cuban Catholics in the United States," in *Puerto Rican and Cuban Catholics in the U.S., 1900–1965*, ed. Jay P. Dolan and Jaime R. Vidal, Notre Dame History of Hispanic Catholics in the U.S. Series, no. 2 (Notre Dame: University of Notre Dame Press, 1994), 158–88. See also Gerald E. Poyo, "Cuban Communities in the United States: Toward an Overview of the Nineteenth-Century Experience," in *Cubans*

in the United States, ed. Miren Uriarte-Gastón and Jorge Cañas Martínez (Boston: Center for the Study of the Cuban Community, 1984). Although it needs to be supplemented for research published after 1983, Lyn MacCorkle's *Cubans in the United States: A Bibliography for Research in the Social and Behavioral Sciences, 1960–1983* (Westport, Conn.: Greenwood, 1984) is a good place to start. On the number of Cuban immigrants between 1859 and 1958 (229,632), see tables 2 and 4 in Lisandro Pérez, "Cuban Catholics," 165, 175. With a few exceptions, much of the research on Cuban migrants before 1959 ignores or underemphasizes religion. In his "Cuban Catholics in the United States" Lisandro Pérez has mentioned an important source for understanding the religious life of Cubans in Ybor City: Federal Writers' Projects, Tampa Staff, "Ybor City," unpublished manuscript, 1935–36, P. K. Yonge Library of Florida History, University of Florida, Gainesville.

24. Lisandro Pérez, "Cuban Catholics," 158; Boswell and Curtis, *Cuban-American Experience*, 71. Here and throughout the book, all estimates of population are from the 1990 census: United States, Department of Commerce, Bureau of the census, 1990 Census of Population and Housing, Dade County. Another piece, although it uses data from the 1980 census, remains valuable as a quantitative study of Cuban migrants: Lisandro Pérez, "Cubans in the United States," *Annals of the American Academy of Political and Social Science* 487 (September 1986): 126–37. Silvia Pedraza's review of the literature on Cuban migrants since 1959 is a useful entry point. See Silvia Pedraza, "Cubans in Exile, 1959–1989: The State of the Research," in *Cuban Studies since the Revolution*, ed. Damián J. Fernández (Gainesville: University Press of Florida, 1992), 235–57. As Pedraza argues, the overwhelming majority of research has dealt with Cubans' success in the labor force.

25. Miguel A. Bretos, *Cuba and Florida: Exploration of an Historic Connection, 1539– 1991* (Miami: Historical Association of Southern Florida, 1991), 3–39. A number of studies have considered U.S.-Cuban relations, and most of those have emphasized politics and economics. One of the most recent and most useful is Louis A. Pérez Jr., *Cuba and the United States: Ties of Singular Intimacy* (Athens: University of Georgia Press, 1990). For an overview of the literature on the history of relations between the United States and Cuba, see Louis A. Pérez Jr., "History, Historiography, and Cuban Studies: Thirty Years Later," in Fernández, *Cuban Studies since the Revolution*, 64–65. On the religious affiliations of Miami's leaders during the early years see Thomas A. Tweed, "An Emerging Protestant Establishment: Religious Affiliation and Public Power on the Urban Frontier in Miami, 1896–1904," *Church History* 64 (September 1995): 412–37.

26. On these demographic changes in Miami, see Boswell and Curtis, "The Hispanization of Metropolitan Miami," in *South Florida: Winds of Change*, ed. Thomas D. Boswell, prepared for the Annual Conference of The Association of American Geographers (Miami 1991), 140–61.

27. Florida's Miccosukee Indians, who live along the Tamiami Trail just south of Miami, organized themselves as a separate tribe in 1961. They would disagree with my account here: they distinguish themselves as the aborigines of Florida and see the Seminoles as migrants from the north. In an interesting twist, the Miccosukee sent representatives to visit Fidel Castro in 1959. See Charles Hudson, *The Southeastern Indians* (Knoxville: University of Tennessee Press, 1976), 487. On the meaning of the Muskogee term *Simanoli* see William C. Sturtevant, "Creek into Seminole," in *North American Indians in Historical Perspective*, ed. Eleanor Burke Leacock and Nancy Oestreich Lurie (New York: Random House, 1971), 105. On African migrants from the Bahamas, see Raymond A. Mohl, "Black Immigrants: Bahamians in Early Twentieth-Century Miami," *Florida Historical Quarterly* 65 (January 1987): 271–97. On the South Florida Jewish diaspora see Henry S. Marks, "Jewish Pioneer in Miami, 1896–1906" (M.A. thesis, University of Miami, 1956); Charlton W. Tebeau, *Synagogue in the Central City: Temple Israel of Greater Miami* (Coral Gables, Fla.: Temple Israel,

1972); Ira M. Sheskin, "The Jews of South Florida," in Boswell, *South Florida*, 163–80; Deborah Dash Moore, *To the Golden Cities: Pursuing the American Jewish Dream in Miami and L.A.* (New York: Free Press, 1994). My estimates of the number of Jews in metropolitan Miami come from Martin B. Bradley et al., *Churches and Church Membership in the United States, 1990* (Atlanta: Glenmary Research Center, 1992), 84–85. According to that study, Catholics constitute 18.8 percent of local church attenders, and Protestants made up 17.3 percent. The population, language, and nativity figures for various groups in 1990 come from the U.S. census. The comparative data about language use from the 1990 census was highlighted in Charles Green and Arnold Markowitz, "One Nation, Many Languages," *Miami Herald*, 28 April 1993, 1A, 4A. The proportion of those who did not speak English at home in the metropolitan Miami area (57.4%) was much higher than the national average (14%). In some portions of the metropolitan area, the proportions were even higher—more than 70 percent in the city of Miami itself and more than 90 percent in the predominantly Spanish-speaking city of Hialeah.

28. Although other groups had begun to have public clout earlier in some ways, the local Anglo-American dominance in politics only changed significantly with the redistricting and elections in the 1990s. For instance, see a local periodical's analysis of the 1993 elections for Dade County Commission, in which the new commission reflected the ethnic makeup of the local population much more closely. Forty-six percent of the new commissioners were Latinos, as opposed to 11 percent on the old commission: Karen Branch and Dexter Filkins, "Residents Voted along Ethnic Lines," *Miami Herald*, 22 April 1993, 1B, 4B. The quotation about the Thai Buddhist community was in Sean Rowe, "Buddhist Temple Plan Criticized in Redland," *Miami Herald*, 20 August 1989, 16. For the outcome of that dispute, in which local Christian and Jewish religious leaders supported the Buddhists, see Paul Sukovsky, "Temple OK'd in Redlands," *Miami Herald*, 10 December 1989, 3, 10. The 25,869 Asians, who hailed from seventeen different nations, remained a small but growing minority in the metropolitan Miami area in 1990. The phrase "parallel social structures" was used by Alejandro Portes and Alex Stepick in *City on the Edge: The Transformation of Miami* (Berkeley: University of California Press, 1993), 8. On the image of Miami in the popular imagination see "Miami: America's Casablanca," *Newsweek*, 25 January 1988, 22–29. Several best-selling books also appeared, starting in the late 1980s: T. D. Allman, *Miami: City of the Future* (New York: Atlantic Monthly Press, 1987); Joan Didion, *Miami* (New York: Pocket Books, 1987); and David Rieff, *Going to Miami: Exiles, Tourists, and Refugees in the New America* (Boston: Little, Brown, 1987).

29. For an intriguing analysis of the baseball diamond as a social space where Cubans made sense of themselves as a nation see Louis A. Pérez Jr., "Between Baseball and Bullfighting: The Quest for Nationality in Cuba, 1868–1898," *Journal of American History* 81 (September 1994): 493–517.

30. Among the many observers who have suggested that institutional piety among Cuban Catholics has increased in exile are Marcos Antonio Ramos, a Protestant minister, and Agustín A. Román, the Catholic auxiliary bishop. They estimate that one in five Cubans in South Florida, or 20 percent, "regularly attend mass." "These figures," they argue, "reflect a higher level of religious practice than in Cuba prior to the revolution." See Agustín A. Román and Marcos Antonio Ramos, "The Cubans, Religion, and South Florida," in *Cuban Exiles in Florida*, ed. Antonio Jorge, Jaime Suchlicki, and Adolfo Leyva de Varona (Miami: North-South Center, University of Miami, 1991), 121. The analysis of national figures on Catholic church attendance is in Mark Chaves and James C. Cavendish, "More Evidence on U.S. Catholic Church Attendance," *Journal for the Scientific Study of Religion* 33, no. 4 (1994): 376–81. Only Reno–Las Vegas had a lower weekly church attendance rate (15.9%) among the forty-eight American dioceses reported in the study. The most reliable survey of the atti-

tudes and practices of South Florida's Roman Catholics was conducted by a non-Catholic geographer who was commissioned by the Archdiocese, and this is the source for my estimates for metropolitan Miami: Ira M. Sheskin, *The Synod Survey Summary Report: The Archdiocese of Miami* (Miami: Archdiocese of Miami, 1986). For a summary of another Catholic-sponsored survey of 4,676 Cuban exiles in the United States and elsewhere, see Juan Clark, "Una encuesta sobre la diáspora Cubana," *Ideal* 21, no. 262 (1993): 9–11. Many observers also have noted the increased presence of Santería in the Miami area. See Mercedes Cros Sandoval, *La religión afro-cubana* (Madrid: Playor, 1975), 271–72.

31. The estimate of practicing Catholics among the first wave of immigrants is cited in Moisés Sandoval, ed., *On the Move: A History of the Hispanic Church in the United States* (Maryknoll, N.Y.: Orbis, 1990), 106–7. All interpreters agree that the number of practicing Catholics—i.e., those who attend church—in contemporary Cuba is quite low. Reliable estimates range from less than 2 percent to less than 4 percent. Citing an estimate from an official of the Cuban Conference of Bishops, one scholar reports that as few as 150,000 (3.7%) out of a national population of more than 10,000,000 might be practicing, even though the official statistics from the *Anuario Pontificio* claimed 37.8 percent of the population as Catholic in 1985. Crahan, "Cuba," 335. Before the 1959 revolution, more than 85 percent of Cubans were baptized. By the 1990s that figure was less than 2 percent, according to some estimates. On this, and Catholic weekly attendance figures, see Barbara E. Joe, "The Church in Cuba—A Dawn?," *America*, 7 December 1991, 428–31. For the official estimates of Cuban Catholics from *Anuario Pontificio* for 1960 and 1983, see Fernández, *Religión y revolución*, 185. Those indicate that the number of nominal Catholics declined in those twenty-three years from 89.3 percent to 38.8 percent of the national population.

32. On Carroll and national parishes, archdiocesan spending on immigrants, and Operation Peter Pan, see McNally, *Catholicism*, 143–51. For useful accounts of the archdiocesan responses to the Cuban migration by one of the participants, who served as Episcopal Vicar for Spanish-Speaking Peoples, see Bryan O. Walsh, "Cubans in Miami," *America*, 26 February 1966, 286–89, and Bryan O. Walsh, "The Spanish Impact Here: How the Archdiocese Is Meeting the Challenge," *The Voice*, 18 July 1975, 1A–3A. On Operation Peter Pan see Bryan O. Walsh, "Cuban Refugee Children," *Journal of Inter-American Studies and World Affairs* 13 (July–October 1971): 378–415. Monsignor Walsh, who directed Operation Peter Pan and had regular contact with Bishop Carroll, also gave me a great deal of information about Carroll and the early years of the diocese in personal interviews. Interview, Monsignor Bryan O. Walsh, 1 June 1993, Miami; Interview, Monsignor Bryan O. Walsh, 17 June 1993, Miami. For the orientation booklet for the Marielitos see El Centro Cristiano de Medios de Comunicación y Juan Clark y Roberto Hernández, *Manual de orientación para refugiados* (Miami: Archdiocese of Miami, 1980). Several works deal with the Puerto Rican experience in New York and elsewhere. For example, see Ana María Díaz-Stevens, *Oxcart Catholicism on Fifth Avenue: The Impact of Puerto Rican Migration upon the Archdiocese of New York* (Notre Dame: University of Notre Dame Press, 1993), and Jaime R. Vidal, "Citizens yet Strangers: The Puerto Rican Experience," in Dolan and Vidal, *Puerto Rican and Cuban Catholics* 88–111.

33. Interview, T.N., 23 June 1992, female, age 46, Miami; Interview, "Ricardo," 11 March 1994, Miami. Ricardo, who arrived in Miami in 1960, was the leading member of the committee that constructed the "provisional chapel" in Miami. On the idiomatic expression "I am Catholic in my own way," see also Mercedes Cros Sandoval, *Mariel and Cuban National Identity* (Miami: Editorial SIBI, 1985), 38.

34. As Portuondo notes, exiled wives of *los mambises* who were living in the United States during the 1890s petitioned the Virgin "for the independence of the nation" (*Virgen de la Caridad*, 228). For an example of this devotion by exiles in the 1890s see Fermín Valdés

Domínguez, "Virgen de la Caridad," *Patria* (New York), 9 June 1894 (dated in Key West, 25 May 1894).

35. Interview #83, 1 August 1991, female, age 51, born Havana, arrived 1960; Eduardo Boza Masvidal, "Una imagen que es un símbolo," in *Ermita de la Caridad*, 9–10.

36. The *balsero* in the photograph came as one of the tens of thousands of migrants who set out from the shores of Cuba in makeshift rafts and boats after a new "crisis"—as the Spanish language press called it—began in August 1994. The rafter was found by the U.S. Coast Guard floating twenty miles from the coastline of Havana. See Evelyn Larrubia, "Pasaje a la libertad tiene alto precio para balseros," *El Nuevo Herald*, 6 September 1994, 1A, 4A.

37. The account of the 1960 feast-day mass appeared in *The Voice*, 16 September 1960. See also McNally, *Catholicism*, 160. The secular press estimated that the crowd for the 1961 feast-day mass totaled 25,000; the Catholic estimates were slightly higher, 30,000. See Underwood, "Exiles Pray." The stadium where the 1961 mass was held was then called Miami Stadium. It is now called Bobby Maduro Stadium.

38. Interview, Monsignor Bryan O. Walsh, 17 June 1993, Miami; McNally, *Catholicism*, 150–51.

39. Interview, "Ricardo," 11 March 1994, Miami. Ricardo did the first regular Spanish-language newscast on a Miami television station (channel 4). That early-morning program, "News in Español," ran from 1960 to 1978. As his work for the shrine and his conversation with me indicated, he also had devotion to Our Lady of Charity. Bishop Coleman F. Carroll to The Reverend Eugenio Del Busto, 7 April 1964, "Shrine of Our Lady of Charity (1966–1973)," File, Archdiocese of Miami Archives, Pastoral Center, Miami Springs.

40. Interview, Monsignor Bryan O. Walsh, 1 June 1993, Miami. Walsh indicated that another reason for many Cuban priests' opposition was that it seemed to be advocating "superstition." Walsh's judgments have some authority because he was intimately involved in the church's dealings with Cubans. His name later even appeared as one of only eight "incorporators" on the certificate of incorporation for the shrine: "Certificate of Incorporation of the Shrine of Our Lady of Charity, Inc. A Non-Profit Corporation," 17 November 1967, Files of Agustín Román, Archdiocese of Miami Pastoral Center, Miami Springs. The surviving correspondence concerning the shrine also confirms Walsh's assessment. For instance, in one letter to an archdiocesan official in 1973 Agustín Román implicitly acknowledged the issue as he asked for permission to celebrate mass on all days except Sundays: "I am not referring to Sundays because I understand that people must go to their own Parish, as you have informed me." Monsignor Agustín Román to Monsignor Orlando Fernández, 5 February 1973, "Shrine of Our Lady of Charity (1966–1973)," File, Archdiocese of Miami Archives, Pastoral Center, Miami Springs.

41. The full text of Bishop Carroll's announcement at the 1961 mass is preserved in an untitled typed manuscript that begins, "Monsignori, Reverend Fathers, and Friends of Our Lady of El Cobre." "Shrine of Our Lady of Charity (1966–1973)," File, Archdiocese of Miami Archives, Pastoral Center, Miami Springs.

42. The letter appointing Román, then a parish priest, as shrine director can be found in the archdiocesan archives: Coleman F. Carroll to Agustín Román, 6 September 1967, "Shrine of Our Lady of Charity (1966–1973)," File, Archdiocese of Miami Archives, Pastoral Center, Miami Springs.

43. This list of the obligations of confraternity members is taken from "By-Laws of the Confraternity or Brotherhood of Our Lady of Charity of Cobre," Files of Agustín Román, Archdiocese of Miami Pastoral Center, Miami Springs. This is a typed but undated four-page document on shrine stationery. After the establishment of the confraternity, the shrine, under the direction of Román, produced a number of printed appeals to join the group. Many of these have been collected in the Cuban Archives at the University of Miami. For example,

see "Cofradía: Nuestra Señora de la Caridad," n.d. [between 1968 and 1973], "Ermita de la Caridad," File, Cuban Archives, Richter Library, University of Miami, Coral Gables.

44. "Certificate of Incorporation," Files of Agustín A. Román, Archdiocese of Miami Pastoral Center, Miami Springs. On the dedication ceremony in 1973 see Chuck Gómez and Miguel Pérez, "Cubans Flock to Dedication of Shrine," *Miami Herald*, 3 December 1973, 1B, 2B, and Gustavo Pena Monte, "Miles de cubanos en la dedicación de la Ermita," *La Voz Católica*, (Spanish suppl.) 7 December 1973, 16. One of the printed pleas for donations to construct the permanent shrine was in the form of a public letter, addressed to exiled Cubans. "Comité Pro Monumento–Ermita a la Virgen de la Caridad," typed letter signed by the Reverend Agustín Román and Dr. José Miguel Morales Gómez, "Ermita de la Caridad," File, Cuban Archives, Richter Library, University of Miami, Coral Gables. This document linked the Virgen, and the building of the shrine, directly with Cuban nationalism. It emphasized her role as "patrona de Cuba," and it claimed that the shrine would be "an unequivocal manifestation of the struggle [*la lucha*] of a community that loves liberty and democracy." That document was written on letterhead that listed twenty-five members of the construction committee, including eleven who had official titles and roles: Coleman F. Carroll, the archbishop of Miami; the Reverend Agustín Román, the shrine director; José Miguel Morales Gómez, committee president. The list also included three vice presidents: Elda Romanach, Luis Botifol, and Ernesto Freyre. The others were Leticia De Amblada, treasurer; Tarcisio Nieto, vice treasurer; the Reverend P. Eugenio Del Busto, secretary; Raúl Valdes Fauly, vice secretary; and Juan Victor Tapia, accountant.

45. For an account of the attempted theft, and the arrest of one of the two men, see the reports published in the local newspapers: Jorge Dávila Miguel, "Intentan robar estatua de la Virgen," *El Nuevo Herald*, 24 November 1994, 1A; and Karen Branch, "A Symbol of Faith Desecrated," *Miami Herald*, 24 November 1994, 1A. William A. Gralnick, "'Our Lady of Charity': You Don't Have to Be Cuban to Love Ermita," *Miami Today*, 1 December 1983, 16. That periodical was a weekly that was delivered to the Brickell corridor of Miami, an area adjoining the shrine.

46. Emphasis mine. Reverend Agustín Román to Monsignor Orlando Fernández, 5 February 1974, "Shrine of Our Lady of Charity (1966–1973)," File, Archdiocese of Miami Pastoral Center, Miami Springs. Many other sermons and writings by Cuban clergy over the years also have emphasized that the shrine is a place for evangelization of unchurched Cubans, as I note in the next chapter. See Agustín A. Román, "The Popular Piety of the Cuban People" (M.A. thesis, Barry University, 1976). One account of the shrine, which was written under the auspices of the Committee on Evangelization of the National Conference of Catholic Bishops, highlighted the same theme: Cecilio J. Morales Jr., *Hispanic Portrait of Evangelization: The Shrine of Our Lady of Charity*, no. 5 (Washington, D.C.: Committee on Evangelization, National Conference of Catholic Bishops, 1981).

CHAPTER TWO

1. Fieldnotes, 8 June 1994, Shrine of Our Lady of Charity. "Mirta" is a pseudonym. The principal actors in this drama—including the nuns and priests at the shrine—know her. So do many others in the Cuban community, since she has even appeared on local television. But I thought it best to protect her identity as much as possible. An *iyawó* is a novice initiated in the week-long "coronation" of the *asiento* ritual, in which the *orisha* is "seated" (*asentado*) or "put on the head." On the *asiento* see Lydia Cabrera, *El monte* (Miami: Ediciones Universal, 1992), especially 397–98, and Joseph M. Murphy, *Santería: An African Religion in America* (Boston: Beacon, 1988), 84–91. As a "bride of the *orisha*," the initiate observes strict taboos for one year, called the "Year of White." It could have been a coincidence that

Mirta wore all white that day. On subsequent occasions, however, I confirmed that she dressed in white as a regular practice. Fieldnotes, 8 September 1994, Shrine of Our Lady of Charity. For a helpful glossary of key terms in Santería, including *asiento* and *iyawó*, see David Hilary Brown, "Garden in the Machine: Afro-Cuban Sacred Art and Performance in Urban New Jersey and New York," 2 vols. (Ph.D. diss., Yale University, 1989), 514–19, and Murphy, *Santería*, 175–82.

2. Interview #230, "Mirta," 8 June 1994, female, age 41; fieldnotes, 8 June 1994, Shrine of Our Lady of Charity.

3. The understanding of "identity" that informs my analysis here has been shaped by scholarship in several fields, especially the literature on collective memory, ethnicity, and nationalism. For instance, see Benedict Anderson's *Imagined Communities* and the works he cites in the preface to the revised edition (New York and London: Verso, 1991), xiv–xv. For other citations see note 20 in chapter 3 and notes 2 and 5 in chapter 4. The view of identity that I advocate is in opposition to that expressed in Hans Mol, ed., *Identity and Religion: International, Cross-Cultural Approaches* (London: Sage Publications, 1978). There Mol characterizes the position of the contributors: "Generally the authors use 'identity' in the sense of a stable niche rather than in the sense of something to be negotiated" (1). For me, identity is dynamic, not stable; negotiated, not given. There are multiple forms of collective identity—national, regional, ethnic, racial, and religious—and all are constructed in ongoing contests among members of a group. These contests for identity often focus on shared symbols. On the struggle over religious identity or "orthodoxy" I have found the writings of Bourdieu helpful: Pierre Bourdieu, *Outline of a Theory of Practice*, trans. Richard Nice (1972; reprint, Cambridge: Cambridge University Press, 1977), 168–69.

4. Catholic clergy often have appealed to popular piety as a means of moving the laity toward orthodoxy and orthopraxis. On this practice in the nineteenth century, see Ann Taves, *The Household of Faith: Roman Catholic Devotions in Mid-Nineteenth-Century America* (Notre Dame: University of Notre Dame Press, 1986), 89–111. I learned of the bishop's interest in Mirta in a conversation the day after I saw the "parallel ritual" at the shrine. Interview, Agustín Román, 9 June 1994, Miami. There are many signs of Mirta's local popularity. One woman, for instance, wrote to Bishop Román to suggest that Mirta be invited to preach at a mass broadcast over Radio Martí for the Cuban rafters being detained in camps in Guantanamo and other sites. Mirta, this woman from Hialeah suggested, was the perfect speaker "for this moment." It was a moment of, as many called it, "crisis," in which thousands of rafters had taken to the sea to find their way to America. C.R. to Agustín Román, 26 August 1994, in the author's files. As other scholars have emphasized, the clergy in the United States also have tried to bring other Latinos into the institutional Church. The parallels with the experience of Puerto Ricans in New York are especially illuminating, even if the case of Cubans in Miami differs in important ways. On the Archdiocese of New York's response to the Puerto Rican migration of 1946–64—including its use of the fiesta of the patron saint (Saint John the Baptist) as a tool of evangelization—see Ana María Díaz-Stevens, *Oxcart Catholicism on Fifth Avenue: The Impact of the Puerto Rican Migration upon the Archdiocese of New York* (Notre Dame: University of Notre Dame Press, 1993). See also Jaime R. Vidal, "Citizens yet Strangers: The Puerto Rican Experience," in *Puerto Rican and Cuban Catholics in the U.S., 1900–1965*, ed. Jay P. Dolan and Jaime R. Vidal (Notre Dame: University of Notre Dame Press, 1994), 69, 88–111.

5. The literature on Santería in Spanish and English is increasing. Fernando Ortiz and Lydia Cabrera lead the way. For instance, see Fernando Ortiz, *Los bailes y el teatro de los negros en el folklore de Cuba* (Havana: Ediciones Cardenas, 1951), and Cabrera, *El monte*. My account of the formation of Santería is profoundly influenced by their work, and I also found more recent scholarship helpful. I have especially drawn on Jorge Castellanos and

Isabel Castellanos, *Cultura afrocubana,* vol. 3: *Las religiones y las lenguas* (Miami: Ediciones Universal, 1992), and George Brandon, *Santería from Africa to the New World: The Dead Sell Memories* (Bloomington: Indiana University Press, 1993). The latter presents one of the most nuanced historical accounts available in English. I also have learned from Brown, "Garden in the Machine," and Murphy, *Santería.* The bibliography in Brandon's book is very helpful: Brandon, *Santería,* 187–202. For a solid overview of the literature, which needs updating, see Diana González Kirby and Sara María Sánchez, "Santería: From Africa to Miami via Cuba: Five Hundred Years of Worship," *Tequesta* 48 (1988): 36–48. Other works, which also consider Miami, are Mercedes Cros Sandoval, *La religión afro-cubana* (Madrid: Playor, 1975), and Stephan Palmié, "Afro-Cuban Religion in Exile: Santería in South Florida," *Journal of Caribbean Studies* 5 (Fall 1986): 171–79. A former "insider" who then did graduate work in religious studies has offered a valuable account: Raúl J. Cañizares, *Walking with the Night: The Afro-Cuban World of Santería* (Rochester, Vt.: Destiny Books, 1993).

6. The classic discussion of the *cabildos* is Fernando Ortiz, "Los cabildos afro-cubana," *Revista Bimestre Cubana* 16, no. 1 (January–February 1921): 5–39. See also Brandon, *Santería,* 70–74.

7. Paul VI, "Evangelii Nuntiandi," apostolic exhortation, in *On Evangelization in the Modern World* (Washington, D.C.: USCC Office for Publishing and Promotion Services, 1975), 7. Pope John Paul II and many other church leaders also celebrated the "new evangelization" that was popularized by Pope Paul VI's document. For instance, see John Paul II's unofficial championing of the "new evangelization" in John Paul II, *Crossing the Threshold of Hope,* trans. Jenny McPhee and Martha McPhee (New York: Knopf, 1994), 105–17. Many local Cuban-born clergy at the shrine and in the parishes address Santería and evangelization in Sunday sermons. Several of them have written on the topic for Spanish-language periodicals. Two, Sosa and Román, have even addressed the issues in master's theses. Agustín A. Román, "The Popular Piety of the Cuban People" (M.A. thesis, Barry University, 1976). Sosa wrote two theses, the first in a seminary and the second in an anthropology department. Juan Sosa, "La Santería: The Lucumí Traditions of the Afro-Cuban Religions" (M.Th. thesis, St. Vincent dePaul Seminary, 1972); Juan Sosa, "La Santería: A Way of Looking at Reality" (M.A. thesis, Florida Atlantic University, 1981). In an interview with me, Sosa revealed that he originally selected the topic of Santería at the urging of two local priests, Bryan Walsh and Agustín Román. Interview, Juan Sosa, 9 June 1993, St. Catherine of Sienna Church, Miami. At the time, Román had not been appointed auxiliary bishop in the Archdiocese. Sosa quotes from Paul VI's reflections on evangelization, for example, in "Popular Religiosity and Religious Syncretism: Santería and Spiritism," *Documentaciones sureste* 4 (March 1983): 22. On the clergy's self-defined "moderate" path to evangelization, see Román, "Popular Piety," 74–78.

8. The distinction between religion as prescribed and religion as practiced is drawn by William A. Christian Jr., *Local Religion in Sixteenth-Century Spain* (Princeton: Princeton University Press, 1981), 178.

9. The quotations are from Román, "Popular Piety," 1. Other information here came from interviews. Interview, Agustín Román, 15 July 1991, Miami; Interview, Juan Sosa, 9 June 1993, Miami.

10. Interview, Agustín Román, 15 July 1991, Miami. I later discovered that the bishop used the same image, and the same diagram, in his master's thesis. Román, "Popular Piety," 9. He talked with me at some length about his missionary training and experience in one of the long taped interviews (two hours and thirty minutes) I conducted with him at the shrine in 1993. To restore through oral history some of the past that was lost when Hurricane Andrew destroyed shrine records, I have donated a copy of that tape to the shrine. Interview,

Agustín Román, 7 July 1993, Archives, Shrine of Our Lady of Charity. He told me in that interview, for instance, that he took his two-step evangelization strategy at the shrine ("determine the reality and then the response") from French missionary practices he had learned at a missionary seminary in Canada and then applied in his contacts with southern Chilean Indians at Holy Spirit Church in Temuko from 1962 to 1966.

11. Román, "Popular Piety," 78, 46–48; Interview, Luís Pérez, 9 March 1994, San Lázaro Catholic Church, Hialeah, Florida. The pamphlet or brochure, written in Spanish and distributed by the shrine, includes no author or date: "Verdades de la fe Cristiana" [The Truths of the Christian Faith], brochure (Miami: Ermita de la Caridad, n.d.). Estimating the number of followers of Santería is difficult for several reasons. It is important to distinguish those with interest from those who have gone through the week-long initiation ceremony (*asiento*). Also, since they are highly secretive, they are not counted systematically. All estimates, then, are highly tentative. One of the most judicious discussions of the number of followers is in Brown, "Garden in the Machine," 111–12, note 170. Reliable estimates of Santería followers in metropolitan Miami, or Dade County, vary from 50,000 to 70,000. Based on 1990 census figures, that would mean approximately 9 to 11 percent of the local Cuban population. This number, as David H. Brown notes, fails to distinguish among degrees of involvement. Most would agree that only about 2 percent are actually initiated. The number of those with some interest, however, is higher, as Román and the clergy realize. The key figure in the Supreme Court case regarding Santería sacrifice in the city of Hialeah, Ernesto Pichardo, estimated that there are 70,000 followers in the area: David Hancock, "Judge: City Can Ban Sacrifices," *Miami Herald* 6 October 1989, 1B, 2B.

12. Interview, Agustín Román, 15 July 1991, Miami. One Cuban-born priest in Miami who read this chapter in draft in 1996 was worried that I had presented the Church's leaders as wanting "to purify the people from a detrimental 'curse,' or to 'exorcise' them from a consuming evil." "In reality," he continued, "I look at the complex tension from a diverse philosophical perspective and not from the right/wrong perspective." The "syncretism" is an "expression of a thirst for God." Still, this local priest also went on to suggest that although the Church should "dialogue" with all religious expressions, "the Church should make clear its nature and purpose, its traditions and practices." "In other words, while we can have dialogues with santeros and babalaos, we must still *clarify* for them that Oshun and Our Lady of Charity are not the same" (emphasis mine). He also went on to condemn Santería as leading to "psychological dependency and magic." Christianity, on the other hand, "can offer to people in Santería a true avenue of freedom and growth away from magic." I hope it is clear that I do not mean to offend, or to demean the priests' efforts to evangelize. I try to show that they are sincere expressions of their concern for the people's religious state. Still, it seems undeniable, at least to me, that they want to distinguish orthodox Catholicism from the practices that mix influences from Santería, whether they talk about "clarifying" or "purifying." I take this to be an understandable impulse, even a role-specific obligation. They are, after all, representatives of the Church, which has clear standards of orthodoxy and orthopraxis. In the end, it might be that some priests and I must respectfully disagree on this point.

13. Araceli Cantero, "Shrine—A Place of Popular Worship," *The Voice*, 5 September 1975, 3.

14. On Ochún see Lydia Cabrera, *Yemayá y Ochún*, 2nd ed. (New York: C.R., 1980). Followers of Ochún often are guarded at the shrine, but some confess openly their devotion, as did one woman who told me that she has a room at home filled with "todos los santos de la Santería." Included there is a seven-foot statue of Our Lady of Charity, she said. Interview #95, 28 January 1992, female, age 39, born Havana, arrived 1969. My account of the priest's encounter is in Fieldnotes, 7 June 1994, Shrine. He chastised the couple because they had not

baptized their son (age 12) in the Catholic Church. The quotation from the confraternity member is from T.N., personal interview with the author, 23 June 1992, Miami.

15. The Román quotation appeared in Cantero, "Shrine—A Place of Popular Worship."

16. This official account of Our Lady of Charity is repeated often. For one source, see the brief history found in a pamphlet published by the shrine: Delia Díaz de Villar, "Historia de la Devoción a la Virgen de la Caridad," in *Ermita de la Caridad* (Miami: Ermita de la Caridad) 12–18. It also appeared in various undated public letters, on shrine stationery, that were circulated by the clergy. See "September 8th—Feast of Our Lady of Charity" and "History of the Devotion to Our Lady of Charity of El Cobre," Vertical File "Virgen del Cobre," Library, St. Vincent dePaul Regional Seminary, Boynton Beach, Florida. On 1 April 1687, the young black in the boat, then age eighty-five, offered a sworn testimony to the miraculous events of that day in the Bay of Nipe. That document is found in El Archivo de Indias in Seville, and it has been reprinted in several places. For example, see "Transcripción del documento original de Juan Moreno," in *La Virgen de la Caridad: Patrona de Cuba*, ed. Mario Vizcaíno (Colección: Cultura Cubana; Miami: Instituto pastoral del sureste, 1987), 23–26.

17. This Santería counter-narrative is recorded in several places, with slight variations. See Canizares, *Walking with the Night*, 65–66, and Sandoval, *La religión Afro-Cubana*, 11–12. Other narratives are told by Cuban Americans of all sorts. Of course, followers of Santería tell stories of their interactions with Ochún, tales about her help with love or health or money. The links between the Virgin and the *orisha* appear also in narratives by Cuban American poets and novelists. For example, note that the Virgin of Cobre often appears associated with Santería, not Catholicism, in fictional narratives by Cuban Americans. See Cristina García, *Dreaming in Cuban* (New York: Knopf, 1992), 199.

18. A number of sources discuss the use of holy water in Santería ritual practice. For example, see Cañizares, *Walking with the Night*, 43. The couple whom the priest chastised at the shrine in 1994 for their leanings toward Santería had, by the way, come to the shrine office to get more holy water. That is how their encounter with the priest began.

19. For a helpful overview of Babalú Ayé/San Lázaro see Lydia Cabrera, "Babalú Ayé–San Lázaro," in *La enciclopedia de Cuba*, 6:268–82.

20. Pedro Luís Pérez, "Vida de San Lázaro, amigo de Jesucristo," pamphlet (n.p., n.d.). The author of this pamphlet is the pastor of San Lázaro Catholic Church in Hialeah. He also is the priest who says the rosary at the annual feast-day mass. The information about Father Pérez's catechetical efforts at his parish are recorded in a taped interview: Interview, Luís Pérez, 9 March 1994, San Lázaro Catholic Church, Hialeah, Florida. For other clerical attempts to deal with the confusions between the Catholic saint and the African *orisha*, see Juan J. Sosa, "Devociones populares: Santa Bárbara y San Lázaro," *Cuba diáspora* (1976): 101–3.

21. El Rincón, also known as Iglesia Católica Apostólica de San Lázaro, is an independent "Catholic" Church, not affiliated with any other body. Many of the rituals—for example, the regular "masses"—closely parallel celebrations in Roman Catholic parishes, although the large statue of Saint Lazarus to the left of the main altar is the main focus of the people's devotions, and they do not recognize the authority of the pope. Members and leaders of the Church believe that they have been harassed by the Archdiocese and the nearby Roman Catholic Church with the similar name, San Lázaro Catholic Church. As one worshiper at El Rincón told me, "I just think that people should go to Church where they want to." Yet, she claimed, the Roman Catholics continue to be "hostile." Fieldnotes, 9 March 1994, El Rincón, Hialeah, Florida. The other church that claims "Catholic" identity dismisses both El Rincón and the Archdiocese of Miami, as one member told me. The former have no ties with other churches and fail to admonish Santería followers in the congregation, and the Roman Catholics err in many ways—theologically, ethically, and ritually. Members of Santuario del Cobre deny the authority of the pope, for instance, and their priest says the consecration of

the mass in Latin. It is a "traditionalist" church, one member told me, emphatically not affiliated with Santería. She proudly handed me a printed sheet documenting the "apostolic succession" of their community and its links with other churches in a body they call the "American Catholic Church." It has churches and leaders in the United States (Seattle), in Mexico, and throughout the Americas. In direct opposition to the authority of the shrine in Miami, El Santuario del Cobre even has organized a "Cofradía de la Caridad del Cobre." On the latter, see *Boletín Mensual*, Santuario de Nuestra Señora de la Caridad del Cobre, vol. 2, no. 3, (March 1994): 3. The other information and quotations came from interviews and fieldwork at the Church. Interview, 9 March 1994, female, age 42, born in Camagüey, Santuario del Cobre, Hialeah, Florida. I compiled information on the gravestones during a visit in 1994: Fieldnotes, Woodlawn Cemetery, 5 September 1994, Miami. The primitive painting, "La Virgen del Cobre," was executed by Angelo Romano and commissioned by Mrs. Carlotta Callas. It was originally presented to the shrine in 1969. It now hangs in a second-floor lobby at the Pastoral Center of the Archdiocese of Miami. For a description of the painting and donation, see the untitled image and one-page account in the files of *La Voz Católica* in the Pastoral Center, Miami Shores. For another interesting image, see the print by Victor Gómez entitled "Cachita." Information about him and the image appeared in a cover story: Araceli M. Cantero, "Surge 'Cachita' barroca y guajira," *La Voz Católica*, 30 August 1991, 9, 16. The bumper sticker of Our Lady of Charity is manufactured by J. T. World Decals of Jackson Heights, New York. It is sold at the shrine.

22. The first quotation is from an interview conducted by one of my former Cuban American students at the University of Miami, Roxana Sosa: Interview, 12 December 1991, M.G., female, arrived in 1965, Miami. The second quotation is from my own fieldwork but based on an earlier interview by Roxana Sosa. Interview by Roxana Sosa, 12 December 1991, M.M., female, arrived 1964, Miami. Interview by the author, 8 June 1994, M.M., female, arrived 1964, Miami. On Cuban yard shrines in Miami, see James R. Curtis, "Miami's Little Havana: Yard Shrines, Cult Religion, and Landscape," *Journal of Cultural Geography* 1 (Fall/Winter 1980): 1–15. For interesting parallels in the use of yard shrines among Italian Americans in New York, see Joseph Sciorra, "Yard Shrines and Sidewalk Altars of New York's Italian Americans," in *Perspectives in Vernacular Architecture, III*, ed. Thomas Carter and Bernard L. Herman (Columbia: University of Missouri Press, 1989), 185–98.

23. Interview with the author, 8 June 1994, M.M., female, age 83, arrived 1964, Miami.

24. David Hilary Brown offers a useful list of *botánicas* in the United States, including those in South Florida. Brown, "Garden in the Machine," 491–92. They open and close occasionally, but that list is a good starting point for the study of these local *botánicas*. I refer here in passing to African American and Anglo interest in Santería. However, that seems rather minimal from what I can gather, at least so far. For evidence, even celebration, of African American and Anglo participation in Santería, see Tracy Cochran, "Among the Believers: Converts to Santería," *New York*, 12 October 1987, 33–34; "African Religion Finding Following in America," *Religion Watch* 9 (December 1993): 4; and Cañizares, *Walking with the Night*, 122–25. A fuller study is needed.

25. I learned about the private vigil and offerings of flowers in the yard shrine owner's home in an interview I conducted at her residence: Interview by the author, 8 June 1994, M.M., female, age 83, arrived 1964, Miami. The description of the "block party" is from Interview #133, 2 March 1992, male, age 59, born Camagüey (raised Havana), arrived 1961. The information on the ritual in the backyard pool came from an interview with a yard shrine owner in Little Havana, conducted by Roxana M. Sosa: Interview with M.C., 12 December 1991, female, arrived 1962, Miami. In that interview M.C. identified herself as a follower of Santería.

26. Fieldnotes, 8 September 1994, Hialeah, Florida. Interview with church member, San-

tuario del Cobre, 8 September 1994, Hialeah, Florida. The church member continually dismissed the mass at the racetrack, in which the Virgin was transported by helicopter by Hermanos al Rescate (Brothers to the Rescue), as a "big show."

27. Fieldnotes, 8 September 1994, annual feast-day mass, Hialeah Racetrack, Hialeah, Florida. Of course, this was not the first warning about Santería to be offered at a festival mass. For instance, during the rosary in 1992 Father Luís Pérez reminded the crowd that Santa Bárbara, San Lázaro, and Ochún are "not in communion with the pope," not Catholic. Fieldnotes, 8 September 1992, annual feast-day mass, Bayfront Park, Miami. The official estimate of the 1994 crowd at "more than 12,000" appeared in the local newspaper account: Betty Cortina, "12,000 Attend Special Mass," *Miami Herald*, 9 September 1994, 19A. That estimate seemed accurate to me. It was one of the larger crowds I had seen at the annual festival. See also the account in the Spanish-language diocesan periodical: María Vega, "No teman, la tormenta va a pasar," *La Voz Católica*, 23 September 1994, 10.

CHAPTER THREE

1. "Yvonne": Interview #17, 3 February 1992, female, age 24, born U.S., resides Hollywood, California. "Manuel": Interview #18, 3 February 1992, male, age 51, born Oriente, arrived 1961, resides Hollywood, California. Fieldnotes, 3 February 1992, Shrine of Our Lady of Charity, Miami.

2. Fieldnotes, 22 May 1993, Peregrinación, St. Kieran's Church and the Shrine of Our Lady of Charity, Legion de María, Curia de Miami, Miami. On the Legion of Mary see Richard P. McBrien, ed., *The HarperCollins Encyclopedia of Catholicism* (San Francisco: Harper San Francisco, 1995), 763. The membership of the Legion of Mary in the United States has increased since the 1960s. On that point see James J. Kenneally, *The History of American Catholic Women* (New York: Crossroad, 1990), 199.

3. Sandra L. Zimdars-Swartz explores the apocalyptic tone of Marian devotion, and modern Marian devotion more generally, in *Encountering Mary: Visions of Mary from La Salette to Medjugorje* (New York: Avon Books, 1992). She focuses on the United States in "The Marian Revival in American Catholicism: Focal Points and Features of the New Marian Enthusiasm," in *Being Right: Conservative Catholics in America*, ed. Mary Jo Weaver and R. Scott Appleby (Bloomington: Indiana University Press, 1995), 213–40. The quotation is from Interview #121, 18 February 1992, female, age 25, born United States (to Cuban parents).

4. Interview #14, 29 January 1992, female, age 45, born Cuba, arrived ? (no answer).

5. On the Latino Catholic population of metropolitan Miami see Ira M. Sheskin, *The Synod Survey Summary Report: The Archdiocese of Miami* (Miami: Archdiocese of Miami, 1986),

6. Interview #239, 10 June 1994, male, age 49, born Venezuela, arrived 1969.

6. "Peregrinaciones a la ermita de la Caridad 1992," annual calendar, mailing, vol. 20, no. 119, Ermita de la Caridad, Miami, author's files.

7. Interview #299, 8 September 1994, female, age 45, born Haiti, arrived 1989. On Haitian Vodou, the Ezili, and the connections with Our Lady of Charity, see Karen McCarthy Brown, *Mama Lola: A Vodou Priestess in Brooklyn* (Berkeley: University of California Press, 1991), 220–25; and Leslie G. Desmangles, *The Faces of the Gods: Vodou and Roman Catholicism in Haiti* (Chapel Hill: University of North Carolina Press, 1992), 131–45.

8. Interview #293, 7 September 1994, female, age 55, born Haiti, arrived 1969.

9. Interview #298, 8 September 1994, female, age 42, born Haiti, arrived 1980.

10. On the predominance of women in United States religious history, see Ann Braude, "Women's History *Is* American Religious History," in *Retelling U.S. Religious History*, ed.

Thomas A. Tweed (Berkeley: University of California Press, 1997). Ann Taves argued that "women made up the bulk of the members of the various devotional organizations" in the United States during the nineteenth century: *The Household of Faith: Roman Catholic Devotions in Mid-Nineteenth-Century America* (Notre Dame: University of Notre Dame Press, 1986), 18. The quotations from travelers are from, in order: Alexander Gilmore Cattel, *To Cuba and Back in 22 Days* (Philadelphia: The Times Printing House, 1874), 33–35; Richard Burleigh Kimball, *Cuba and the Cubans* (New York: Samuel Hueston, 1850), 152–57; James Williams Steele, *Cuban Sketches* (New York: G. P. Putnam's Sons, 1881), 174–81. These travel accounts also are excerpted in Louis A. Pérez Jr., ed., *Slaves, Sugar, and Colonial Society: Travel Accounts of Cuba, 1801–1899* (Wilmington, Del.: Scholarly Resources Books, 1992), 147–78. Interview, Father Juan Sosa, 9 June 1993, St. Catherine of Siena Church, Miami. My thinking about gender and religion has been shaped by a wide range of scholars, too many to mention here. In defining gender I follow Joan W. Scott: "Gender: A Useful Category of Historical Analysis," *Journal of American History* 91 (December 1986): 1053–75. Gender involves, Scott argues, two related propositions: "Gender is a constitutive element of social relationships based on perceived differences between the sexes, and gender is a primary way of signifying relationships of power" (1067). Scott goes on to explain that the first assertion involves four secondary elements—available symbols (e.g., Mary), normative interpretations of those symbols, social institutions and organizations, and subjective identity. Scott has little to say about religion. On gender and religion, still useful is Caroline Walker Bynum, Steven Harrell, and Paula Richman, eds., *Gender and Religion: On the Complexity of Symbols* (Boston: Beacon, 1986). For an introduction to the scholarship and issues concerning religion and gender in the United States, see Ann Taves, "Women and Gender in American Religion(s)," *Religious Studies Review* 18, no. 4 (October 1992): 263–70; Rosemary Skinner Keller, Ann Braude, Maureen Ursenback Beecher, and Elizabeth Fox-Genovese, "Forum: Female Experience in American Religion," *Religion and American Culture* 5 (Winter 1995): 1–21; David G. Hackett, "Gender and Religion in American Culture, 1870–1930," *Religion and American Culture* 5 (Summer 1995): 127–57. Susan Juster's provocative book on Protestants in revolutionary New England offers an interesting model for gender analysis: Susan Juster, *Disorderly Women: Sexual Politics and Evangelicalism in Revolutionary New England* (Ithaca: Cornell University Press, 1994). On American Catholic women see Karen Kennelly, ed., *American Catholic Women: A Historical Exploration* (New York: Macmillan, 1989), and Kenneally, *History of American Catholic Women*. There still is a great deal of historical and ethnographic work to do on Latina Catholicism. On devotion to the Mexican national Virgin see Jeanette Rodriguez, *Our Lady of Guadalupe: Faith and Empowerment among Mexican-American Women* (Austin: University of Texas Press, 1994). In *Hispanic Women: Prophetic Voice in the Church* (San Francisco: Harper and Row, 1988), Ada María Isasi-Díaz and Yolanda Tarango offer a theological essay that includes, and is grounded in, conversations with Latinas, including Cubans.

11. Bishop Pfeifer was quoted in a story about the National Conference of Catholic Bishops in the *News and Observer* (Raleigh), 17 November 1994, 6A. Interview #86, 11 July 1993, male, age 31, born Matanzas, arrived 1970.

12. Interview, Father Juan Sosa, 9 June 1993; Interview, Dr. Mercedes Cros Sandoval, 15 June 1993, Miami.

13. On *exilio* as a male noun see Ruth Behar, ed., *Bridges to Cuba/Puentes a Cuba* (Ann Arbor: University of Michigan Press, 1995), 13. The quotation is from Interview #238, 9 June 1994, male, age 69, born Havana, arrived 1962. On shrines as spaces at the intersection of the public and private realms, see Robert A. Orsi, " 'He Keeps Me Going': Women's Devotion to Saint Jude Thadeus and the Dialectics of Gender in American Catholicism, 1929–1965," in *Belief in History: Innovative Approaches to European and American Religion*, ed. Thomas

Kselman (Notre Dame: Notre Dame University Press, 1991), 143–44. Interview, Father Juan Sosa, 9 June 1993. Father Sosa also told me that he conducted a survey of shrine visitors, while he served there, and that survey supported his observations: women visit more often in "ordinary time."

14. I am indebted to Caroline Walker Bynum's scholarship for highlighting the ways that women and men can experience and interpret symbols differently. She made that point in her introduction to *Gender and Religion* (13) and in her other historical work as well.

15. On the age distribution of Catholics in the Archdiocese of Miami see Sheskin, *Synod Survey*, 5. A useful summary of a survey of 4,676 Cuban exiles, which was sponsored by the exiled clergy, is found in "Sumario de la encuesta de la reflexión cubana en la diáspora," *Ideal* 20, no. 261 (1992): 4–5. That includes data on age distribution. On the age of Cuban migrants compared with other Spanish-speaking and non-Spanish-speaking Americans, see Thomas D. Boswell and James R. Curtis, *The Cuban-American Experience: Culture, Images, and Perspectives* (Totowa, N.J.: Rowman and Allanheld, 1983), 100–102. See also Thomas D. Boswell and Manuel Rivero, *Demographic Characteristics of Pre-Mariel Cubans Living in the United States: 1980* (Miami: Research Institute for Cuban Studies, University of Miami, [1985]), 19–22. The Marielitos were about ten years younger than the pre-1970 Cuban migrants. On this see María Cristina García, *Havana USA: Cuban Exiles and Cuban Americans in South Florida, 1959–1994* (Berkeley: University of California Press, 1996), 68.

16. Fieldnotes, 10 June 1994, Shrine of Our Lady of Charity. On church attendance see Sheskin, *Synod Survey*, 16. Interview #114, 15 February 1992, female, age 62, born Havana, arrived 1963.

17. The grandmother: Interview #277, 6 September 1994, female, age 67, born Havana, arrived 1959. The daughter, and mother of the toddler: Interview #278, 6 September 1994, female, age 27, born U.S. (Hialeah). Fieldnotes, 6 September 1994, Shrine of Our Lady of Charity.

18. Interview #232, 9 September 1994, female, age 24, born Havana, arrived 1980; Interview, Bishop Agustín Román, 15 July 1991, Shrine of Our Lady of Charity. The young woman who said that she was "half Cuban" is still rather devout. She told me that she visits the shrine "three times each month." Interview #204, 11 March 1994, female, age 24, born Puerto Rico (to Cuban parents), arrived 1979.

19. Many studies of European migrants—Catholics, Protestants, and Jews—have noted intergenerational differences in religious practice. Similar patterns have held among migrants from Asia, including those who have arrived since the changes in the 1965 immigration laws. For example, see Raymond Brady Williams, *Religions of Immigrants from India and Pakistan: New Threads in the American Tapestry* (Cambridge and New York: Cambridge University Press, 1988).

20. As many scholars in the humanities and social sciences have argued since the 1970s, the traditional racial categories have no biological basis, no essentialized meaning, and therefore little descriptive value. "Race" is a cultural construct, formed in a particular historical context and (more recently) challenged in another. Some scholars have abandoned the term, choosing instead to focus on "ethnicity." As the social historian Peter H. Wood put it, "Race is an idea whose time has almost passed." Peter H. Wood, "Race," *Encyclopedia of American Social History*, vol. 1, ed. Mary Kupiec Cayton, Elliott J. Gorn, and Peter W. Williams (New York: Scribner's, 1993), 437. However, "ethnicity," another socially created category, is not free from conceptual problems. Further, attending to the discourse about race (as part of the discourse about ethnicity) can be useful, as one anthropologist has argued persuasively: "Concepts of race can nevertheless be important to the extent that they inform people's actions; at this level, race exists as a cultural construct, whether it has 'biological' reality or not." Thomas Hylland Eriksen, *Ethnicity and Nationalism: Anthropological Perspectives*

(London and Boulder: Pluto Press, 1993), 4–5. For me, race (like ethnicity) is a social construct that serves to distinguish groups which have some regular interaction by creating a shared social identity characterized by metaphoric kinship. It is through the discourse about race, then, that people make meaning (since it defines "us" and "them") and negotiate power (since it usually privileges "us"). My thinking about race has been shaped not only by Eriksen (see pp. 4–6, 12) but also by other scholars. For an interesting overview see Richard H. Thompson, *Theories of Ethnicity: A Critical Appraisal*, Contributions in Sociology, no. 82 (Westport, Conn.: Greenwood, 1989). For a helpful collection, see Werner Sollors, ed., *The Invention of Ethnicity* (New York and Oxford: Oxford University Press, 1989). For an exploration of the issue of how we classify social groups, see Cynthia K. Mahmood and Sharon L. Armstrong, "Do Ethnic Groups Exist?: A Cognitive Perspective on the Concept of Cultures," *Ethnology* 31 (January 1992): 1–14. Barbara Jeanne Fields focuses on the history of the ideology of "race" in the United States in "Slavery, Race, and Ideology in the United States of America," *New Left Review*, no. 181 (May/June 1990): 95–118. Gastón Baquero offers a useful overview of race and slavery in Cuba: "El negro en Cuba," *La enciclopedia de Cuba*, vol. 5 (San Juan and Madrid: Enciclopedia y Clásicos Cubanos, 1974), 415–53.

21. Julia Ward Howe, *A Trip to Cuba* (Boston: Ticknor and Fields, 1860), 216. The assessment of white exiles' attitudes is from Baquero, "El negro en Cuba," 415. Raúl J. Cañizares, "Cuban Racism and the Myth of the Racial Paradise," *Ethnic Studies Report* 8, no. 2 (July 1990): 27–32. Cañizares also discusses the system of racial typing in that article, and he argues that racism was an "integral part of Cuban society," even before United States attitudes had influence in the early twentieth century. For a study of race relations and racial discourse during the late nineteenth and early twentieth centuries, see Aline Helg, *Our Rightful Share: The Afro-Cuban Struggle for Equality, 1886–1912* (Chapel Hill: University of North Carolina Press, 1995).

22. The quotation is from Olga Portuondo Zúñiga, *La Virgen de la Caridad del Cobre: Símbolo de cubanía* (Santiago de Cuba: Editorial Oriente, 1995), 33. Portuondo emphasizes the importance of Our Lady of Charity as creole and the significance of her legend for constructing ethnic and cultural unity. On this point see also 45–47, 170–73, 246.

23. Ermita de la Caridad, "By-Laws of the Confraternity or Brotherhood of Our Lady of Charity of Cobre," n.d., Files of Bishop Agustín Román, Archdiocese of Miami, Pastoral Center, Miami Springs; Fieldnotes, 5 June 1994, Haitian Catholic Center, Miami.

24. On the racial composition of the exile population, before and after the 1980 Mariel boatlift, see Boswell and Curtis, *Cuban-American Experience*, 102–4; James S. Olson and Judith E. Olson, *Cuban Americans: From Trauma to Triumph* (New York: Twayne, 1995), 61, 84; Mercedes Cros Sandoval, *Mariel and Cuban National Identity* (Miami: Editorial SIBI, 1986), 18; Boswell and Rivero, *Demographic Characteristics of Pre-Mariel Cubans*, 22–24; García, *Havana USA*, 44, 68. See also Heriberto Dixon, "The Cuban-American Counterpoint: Black Cubans in the United States," *Dialectical Anthropology* 13 (1988): 227–39. As these authors realize, census data for Cubans can be misleading because they are based on self-identification. For instance, in the 1980 census, interpreting race as ethnic or cultural background, many "Hispanic" and mixed-race Cubans identified themselves as "Spanish" (not white or black), writing in this label rather than choosing one of those available. All these statistics, then, should be approached with caution.

25. Interview #199, 10 March 1994, female, age 64, born Matanzas, arrived 1970.

26. Interview, Father Juan Sosa, 9 June 1993, St. Catherine of Siena Church, Miami.

27. The occupational statistics about the 1960s migrants are cited in Olson and Olson, *Cuban Americans*, 61. On class and Cuban migrants, before and after the Marielitos, see also Boswell and Rivero, *Demographic Characteristics of Pre-Mariel Cubans*, 49–61; Boswell and Curtis, *Cuban-American Experience*, 104–6; and García, *Havana USA*, 20, 68. For an

interesting collection of sources that explore the interconnections of race and class (and gender), see Margaret L. Andersen and Patricia Hill Collins, ed., *Race, Class, and Gender: An Anthology* (Belmont, Calif.: Wadsworth, 1995).

28. Lydia Cabrera, *Yemayá y Ochún*, 2nd ed. (New York: C.R., 1980). For example, there are Catholic parishes dedicated to the Virgin of Cobre in the western provinces of Havana and Matanzas. On these parishes, see Ismael Testé, *Historia eclesiástica de Cuba*, 3 vols. (Burgos: Editorial El Monte Carmelo, 1969), 2:519-25, 3:183. The early Cuban migrants also were disproportionately urban. As Olson and Olson note, "Although only 31 percent of Cuban society in 1959 lived in a large city, more than 83 percent of the immigrants came from major metropolitan areas" (*Cuban Americans*, 61). In exile, too, the Cubans are highly urban, as most other migrants have been. As many as 98 percent of Cubans in the United States have lived in large metropolitan areas. The majority of those Cubans live in Miami. On this point see Boswell and Rivero, *Demographic Characteristics of Pre-Mariel Cubans*, 17.

29. Interview #155, 6 June 1993, female, age 50, born Cuba, arrived 1970. As I suggested in an earlier note, Robert Orsi has suggested that shrines can stand at the intersection of the private and the public: Orsi, " 'He Keeps Me Going,' " 144.

30. Two students of Christian pilgrimage have identified seven types of modern Catholic shrines, or really types of origin stories for shrines: significant site shrines, ex-voto shrines, devotional shrines, spontaneous miracle shrines, acquired object shrines, found object shrines, and apparitional shrines. See Mary Lee Nolan and Sidney Nolan, *Christian Pilgrimage in Modern Western Europe*, Studies in Religion (Chapel Hill: University of North Carolina Press, 1989), 216-90. See especially table 7.1 on page 218. On "devotional shrines" see Nolan and Nolan, *Christian Pilgrimage*, 237-41. They do not identify diasporic nationalist shrines, as I do here.

31. Interview #49, 1 March 1992, female, age 47, born Havana, arrived 1974.

32. In chapter 6, note 2, I set out my understanding of ritual practice. Here I offer only three proposals to clarify my approach: (1) rituals, as I view them, are embodied social practices that place participants temporally and spatially and thus negotiate meaning and power; (2) interpreting rituals is more like making sense of gestures than reading texts: it involves attending to the multiple and ambiguous significations of bodily practices—like kneeling; (3) ritual practices are both verbal and nonverbal. In the remainder of this chapter I attend to the different kinds of pilgrimage practices.

33. Fieldnotes, 30 December 1995, Mary's Central Shrine of the Miraculous Medal, St. Vincent's Seminary, Philadelphia. The organization dedicated to the Miraculous Medal was founded in 1915, and the Philadelphia shrine was built in 1927. For a brief description of the Philadelphia shrine see J. Anthony Moran, *Pilgrims' Guide to America: United States Catholic Shrines and Centers of Devotion* (Huntington, Ind.: Our Sunday Visitor Publishing Division, 1992), 62-63. The priests at Our Lady of Charity's shrine in Miami have tried to modify the practice of bringing flowers. As I noticed on a visit in 1994, a sign in Spanish encouraged devotees to "bring food for the poor as an offering to the Virgin, instead of flowers." Fieldnotes, 7 June 1994, Shrine of Our Lady of Charity.

34. I noticed the posing and photographing on a Sunday afternoon in 1992 and on many subsequent visits: Fieldnotes, 26 January 1992, Shrine of Our Lady of Charity; Diana Eck, *Darśan: Seeing the Divine Image in India*, 2nd rev. and enl. ed. (Chambersburg, Pa.: Anima Books, 1985), 1-10, 59-75.

35. I recorded my observations of and conversations with the tourists from North Carolina in Fieldnotes, 9 July 1994, Shrine of Our Lady of Charity. The tourist couple from New York provided their views in two interviews that day: Interview #245, 10 June 1994, female, age 57, born Havana, arrived 1978 (resides New York); Interview #246, 10 June 1994, male, age

? (no answer), born Oriente, arrived 1962 (resides New York). The quotation here is from Interview #245.

36. Nancy: Interview #262, 11 June 1994, female, age 23, born New York (to Puerto Rican parents). Robert: Interview #263, 11 June 1994, male, age 23, born United States (to Cuban parents). The first quotation is from Interview #263; the second, longer one is from Interview #262.

37. One of these two young Cubans was the only sixteen-year-old to slip into my sample. I talked informally to many other Cubans under eighteen, but he was the only one with whom I did a structured interview. I misjudged his age: he looked much older. Interview #8, 29 January 1992, male, age 16, born United States (Miami); Interview #9, 29 January 1992, female, age 20, born United States (Miami). I recorded my observations of and conversations with the elderly walker in Fieldnotes, 7 June 1994, Shrine of Our Lady of Charity.

38. Rosa's performance: Fieldnotes, 12 March 1994, Shrine of Our Lady of Charity. All rituals are created over and over again by participants in some sense, but Rosa's is an especially interesting example of an invented ritual. On this see Ronald L. Grimes, "Reinventing Ritual," *Soundings* 75 (Spring 1992): 21–41.

39. In his study of Catholic religious practice in a mountainous valley in northern Spain, William Christian Jr. distinguished five kinds of prayers: generalized affective prayers, prayers for the fulfillment of the annual round, prayers for forgiveness, prayers for salvation, and instrumental prayers. William A. Christian Jr., *Person and God in a Spanish Valley*, rev. ed. (Princeton: Princeton University Press, 1989), 114. Here I emphasize only the first and last of Christian's types, since those were most prominent at the Miami shrine. The factory worker was born in Camagüey, arrived in 1951, and now lives in Homestead, Florida, although he spent much of his adult life in New Jersey. I recorded his story during a visit to the shrine on the feast day in 1995: Fieldnotes, 8 September 1995, Shrine of Our Lady of Charity. Others who said that they prayed for money or work included the following: Interview #71, 26 February 1992, male, age 46, born Oriente, arrived 1980 (resides New Jersey); Interview #173, 6 June 1993, female, age 63, born "Cuba," arrived ? (no answer); Interview #201, 10 March 1994, male, age 73, born Las Villas, arrived 1961.

40. On Lourdes and La Salette see Zimdars-Swartz, *Encountering Mary*, 27–67. On Chimayó see Ramón A. Gutiérrez, "El Santuario de Chimayó: A Syncretic Shrine in New Mexico," in *Feasts and Celebrations in North American Ethnic Communities*, ed. Ramón A. Gutiérrez and Geneviève Fabre (Albuquerque: University of New Mexico Press, 1995), 71–86. On St. Jude's shrine see Robert A. Orsi, *Thank You, St. Jude: Women's Devotion to the Patron Saint of Hopeless Causes* (New Haven: Yale University Press, 1996). The hospital shrine in Illescas, Spain, is described in Carmelo Viñas and Ramón Paz, eds., *Relaciones histórico-geográfico-estadísticas de los pueblos de España: Hechas por iniciativa de Felipe II, Reino de Toledo*, vol. 2, part 1 (Madrid: Consejo superior de investigaciones científicas, 1951), 497. On the enshrinement of Our Lady of Charity in the hospital chapel in Cobre, see Portuondo, *Virgen de la Caridad*, 104. On the Cuban shrine as "the Lourdes of Cuba" see Gerrado Castellanos, *Huellas del pasado* (Havana: Editorial Hermes, 1925), 318. Quoted in Portuondo, *Virgen de la Caridad*, 250.

41. Interview #118, 16 February 1992, female, age 52, born Havana, arrived 1962.

42. For instance, fifty persons attended a healing mass in March 1994: Fieldnotes, healing mass, 12 March 1994, Shrine of Our Lady of Charity. The woman who accompanied her ill husband to the shrine was Interview #191, 10 March 1994, female, age 64, born Havana, arrived 1962.

43. The woman with the mauled daughter: Interview #30, 7 February 1992, female, age 48, born Las Villas, arrived 1970. José, the man in the wheelchair who brought his two friends: Interview #226, 7 June 1994, male, age 36, born U.S. (New York).

44. Prayer card, blue ink on white paper, 3.5" × 4.5", "Oración de la madre que espera un hijo," La Ermita de la Caridad, Miami. The quotations from pilgrims are, in order, from: Interview #113, 15 February 1992, female, age 42, born Oriente, arrived 1972; Interview #129, 1 March 1992, female, age 28, born Chile, arrived 1986.

45. John and Jeannette, the engaged couple: Interview #4, 26 January 1992, male, age 28, born Colombia, arrived 1988; Interview #5, 26 January 1992, female, age 22, born Havana, arrived 1988. Interview, Ricardo, 11 March 1994, Miami.

46. Eduardo Boza Masvidal, Agustín A. Román, and Enrique San Pedro, S.J., *CRECED: Documento final* (Miami: Comunidades de reflexión eclesial Cubana en la diáspora [CRECED], 1993), 89–90. On Cuban American family life see also Boswell and Curtis, *Cuban American Experience*, 180–87, 190–91; Tina Bucavalas, Peggy A. Bulger, and Stetson Kennedy, *South Florida Folklife* (Jackson: University Press of Mississippi, 1994), 69–74. The latter is especially illuminating on the rituals that mark the changes in the life cycle. "Noche Familiar," the reverse side of "Peregrinaciones a la Ermita de la Caridad 1992," the mailing that lists the collective rituals for the year, blue ink on white paper, 14" × 8.5" (folded into a mailing that is 4.5" × 8.5"), vol. 20, no. 119, Ermita de la Caridad, Miami, author's files.

47. Pilar: Interview #144, 6 June 1993, female, age 31, born Havana, arrived 1981.

48. The quotations are from, in order: Interview #227, 7 June 1994, female, age 21, born Havana, arrived 1984; Interview #122, 18 February 1992, female, age 63, born Oriente, arrived 1956; Interview #208, 12 March 1994, female, age 21, born Havana, arrived 1989. As William Christian Jr. has argued in *Local Religion in Sixteenth-Century Spain* (Princeton: Princeton University Press, 1981), "The importance of vows in the daily life of Catholic laity has been insufficiently appreciated, perhaps precisely because most personal vows were made and fulfilled without clerical intervention" (31). On vows see Christian's discussion in that book (23–69).

49. The recent arrival who suggested that all recent migrants make vows to visit: Interview #276, 6 September 1994, male, age 47, born Las Villas, arrived 1994. The Cuban resident: Interview #149, 6 June 1993, female, age 65, born Havana (resides Havana). The man who promised to visit the Cobre shrine if communism falls: Interview #201, 10 March 1994, male, age 73, born Las Villas, arrived 1961.

50. Interview #30, 7 February 1992, female, age 48, born Las Villas, arrived 1970; Interview #227, 7 June 1994, female, age 21, born Havana, arrived 1984; Interview #18, 3 February 1992, male, age 51, born Oriente, arrived 1961.

CHAPTER FOUR

1. *Oxford English Dictionary*, 2nd ed., s.v. "diaspora." Many works construct groups as "diasporic," for example, Martin L. Kilson and Robert I. Rotberg, eds. *The African Diaspora* (Cambridge: Harvard University Press, 1976); and Richard Harvey Brown and George V. Coelho, eds., *Migration and Modernization: The Indian Diaspora in Comparative Perspective*, Studies in Third World Societies (Williamsburg, Va.: Department of Anthropology, William and Mary College, 1987). One volume explores the continuities and discontinuities between Jewish and African diasporas. See especially the essay by John Gibbs St. Clair Drake, "African Diaspora and Jewish Diaspora: Convergence and Divergence," in *Jews in Black Perspectives: A Dialogue*, ed. Joseph R. Washington Jr. (Rutherford, N.J.: Fairleigh Dickinson University Press, 1984), 19–41. Sometimes the term has been applied more loosely. See Lawrence J. McCaffrey, *The Irish Diaspora in America* (Bloomington: Indiana University Press, 1976), and Glenn Hendricks, *The Dominican Diaspora: From the Dominican Republic to New York City* (New York and London: Teachers College Press, 1974).

2. James Clifford, "Diasporas," *Cultural Anthropology* 9 (August 1994): 302–38; William Safran, "Diasporas in Modern Societies: Myths of Homeland and Return," *Diaspora* 1, no. 1 (1991): 83–99. My understanding of collective identity (which I define in note 3, chapter 2) has been formed in relation to scholarship in several fields. On the transtemporal processes of diasporic identity, I have applied scholars' reflections on collective memory: Maurice Halbwachs, *The Collective Memory*, trans. Francis J. Ditter Jr. and Vida Yazdi Ditter (1950; reprint, New York: Harper and Row, 1980); Marie-Noëlle Bourguet, Lucette Valensi, and Nathan Wachtel, eds., *Between Memory and History* (Chur, Switzerland: Harwood Academic Publishers, 1990); Eric Hobsbawm and Terrance Ranger, eds., *The Invention of Tradition* (Cambridge: Cambridge University Press, 1983); Paul Connerton, *How Societies Remember* (Cambridge: Cambridge University Press, 1989); and Michael G. Kammen, *Mystic Chords of Memory: The Transformation of Tradition in American Culture* (New York: Knopf, 1991). On the spatial dimensions of collective identity, I have learned from scholars in human geography and cultural studies: Yi-Fu Tuan, *Space and Place: The Perspective of Experience* (Minneapolis: University of Minnesota Press, 1977); Edward Soja, *Postmodern Geographies: The Reassertion of Space in Critical Social Theory* (New York and London: Verso, 1989); Henri Lefebvre, *The Production of Space*, trans. Donald Nicholson-Smith (Oxford: Blackwell, 1991); Michel Foucault, "Questions on Geography," in *Power/Knowledge: Selected Interviews and Other Writings, 1972–1977*, ed. Colin Gordon (New York: Pantheon Books, 1980), 63–77; Michel de Certeau, *The Practice of Everyday Life*, trans. Steven F. Rendell (Berkeley: University of California Press, 1984).

3. For an interesting exploration of transnational migration that seeks to work toward a new paradigm, see Nina Glick Schiller, Linda Basch, and Cristina Blanc-Szanton, eds., *Toward a Transnational Perspective on Migration: Race, Class, Ethnicity, and Nationalism Reconsidered*, Annals of the New York Academy of Sciences, no. 645 (New York: New York Academy of Sciences, 1992). Many works draw distinctions among types of migrants. A helpful study is William Petersen, "A General Typology of Migration," *American Sociological Review* 23 (June 1958): 256–66. For a more recent overview, see David M. Heer, "Migration," in *The Social Science Encyclopedia*, ed. Adam Kuper and Jessica Kuper (London: Routledge and Kegan Paul, 1985), 524–26.

4. Yi-Fu Tuan, *Topophilia: A Study of Environmental Perception, Attitudes, and Values* (Englewood Cliffs, N.J.: Prentice-Hall, 1974), 99; Tuan, *Space and Place*, 157; Edward Said, "The Mind of Winter: Reflections on Life in Exile," *Harper's* 269 (September 1984): 49; Uva de Aragón Clavijo, *El caimán ante el espejo: Un ensayo de interpretación de lo cubano* (Miami: Ediciones Universal, 1993), 17, 11. For a perceptive account by an Anglo writer who lives in New York, see David Rieff, *The Exile: Cuba in the Heart of Miami* (New York: Simon and Schuster, 1993).

5. Cristina García, *Dreaming in Cuban* (New York: Knopf, 1992), 219; Clavijo, *El caimán ante el espejo*, 17. The dissenting view of national identity is recorded in a letter: J.B. to the author, 8 July 1996. My understanding of nation and nationalism has been shaped by a number of works. Among the most useful are Benedict Anderson, *Imagined Communities: Reflections on the Origin and Spread of Nationalism*, rev. ed. (New York and London: Verso, 1991), and Ernest Gellner, *Nations and Nationalism* (Ithaca: Cornell University Press, 1983). See also works cited in the preface to Anderson, *Imagined Communities*, xii. Especially important for my thinking also have been several articles in a special issue of *Cultural Anthropology*. Akhil Gupta and James Ferguson, "Beyond 'Culture': Space, Identity, and the Politics of Difference," *Cultural Anthropology* 7 (February 1992): 6–22; and Liisa H. Malkki, "National Geographic: The Rooting of Peoples and the Territorialization of National Identity among Scholars and Refugees," *Cultural Anthropology* 7 (February 1992): 24–44. See also Liisa H. Malkki, *Purity and Exile: Violence, Memory, and National Cosmology among Hutu Refugees*

in Tanzania (Chicago: University of Chicago Press, 1995). A number of works in political anthropology also shed light on the subject, including Thomas Hylland Eriksen, *Ethnicity and Nationalism: Anthropological Perspectives* (London and Boulder: Pluto Press, 1993); and Zdzislaw Mach, *Symbols, Conflict, and Identity: Essays in Political Anthropology* (Albany: State University of New York Press, 1993). A special issue of the journal published by the National Museum of Ethnography in Stockholm is also helpful: *Ethnos* 58 (1993).

6. The term "diaspora nationalism" seems to have been coined by Ernest Gellner. See Gellner, *Nations and Nationalism*, 101–9. The quotations are from Ruth Behar, ed., *Bridges to Cuba/Puentes a Cuba* (Ann Arbor: University of Michigan Press, 1995), 2–3. A number of interpretations of Cuban Miami's political culture have appeared. Among the most interesting are Joan Didion, *Miami* (New York: Pocket Books, 1987); Rieff, *The Exile*; and María Cristina García, *Havana USA: Cuban Exiles and Cuban Americans in South Florida, 1959–1994* (Berkeley: University of California Press, 1996). Didion documents some of the coercion and violence against dissenters in Cuban Miami, including the story of how one radio commentator had his legs blown off in the parking lot of WQBA for editorializing that Cubans should not bomb opponents. Didion, *Miami*, 133, 149.

7. The geographer John Kirkland Wright coined the term "geopiety" to describe the religious dimension of this attachment. See John K. Wright, "Notes on Early American Geopiety," in *Human Nature in Geography: Fourteen Papers, 1925–65* (Cambridge: Harvard University Press, 1966), 250–85. Others have modified and applied the term. See Yi-Fu Tuan, "Geopiety: A Theme in Man's Attachment to Nature and Place," in *Geographies of the Mind: Essays in Historical Geosophy*, ed. David Lowenthal and Martyn J. Bowden (New York: Oxford University Press, 1976), 11–39, and Tuan, *Space and Place*, 149–60.

8. The prediction by the astrologer Mary García was included in a wide-ranging article on the topic: Lydia Martin and Tananarive Due, "Does Pluto's Presence Signal Castro's End?," *Miami Herald*, 28 August 1994, 1J, 5J. Two surveys in 1992 reported on Cuban American attitudes about returning to their homeland. The first was conducted by pollsters with Bendixen and Associates for a local Spanish-language television station (WLTV). The second was designed by sociologist Juan Clark of Miami Dade Community College and conducted under the auspices of the Archdiocese of Miami. The first survey found that 24 percent said they would return to a free Cuba. The second reported that 45 percent were unsure, and only 10 percent said they definitely would do so. "Poll: Optimism Dips over Quick Castro Fall," *Miami Herald*, 5 May 1992, 1B, 2B. "Sumario de la encuesta de la reflexión cubana en la diáspora," *Ideal* 20, no. 261 (1992): 4–5. The expression about Christmas Eve dinner was mentioned by shrine visitors and is discussed briefly in María Christina Herrera, "The Cuban Ecclesial Enclave in Miami: A Critical Profile," *U.S. Catholic Historian* 9 (Spring 1990): 212.

9. The passage about the "imaginary island" is from an article that analyzes the transition to a "literature of settlement": Jorge Duany, "Neither Golden Exile nor Dirty Worms: Ethnic Identity in Recent Cuban American Novels," in *Cuban Studies 23*, ed. Jorge Pérez-López (Pittsburgh: University of Pittsburgh Press, 1993), 180. Roberto G. Fernández, *Raining Backwards* (Houston: Arte Público Press, 1988), 12–13. Ricardo Pau-Llosa, "The Map," in his *Cuba* (Pittsburgh: Carnegie Mellon University Press, 1993), 11–13. The first-generation poet I mention is Lourdes Casal, and the phrase is from "La Havana 1968," in *Veinte años de literatura cubanoamericana: Antología 1962–1982*, ed. Silvia Burunat and Ofelia García (Tempe: Bilingual Press/Editorial Bilingüe, 1988), 53. Pura del Prado, "Letanía de la patria," in Burunat and García, *Veinte años de literatura cubanoamericana*, 70–72. Even pre-1959 Cuban migrants could feel that they were political exiles in the United States, as did the poet José María Heredia (1803–38), who had to flee the homeland to avoid prison. For a famous artistic expression of his sentiments from his exile in New York, see "Exiles' Hymn," in his

Poesías líricas (1825; reprint, Paris: G. Hermanos, 1892). I could cite many examples of diasporic nationalism in the visual arts as well. For example, the work of Arturo Rodríguez, a Cuban exile painter in Miami, uses fantasy to explore exilic life. In all of Rodríguez's work, human figures appear in the air, anchored only to moving surfaces such as wheels, ladders, water—or the shoulders of another untethered person. In this way Rodríguez poignantly captures the condition of exile. See, for instance, *Misterioso* (1987), which appeared in the joint exhibition entitled "Crossings" at the Museum of Art in Fort Lauderdale. For an account of the show, see Helen L. Kohen, "Memorable *Crossings* for Painters in Exile," *Miami Herald*, 11 September 1994, 1I, 7I.

10. On the role of ethnic groups in shaping the American cultural landscape, see Michael P. Conzen, "Ethnicity on the Land," in *The Making of the American Landscape*, ed. Michael Conzen (Boston and London: Unwin Hyman, 1990), 221–48. For Cuban influences on Miami's landscape see Thomas D. Boswell and James R. Curtis, *The Cuban American Experience: Culture, Images, and Perspectives* (Totowa, N.J.: Rowman and Allanheld, 1983), 89–96.

11. According to 1990 census records, the population of Little Havana was 69,327. This and a great deal of other information about the area can be found in City of Miami, Planning, Building, and Zoning Department, *La Pequeña Havana: Community Development Target Area*, Neighborhood Planning Program, 1994–96 (Miami: City of Miami, n.d.). Local Cuban leaders drew up design guidelines for the area in 1988 that aimed to preserve the area as "a showcase of Hispanic culture" (1). Toward that end, they exhorted planners and architects and business leaders to use portales, arches, balconies, campaniles, fountains, stucco walls, and barrel tile in construction and renovation. All of that is aimed at preserving the "Spanish/Mediterranean architectural flavor" (15). The Cuban leaders behind this plan aimed to take advantage of the Latino character of the area for the city's economic development, even though the effects of their efforts might be to continue the Cuban influence on the cultural landscape. City of Miami, Planning Department, "Design Guidelines and Standards: Latin Quarter District" (Miami: City of Miami, 1988). For a local dispute that erupted in 1993 over the enforcing of these architectural guidelines, see Peter Whoriskey, "A Matter of Style," *Miami Herald* 17 October 1993, 1B, 5B.

12. *Ecos de Santa Cruz del Sur: Boletín oficial del Municipio de Santa Cruz del Sur en el exilio*, vol. 2, no. 2 (March/April 1994). The headquarters I refer to in Little Havana, near the memorials, is the Municipality in Exile from Santiago de Cuba. Helpful statistical information on these organizations in Miami is included in Thomas D. Boswell and James R. Curtis, "The Hispanization of Metropolitan Miami," in *South Florida: Winds of Change*, ed. Thomas D. Boswell, prepared for the Annual Conference of the Association of American Geographers (Miami, 1991), 140–61. See also Joaquín Freire Díaz, *Historia de los municipios de Cuba* (Miami: La Moderna Poesía, 1985).

13. I interviewed that newsletter editor and confraternity member several times. The first was in 1994 at the shrine. Interview #222, 5 June 1994, male, age 77, born Sagua la Grande, arrived 1961, resides Miami.

14. C. P. Tiele, s.v. "Religions," *Encyclopedia Britannica*, 9th ed. (New York: Charles Scribner's Sons, 1886). A good deal has been written on early scholarly attempts to classify religions. For one helpful overview by an influential student of "comparative religion," see Morris Jastrow Jr., *The Study of Religion*, Classics in Religious Studies Series (1901; reprint, Chico: Scholars Press, 1981), 58–128.

15. Emile Durkheim, *The Elementary Forms of the Religious Life*, trans. Joseph Ward Swain (1915; reprint, New York: Free Press, 1965), 62 (emphasis added); Mircea Eliade, *The Sacred and the Profane*, trans. Willard R. Trask (New York and London: Harcourt Brace Jovanovich, 1959), 20–65.

16. Jonathan Z. Smith, *Map Is Not Territory: Studies in the History of Religions* (Chicago: University of Chicago Press, 1978), 291; Charles H. Long, *Significations: Signs, Symbols, and Images in the Interpretation of Religion* (Philadelphia: Fortress, 1986), 7. On the bonds with places, or geopiety, see Wright, *Human Nature in Geography*, 250–85. The authors of textbooks on the geography of religions explore similar issues in slightly different ways. See David E. Sopher, *Geography of Religions* (Englewood Cliffs, N.J.: Prentice-Hall, 1967), and Chris C. Park, *Sacred Worlds: An Introduction to Geography and Religion* (London and New York: Routledge, 1994).

17. Smith, *Map*, 143.

18. Jonathan Z. Smith used the term "diasporic religion," although as I indicate later I use it here in a slightly different way.

19. Smith, *Map*, xiv, 101–3, 186, 308–9.

20. All quotations are from ibid, xiv.

21. Ibid.

22. The quotations are from, in order, the following structured interviews taken on a single day. These are representative of the responses I received during the several years of interviewing: Interview #279, 7 September 1994, female, age 45, born Havana, resides Havana; Interview #285, 7 September 1994, male, age 45, born Morón, arrived 1993, resides Hollywood, Florida; Interview #284, 7 September 1994, female, age 39, born Havana, arrived 1969, resides Hollywood, Florida; Interview #294, 7 September 1994, female, age 48, born Cabaiguán, arrived 1988, resides Miami.

23. F.N., "Cuba," dated 27 July 1994. The poem was enclosed in a letter to the shrine: F.N. to Agustín Román, 22 September 1994, in the author's files. In that letter this devotee tells Bishop Román that she composed the letter "shortly after having arrived from Cuba." Even though it might not be published, the poem has crossed the boundary into the public realm, both because she sent it to the shrine clergy and because, as the author recounts, she showed it to "various friends." It was they who "insisted" that she send a copy to Román.

24. The five goals of CRECED are repeated in several publications. See, for instance, an issue of *Ideal* devoted mostly to that project: Rafael B. Abislaimán, "CRECED: Una visión panorámica," *Ideal* 21 (1993): 5–7; Eduardo Boza Masvidal, Agustín A. Román, and Enrique San Pedro, S.J., eds., *CRECED: Documento final* (Miami: Comunidades de reflexión eclesial Cubana en la diáspora [CRECED], 1993), 131–32.

25. I met the confraternity member who makes telephone calls at a *romería* at the shrine, and I spoke with her several times after that. Our first meeting was in 1994: Interview #221, 5 June 1994, female, age 72, born Havana, arrived 1961, resides Miami.

26. On the horizontal and vertical dimensions of ritualization, see Catherine Bell, *Ritual Theory, Ritual Practice* (New York: Oxford University Press, 1992), 125.

27. Fieldnotes, 8 Sepember 1992, feast-day mass, Bayfront Park, Miami; Rubén Travieso, *Recuerdos de Cuba: Libro para colorear* (Miami: Rubén Travieso, 1980). The radio station that sponsored the coloring book distribution was WQBA, which promotes itself as "la Cubanísima," the most Cuban. By "artifact" I mean an object made or modified by humans. I treat the topic in greater depth in chapter 5. See note 6 in that chapter for a list of some of the sources that have shaped my view of material culture.

CHAPTER FIVE

1. The quotations are from Chuck Gómez and Miguel Pérez, "Cubans Flock to Dedication of Shrine," *Miami Herald*, 3 December 1973, 1B, 2B. The estimate of the crowd, and other details about that ceremony are included (with photographs) in Bob O'Steen, "Young and Old

Showed Emotion: Flags Waved in 'Silent Applause,'" *The Voice*, 7 December 1973, 13; "Que la Virgen de la Caridad una al Exilio y lo conduzca a la liberación . . . ," and Gustavo Peña Monte, "Miles de cubanos en la dedicación de la Ermita," *La Voz Católica* (Spanish suppl.), 7 December 1973, 16. The dedication mass was concelebrated in front of the shrine by Cardinal John Krol of Philadelphia, president of the United States Conference of Bishops; Archbishop Coleman Carroll of Miami; Auxiliary Bishop René Gracida of Miami; Monsignor Eduardo Boza Masvidal; Father Orlando Fernández; and Monsignor Bryan Walsh, director of the Apostolate for Immigrants and Refugees. On *los taburetes*, the traditional Cuban chairs that are still built by farmers in the Cuban countryside, see the brief pamphlet published by the shrine: "La Virgen de la Caridad en Miami" (Miami: Ermita de la Caridad, n.d.). Agustín Román also mentions the chairs, and other features I describe here, in "La Virgen de la Caridad en Miami," in *Ermita de la Caridad* (Miami: Ermita de la Caridad, 1986), 6–8. As I learned in an interview with the contractor, the tiled image of the Virgin over the central portal was done by a local subcontractor, Rivera Tile Company, from a painting by Teok Carrasco, who also executed the mural inside the shrine. Interview, Donald W. Myers (shrine contractor), 6 September 1994, Miami. I discuss the mural—as well as the busts, statue, and building—later.

2. The interpretation of the shrine as "a place of refuge" for migrants is from Interview #223, male, age 27, born U.S. Several clergy and laity compared the shrine to the Statue of Liberty. For example, Interview #69, 3 January 1992, female, age 66, born Santiago de las Vegas, arrived 1962. Archbishop Coleman Carroll used the same analogy. He predicted in 1973 that the shrine "will be to this area what the Statue of Liberty is to the northeast section of the U.S." Quoted on the back of a photograph that appeared in *The Voice*, 7 December 1973, Archives, *La Voz*, Archdiocese of Miami, Pastoral Center, Miami Springs.

3. The shrine exterior is constructed of poured, reinforced concrete. It has a structured steel shell between the buttresses on the upper walls. The outer walls were finished with sprayed concrete (Gunite), the contractor noted. Interview, Donald W. Myers (shrine contractor), 6 September 1994, Miami. I use the typology of architectural styles employed by Alan Gowans. In his terms, the Miami shrine might be labeled "sculptural modernism," though it shares some features with "geometric modernism" too. My working definition of "modern" architecture also is from Gowans. The Miami shrine fits one of these four characteristics of "modernism" less clearly: there is more ornament than on most modern buildings. As the photographic record shows, the original shrine roof was blue and gold, not the less ornate rust color that appears there now. The tiled image of the Virgin and the three fishermen over the main portal also is not typical of "modern" architectural style. Alan Gowans, *Styles and Types of North American Architecture: Social Function and Cultural Expression* (New York: Icon Editions, HarperCollins, 1992), 307–9, 281–83. I also have profited from Manfredo Tafuri and Francesco Dal Co, *Modern Architecture*, trans. Robert Erich Wolf (New York: Harry N. Abrams, 1979). Besides these and other works on the history of architecture, some studies of religious buildings are helpful: James P. Wind, *Places of Worship: Exploring Their History* (Nashville: American Association for State and Local History, 1990); J. G. Davies, *Temples, Churches, and Mosques: A Guide to the Appreciation of Religious Architecture* (New York: Pilgrim Press, 1982); and J. G. Davies, "Architecture," in *Encyclopedia of Religion*, ed. Mircea Eliade (New York: Macmillan, 1987). Some other sources focus on the United States: Peter W. Williams, "Religious Architecture and Landscape," *Encyclopedia of the American Religious Experience*, ed. Charles Lippy and Peter W. Williams (New York: Scribner's, 1988); John Dillenberger, *The Visual Arts and Christianity in America* (New York: Crossroad, 1988); the editors of *Architectural Record*, *Religious Buildings* (New York: McGraw-Hill, 1979); and Bartlett H. Hayes, *Tradition Becomes Innovation: Modern Religious Architecture in America* (New York: Pilgrim Press, 1983). Le Courbusier's chapel in

Ronchamp is reproduced frequently. See, for example, Vincent Scully Jr., *Modern Architecture* (New York: George Braziller, 1967), figures 138–41. The visitor identified the shrine as "modern" in Interview #204, 11 March 1994, female, age 24, born Puerto Rico (of Cuban exile parents), arrived 1979.

4. On the number of Catholic shrines in the United States, see J. Anthony Moran, *Pilgrims' Guide to America: United States Catholic Shrines and Centers of Devotion* (Huntington, Ind.: Our Sunday Visitor Publishing Division, 1992), 7. Another reference work counts 330 for North America, 973 for Latin America, and 6,150 for Western Europe: Michael Walsh, *Dictionary of Catholic Devotions* (San Francisco: Harper San Francisco, 1993), 242. For an analysis of those European shrines see Mary Lee Nolan and Sidney Nolan, *Christian Pilgrimage in Modern Western Europe*, Studies in Religion (Chapel Hill: University of North Carolina Press, 1989). Helpful anthropological perspectives on Christian pilgrimage are found in the essays in John Eade and Michael J. Sallnow, eds., *Contesting the Sacred: The Anthropology of Christian Pilgrimage*, (London and New York: Routledge, 1991). That work persuasively challenges Victor Turner's understanding of pilgrimage and pilgrimages sites, but the latter's work remains important. Victor Turner and Edith Turner, *Image and Pilgrimage in Christian Culture: Anthropological Perspectives* (New York: Columbia University Press, 1978). So, too, are the historical studies of Catholic devotion in Spain by William A. Christian Jr., including *Local Religion in Sixteenth-Century Spain* (Princeton: Princeton University Press, 1981). For an interesting collection of studies of pilgrimage sites in the United States, mostly by geographers, see Gisbert Rinschede and S. M. Bhardwaj, eds., *Pilgrimage in the United States, Geographia Religionum*, vol. 5 (Berlin: Dietrich Reimer Verlag, 1990). Another geographer offers a useful synthesis of the literature on the topic: Chris C. Park, *Sacred Worlds: An Introduction to Geography and Religion* (London and New York: Routledge, 1994), 245–85. The *Oxford English Dictionary* defines a "shrine" as a "receptacle containing an object of religious veneration," noting that its core meaning is a "box." The meaning of "santuario" which is offered as a synonym for "ermita" (the term that Miami's Cubans use for the building that enshrines their patroness) is similar. S.v. "ermita" in *Diccionario de la Lengua Española* (Madrid: Real Academia Española, 1992). A helpful overview of the meaning and function of shrines in various cultures is Paul B. Courtright, "Shrines," in *Encyclopedia of Religion*.

5. Gómez and Pérez, "Cubans Flock to Dedication," 1B, 2B; Interview #281, 6 September 1994, male, age 27, born Cuba, arrived 1993.

6. My approach here, and throughout this chapter, has been informed by recent literature in material culture studies, which includes scholarship from folklore, art and architectural history, religious studies, anthropology, and geography. It is characterized, as Thomas J. Schlereth has suggested, by its focus on a type of evidence—artifacts. Thomas J. Schlereth, *Cultural History and Material Culture: Everyday Life, Landscapes, and Museums* (Ann Arbor: UMI Research Press, 1990), 27. Schlereth's prologue to that collection of his essays, "Material Culture or Material Life? Discipline or Field? Theory or Method?," is a useful introduction to material culture studies. So is Thomas J. Schlereth, ed., *Material Culture: A Research Guide* (Lawrence: University Press of Kansas, 1985). By "artifact" I mean an object made or modified by humans, as Jules David Prown defines it in his contribution to another helpful volume on the topic, *History from Things: Essays on Material Culture*, ed. Steven Lubar and W. David Kingery (Washington and London: Smithsonian Institution Press, 1993). That volume considers all four types of artifacts I identify here—art, utilitarian objects, architecture, and landscapes. On reading cultural landscapes see the chapter in that volume by Pierce Lewis, "Common Landscapes as Historic Documents." Geographers, like Lewis, have been especially helpful in analyzing these landscapes. On this see also D. W. Meinig, ed., *The Interpretation of Ordinary Landscapes: Geographical Essays* (New York: Oxford

University Press, 1979), and Michael P. Conzen, ed., *The Making of the American Landscape* (Boston and London: Unwin Hyman, 1990).

7. Bishop Coleman F. Carroll to the Reverend Eugenio Del Busto, 7 April 1964, "Shrine of Our Lady of Charity (1966–1973)," File, Archives, Archdiocese of Miami, Miami Shores. In that memorandum, Carroll reported that he was "sounding out" the idea of a Cuban shrine with "three or four reliable and dependable people."

8. Interview, Monsignor Bryan Walsh, 17 June 1993, Miami. Walsh was the first to tell me what I later learned from other sources—that the site of the shrine had been intended for another use by Archbishop Hurley. Hurley had served in Yugoslavia from 1945 to 1950. When he took over his pastoral work in Florida he decided to build a shrine to Catholic martyrs to communism. Filled with the anticommunist spirit of the 1950s, Walsh recalled, Hurley made plans for the site. He commissioned the refugee sculptor Ivan Mestrovic to execute a pietá and granite reliefs of six "heroes of the faith." The pietá and those images now adorn the Pastoral Center of the Archdiocese of Miami, where a plaque there explains their history and intention—"to commemorate the sufferings of the Church under atheistic communism." The plan was aborted, Walsh suggested, when the diocese was split and Carroll took control of the Catholics in South Florida. Financial problems and other obstacles prevented that monument from being installed on the grounds beside Mercy Hospital, where the Cuban shrine now stands.

9. The quotation is from Interview #130, 1 March 1992, female, age 67, born Havana, arrived 1960. Thirty-one visitors used the exact phrase "frente a Cuba" to describe the significance of the site. For example, Interview #138, 3 March 1992, male, age 57, born Ciego de Avila, arrived 1969.

10. In structured interviews sixty-five visitors specifically mentioned the significance of the shrine's placement by the sea. Many others said the same in unstructured interviews. The structured interviews quoted or cited in this paragraph are, in order, from the following interviews: Interview #84, 31 July 1991, female, age 43, born Havana, arrived 1955; Interview #219, 4 June 1994, female, age 34, born Pinar del Río, arrived 1960; Interview #212, 12 March 1994, female, age 53, born Havana, arrived 1993; Interview #232, 9 June 1994, female, age 24, born Havana, arrived 1980; Interview #228, 7 June 1994, female, age 20, born Havana, arrived 1980; Interview #221, 5 June 1994, female, age 72, born Havana, arrived 1961; Interview #260, 11 June 1994, male, age 54, born Morón, arrived 1973.

11. It might help here, as I begin to interpret the building, to say something about my approach to architecture. Like the art historian Thomas A. Markus, I suggest that to decode a building's meaning is to position oneself in three "domains": those of building, the texts, and the experiencing subjects. To consider the building itself, in turn, involves analysis of its form, function, and space. To consider texts is to examine available verbal and nonverbal representations of the building from a variety of sources, including designer's drawings and writings. The "intentions" of the architect or donors, however, are not privileged sources, though they are part of the record. Their meanings contend with those of others who experience the architectural space. The experience of the building by the interpreter and those who use it, then, are important sources for any attempt to decode its multiple meanings. Although Markus puts it slightly differently, I also believe that all three domains—buildings, texts, and experiencing subjects—must be understood in terms of the wider social context. Buildings, in my view, are social sites at which viewers negotiate meaning and power. Thomas A. Markus, *Buildings and Power* (London and New York: Routledge, 1993), 3–28. The interpretation of the confessional is from "Our Lady of Charity Shrine," pamphlet (Miami: Ermita de la Caridad, n.d.). This freely distributed document is an 8.5" × 11" paper folded three times to form a small pamphlet. It interprets the place for non-Spanish-speaking visitors. The scriptural passage is from Luke 1:47.

12. This list of the committee members is taken from an undated document that was printed on letterhead with the group name and member list (twenty-five participants) and apparently circulated during the first years of their work: "Comité Pro Monumento-Ermita a la Virgen de la Caridad," Cuban Archives, Richter Library, University of Miami, Coral Gables. The membership changed slightly over time, and those who led the drive to build the temporary chapel, now the convent, included others who did not participate in planning the permanent shrine (e.g., Manolo Reyes). For a list of those who served on the committee in the year that the shrine was dedicated, see "Comité de recaudación y construcción pro–Ermita de la Caridad," October 1973, "Shrine of Our Lady of Charity," File, Archives, Archdiocese of Miami, Miami Shores. See also the photograph of twenty committee members reprinted in *Ermita de la Caridad*, 36. One influential member of the committee, Agustín Román, told me that the group made design decisions—not only about the cornerstone but also the six buttresses, which I discuss later. Archbishop Carroll had the final word, of course. Interview, Agustín Román, 7 July 1993, Shrine of Our Lady of Charity.

13. For readers unfamiliar with the term *reredos*, it refers to a wall or screen, usually of wood or stone, that rises behind an altar. It usually is decorated. One exile publication reproduced a photograph of that main altar area in an article recalling Pope Paul VI's naming the site a Minor Basilica. "El Cobre: Basílica Menor," *Cuba diáspora* (1981): 50–51. By identifying the Cobre shrine as "Spanish colonial" I refer to its architectural style, not its dedication date. As I noted in chapter 1, the current shrine in Cobre is relatively recent. It was dedicated on 8 September 1927.

14. Araceli M. Cantero, "Un manto que refleje su blancura," *La Voz Católica*, 24 February 1989, 4.

15. David Freedberg, *The Power of Images: Studies in the History and Theory of Response* (Chicago: University of Chicago Press, 1989), 1.

16. Interview #300, 7 September 1994, male, age 38, born Sancti Spíritus, arrived 1984. The image at the shrine also has evoked more malevolent responses. For example, one weekday morning in 1994 a twenty-seven-year-old man damaged the statue as he tried to steal it. This homeless man, who was drunk when he was arrested, told the police that he agreed to attempt the desecration and theft in exchange for $80 and liquor. The man who hired him to "steal a doll from a church" was a white man in his thirties who had contacted him on a street corner in the northwest section of the city and driven him to the shrine. That man, whose motives remained unclear, escaped in his pickup truck when visitors interrupted the theft in progress. It was then that the statue fell and was damaged slightly. See Jorge Dávila Miguel, "Intentan robar estatua de la Virgen," *El Nuevo Herald*, 24 November 1994, 1A; Karen Branch, "A Symbol of Faith Desecrated," *Miami Herald*, 24 November 1994, 1A. In an interview with me, and in his public statements, Bishop Román was forgiving and conciliatory. He visited the homeless man in jail and concluded that he knew nothing of the statue's significance for Cubans. Agustín A. Román, telephone interview with the author, 7 December 1994. See also Agustín A. Román, "La patrona de la diáspora cubana," *El Nuevo Herald*, November 1994.

17. For a compelling account of the function of secondary images associated with pilgrimage sites, see Freedberg, *Power of Images*, 120–24.

18. For example, wall paintings have been excavated in various sites in Mexico—Teotihuacan in central Mexico, near Oaxca City in southern Mexico, and in Bonampak in the Valley of the Usumacinta River. The Spanish colonists brought their own traditions of mural painting too. See Emily Edwards, *Painted Walls of Mexico: From Prehistoric Times until Today* (Austin: University of Texas Press, 1966). On the mural at the shrine two documents are especially important. The artist offered his own account: Teok Carrasco, "Descripción del mural," in *Ermita de la Caridad*, 38–41. Concepción García described the painting briefly

and, more important, identified the forty-four historical figures on it in "El mural de la Ermita," *Cuba diáspora* 7 (1979): 73–78. That account was reproduced (without attribution) and distributed by the shrine clergy as a pamphlet: "El mural de la Ermita" (Miami: Ermita de la Caridad, n.d.). In a taped interview with the author, the muralist identified the color of the mural as sepia, a brownish gray to dark olive brown. That was the appropriate shade, he told me at his home, because it was "a religious color." Interview, Teok Carrasco, 9 July 1993, Miami. In my analysis of Carrasco's painting at the shrine, I excavate cultural meanings. With Janet Wolff and other art historians, in my analysis I implicitly reject the Romantic notion of art "as the creation of 'genius,' transcending existence, society and time." Janet Wolff, *The Social Production of Art*, 2nd ed. (New York: New York University Press, 1993), 1. Following Wolff, I see the painter as the "non-unitary, provisionally fixed, psychically and socially produced originator of the text" (53). The meanings "intended" by the artist, in my view, compete with those inscribed by viewers. It is in this sense that paintings, like utilitarian objects and buildings, become social spaces with significance for the construction of collective identity.

19. For information on the muralist's life and work, see the obituaries in the secular and religious press: Araceli M. Cantero, "También pintó para la Virgen," *La Voz Católica*, 21 January 1994, 16; "Cuban Artist Carrasco Dies at 77," *Miami Herald*, 30 December 1993. In my interview with the artist cited in the preceding note, he also gave me a packet of clippings, catalogs, brochures, and other biographical material. Among the most useful was a seven-page typed listing of key dates and professional accomplishments. He was especially proud of a typed Spanish-language note signed by Ernest Hemingway on letterhead from La Florida Bar-Restaurant in Havana in which the writer praised Carrasco as "one of the greatest mural painters of the century." Ernest Hemingway to Teok Carrasco, October 1955, the estate of Teok Carrasco.

20. Interview #153, 6 June 1993, male, age 67, born Camagüey, arrived 1960. The quotation from Carrasco is reprinted in a biographical pamphlet for an unidentified exhibition, "Teok Carrasco: Exposición," undated, in author's files. It is undated, but from the contents it is clear that it was printed after November 1990. In that same pamphlet, the artist compared his work not only to that of a historian but also to that of a religious leader: "The profession of painter is like a priest's." The murals of Diego Rivera have been analyzed and reproduced widely. For one reproduction of this historical mural see Edwards, *Painted Walls*, 206–8.

21. Quoted in García, "El mural," 73. Carrasco told me in an interview that he modeled the face of the Virgin after his daughter's. That added emotional power to the image for him, apparently: his eyes filled with tears as he relayed that. Interview, Teok Carrasco, 9 July 1993, Miami.

22. The quotation is from Carrasco, "Descripción del mural," 39. Las Casas is well-known to students of Latin America. For his historical treatment of Cuba see the relevant passages in his "Historia de las Indias," in *Obras escogidas*, ed. J. Pérez de Tudela, vols. 1–2 (Madrid: Biblioteca de Autores Españoles, 1957–58). Las Casas condemned Spanish treatment of the natives in several works. See, for instance, the several pages on Cuba in the English translation of his *Short Account of the Destruction of the Indies*, trans. Nigel Griffin (London: Penguin Books, 1992), 27–30. On Father Miguel Velázquez, the nephew of the more famous Diego Velázquez, see Mercedes García Tudurí, "La educación de Cuba," in *La enciclopedia de Cuba*, ed. Vincente Báez (San Juan and Madrid: Enciclopedia y Clásicos Cubanos, 1974): 6:521. See also Ismael Testé, *Historia eclesiástica de Cuba*, 3 vols. (Burgos: Editorial El Monte Carmelo, 1969) 1:78, 83. The legend of Apolonia, which I alluded to in chapter 1, is recounted in several historical overviews printed by the shrine over the years. One such account, on shrine letterhead, narrated the apparition this way: After the discovery of the image in the Bay of Nipe in the seventeenth century, the image was taken to Barajagua. It

appeared and disappeared several times at its shrine there. "Again it disappeared and appeared several times," that account continued, "and finally was seen by a little girl named Apolonia on El Cobre Hill. The people decided to place it on the top of the hill, where they later built a shrine." "September 8th: Feast of the Nativity of the Blessed Virgin Mary . . . ," public letter distributed by the Shrine of Our Lady of Charity, n.d., Vertical File "Virgen del Cobre," Library, St. Vincent dePaul Regional Seminary, Boynton Beach, Florida. See also Testé, *Historia eclesiástica*, 3:369. For a brief history of the shrines, including the earliest one, see Testé, *Historia eclesiástica*, 3:399–400. Readers who are unfamiliar with the historical figures I discuss here and later might consult Jaime Suchlicki, *Historical Dictionary of Cuba* (Metuchen, N.J.: Scarecrow Press, 1988). That contains brief biographical entries. Those who are unfamiliar with Cuban history might consult Leslie Bethell, ed., *Cuba: A Short History* (Cambridge: Cambridge University Press, 1993); or Jaime Suchlicki, *Cuba: From Columbus to Castro* (Washington: Pergamon-Brassey's, 1990).

23. On Jesús Rabí, see Máximo Gómez's account of the wars for independence, "Diario de campaña," which is reproduced in *La enciclopedia de Cuba*, 4:573–76. Rabí, who is less known than Gómez and some other figures on the mural, also is pictured on an another page in the same volume of the encyclopedia (p. 516).

24. John Farina mentions the political science award and notes the struggle for the meaning of Varela in his introduction to *Félix Varela: Letters to Elpidio*, ed. Felipe J. Estévez (New York: Paulist Press, 1989), xv–xvii.

25. See *The Religious Controversy between the Reverend Dr. W. C. Brownlee and the Reverend Drs. John Power, Thos. C. Levins, and Félix Varela* (Philadelphia: Boyle and Benedict, 1833); W. C. Brownlee, *Letters in the Roman Catholic Controversy* (New York: J. Whitmans, 1834); and Félix Varela, "Address to Protestants," *Catholic Observer*, 15 December, 22 December, 29 December 1836, 12 January 1837. A number of scholarly biographies and devotional homages have been published since the first biography of Varela appeared. That work was José Ignacio Rodríguez, *Vida del presbítero Don Félix Varela* (Havana: O Novo Mundo, 1878). Clergy at the shrine have praised him from the pulpit and in print. See Agustín Román, "Padre Félix Varela y Morales," in *El Habanero*, ed. Félix Varela (Miami: Ideal, 1974), iv–ix. See also the twenty-eight-page biographical portrait sometimes sold at the shrine, which holds up his life as a model of virtue and faith: Monseñor Teodoro de la Torre, *Félix Varela: Vida ejemplar* (Miami: Padre Félix Varela Foundation, n.d.); "Un poema de Martí a la Virgen," *Cuba diáspora* (1978): 77–78; "El mural de la Ermita" (pamphlet); John Kirk, *José Martí: Mentor of the Cuban Nation* (Tampa: University Presses of Florida, 1983), 119–25.

26. Zdzislaw Mach, *Symbols, Conflict, and Identity: Essays in Political Anthology* (Albany: State University of New York Press, 1993), 198; Román, "La Virgen de la Caridad en Miami," 7.

27. Interview #252, 10 June 1994, female, age 35, born Havana, arrived 1962. Others also noticed the significance of the six buttresses. For example, Interview #48, 1 March 1992, female, age 53, born Trinidad (in Las Villas), arrived 1971. The quotation about the "pain of exile" comes from Interview #99, 3 March 1992, female, age 53, born Guanabacoa, arrived 1980.

28. On the history of Cuban colonial architecture see Joaquín E. Weiss, *La arquitectura colonial cubana: Siglos XVI/XVII* (Havana: Editorial letras Cubanas, 1979) and *La arquitectura colonial cubana: Siglo XVIII* (Havana: Editorial letras Cubanas, 1979). See also Nicolás Quintana, "Evolución histórica de la arquitectura en Cuba," in *La enciclopedia de Cuba*, 5:1–114. Monsignor Walsh told me that financial factors played some part in the conversations about the shrine's style: Interview, Bryan O. Walsh, 17 June 1993, Miami. The contractor did too: Interview, Donald W. Myers, 6 September 1994, Miami. In the same interview,

the contractor also told me that "it was a difficult building. It's round and the walls taper in. That creates a form problem." That problem might have been solved too, then, by using a different, more traditional, exterior shape. But the construction committee was drawn to the conical shape, for reasons that I explore later.

29. Interview #273, 6 September 1994, male, age 27, born Villa Clara, arrived 1993.

30. Interview #241, 10 June 1994, female, age 61, born Marianao, arrived ? (no answer); Interview #156, 6 June 1993, female, age 65, born Pinar del Río, arrived 1958; Irving Rouse, *The Taínos: Rise and Decline of the People Who Greeted Columbus* (New Haven: Yale University Press, 1992), 9–10, 13–14, 18, 21, 23, 118–21. On Taíno religion see also Roberto Cassá, *Los indios de las Antillas* (Madrid: Editorial MAPFRE, 1992), 133–48. The Cuban anthropologist Fernando Ortiz was preoccupied with the indigenous parallels and influences, including the parallels with Atabey, as Olga Portuondo Zúñiga argues. She discusses his unpublished notes on the subject and her own views in *La Virgen de la Caridad del Cobre: Símbolo de cubanía* (Santiago de Cuba: Editorial Oriente, 1995), 53–80. On the Taíno *caney* see also Quintana, "Evolución histórica de la arquitectura," 4–5, and Weiss, *Arquitectura colonial cubana: Siglos XVI/XVII*, 5–7, 190. Another scholar who has studied the religion of the Taínos, Anthony M. Stevens-Arroyo, has identified other parallels: he argues that the Virgin of Cobre evokes images of another Taíno female spirit, Guabonito (not Atabey). Either way the possible continuities are intriguing. See two works by Anthony M. Stevens-Arroyo, *Cave of the Jagua: The Mythological World of the Taínos* (Albuquerque: University of New Mexico Press, 1988), 191–94, 216–19; and "The Persistence of Religious Cosmovision in an Alien World," in *Enigmatic Powers: Syncretism with African and Indigenous People's Religions among Latinos*, ed. Anthony M. Stevens-Arroyo and Andres I. Pérez y Mena, Program for the Analysis of Religion among Latinos Studies Series, no. 2 (New York: Bildner Center for Western Hemisphere Studies, 1995), 113–35. Historical sources and popular legend indicate that some of the indigenous peoples of Cuba had Marian devotion. At the same time, compared to the history of the Guanaches's devotion to Our Lady of Candalaria in the Canary Islands, the Taíno Marian devotion did not endure very long. Nor did it become nearly as significant a unifying practice. This can be explained in part by the lower number of Taíno converts and the quicker subjugation and horrific decline of the natives in the Caribbean. On this point see Anthony M. Stevens-Arroyo, "The Inter-Atlantic Paradigm: The Failure of Spanish Medieval Colonization of the Canary and Caribbean Islands," *Comparative Studies in Society and History* 35, no. 3 (July 1993): 515–43.

31. For a photograph of this shrine in Benin see Robert Farris Thompson, *Face of the Gods: Art and Altars of Africa and the African Americas* (New York: Museum for African Art; Munich: Prestel, 1993), 175. The first person to call my attention to the stylistic parallels with African shrines was an African specialist who attended a public lecture I gave on the topic at the University of Florida, Gainesville, on 29 March 1993. I am grateful to him. On African architectural influences in the Americas, see also Robert Farris Thompson, *Flash of the Spirit: African and African-American Art and Philosophy* (New York: Vintage Books, 1983), 195–206.

32. Gómez and Pérez, "Cubans Flock to Dedication," 2B. Construction Committee of the Shrine and Monument to Our Lady of Charity, "Shrine and Monument to Our Lady of Charity," fundraising mailing, n.d. [26 December 1969], Cuban Archives, Richter Library, University of Miami, Coral Gables. Note that the committee described the structure as a "monument" here, and that document also included a photograph of a model that was not accepted. The architect who won the contract drew two plans for the building—the one that was built ("plan B") and another that was rejected ("plan A"). Design A, which was rejected by Archbishop Carroll, was drawn in 1969. It called for a larger building with an elevator ascending to a small shrine at the top and a large hall at the bottom. According to Román, Carroll

rejected it for several reasons: it was too large, too impractical (only fifty seats above), and too unsafe (not hurricane-proof). Interview, Agustín Román, 9 March 1994, Shrine of Our Lady of Charity. The architect's designs for both buildings are among the few documents to survive in the archives at the shrine. An image of plan A, with a full description of it, also survives in other documents. For example, "Proyecto de Monumento-Ermita a la Virgen de la Caridad," fundraising pamphlet, n.d. [after October 1969], Cuban Archives, Richter Library, University of Miami, Coral Gables; Román, "La Virgen de la Caridad en Miami," 7; Interview #223, 5 June 1994, male, age 27, born U.S.; Interview #109, 11 February 1992, female, age 55, born Guanajay, arrived 1966. Others who offered very similar interpretations included: Interview #89, 18 January 1992, male, age 24, born Havana, arrived 1991; Interview #104, 4 February 1992, age 22, born U.S.; Interview #245, 10 June 1994, female, age 57, born Havana, arrived 1978.

33. Interview #137, 3 March 1992, female, age 51, born Puerto Padre, arrived 1960. Like the Mayan temple at Tikal, Guatemala, its exterior form alludes to a mountain. At the same time, the design creates an interior space that recalls the dark, closed area of cave temples in India. On architectural expressions of the sacred mountain in the Americas, Mesopotamia, and Egypt, see Vincent Scully Jr., *Architecture: The Natural and the Manmade* (New York: St. Martin's, 1991), 1–38. On Hindu cave temples, and allusions to caves in free-standing structures, see George Michell, *The Hindu Temple* (1977; reprint, Chicago: University of Chicago Press, 1988), 69–71. Although I take my interpretation in different directions, it is shaped by Mary Douglas's reflections on natural symbols, especially on how the "physical body" is associated with the "social body." Mary Douglas, *Natural Symbols* (1970; reprint, New York: Pantheon Books, 1982). On Greek temples see Scully, *Architecture*, 39–63, and Davies, *Temples*, 41–65. On Byzantine Christian structures, see Davies, *Temples*, 90–117. On architecture and the body see also Joel Brereton, "Sacred Space," in *Encyclopedia of Religion*, 12:532. One invitation to a mass celebrating Cuban independence day in 1967 called her "Madre de la Caridad." "Madre de la Caridad, Salva a Cuba," Mailing for procession and mass (6:30 P.M., 20 May 1967), Cuban Archives, Richter Library, University of Miami, Coral Gables. The young exile who interpreted the shrine's form as the mantle of the Virgin also told me that he prayed to her for "motherly advice." Interview #230, 5 June 1994, male, age 27, born U.S. On the Virgin as "my mother": Interview #155, 6 June 1993, female, age 70, born Camagüey, arrived 1966. Ann Taves, for example, emphasized family metaphors in her study *The Household of Faith: Roman Catholic Devotions in Mid-Nineteenth-Century America* (Notre Dame: University of Notre Dame Press, 1986), 48–51. On the Virgin as "*our* mother": Interview #126, 23 February 1992, female, age 22, born Havana, arrived 1988. The homilist at the annual feast-day mass in 1985, Father José Luis Hernando, used the same language ("our mother"): "La Virgen es Nuestra Señora de los Mandados," *La Voz Católica*, 13 September 1985, 15.

34. Thomas Hylland Eriksen, *Ethnicity and Nationalism: Anthropological Perspectives* (London and Boulder: Pluto Press, 1993), 107–8. Jonathan Z. Smith also has made connections between exile and return, death and rebirth. "To be exiled," he argued, "is to be in a state of chaos, destruction, and death; to return from exile is to be recreated and reborn." Jonathan Z. Smith, *Map Is Not Territory: Studies in the History of Religions* (Chicago: University of Chicago Press, 1978), 120. Here I interpret entering the shrine as symbolic return to the homeland. Quoting an eighteenth–century Polish Jew, Smith explicitly links return to the sanctuary with return to "mother's womb" and bonding with the land: Smith, *Map*, 127.

35. In interpreting the shrine as a "crossing place" I am extending a northern Indian understanding of a *tirtha*. As George Michell notes of the Hindu temple; "The temple is conceived as a place of transit, a ford, or crossing place (*tirtha*)." Michell, *Hindu Temple*, 66. I offer a fuller analysis on this point in the postscript.

36. In emphasizing here that the meanings of buildings arise from the practices held within them, I am extending James W. Fernandez's analysis of the "architectonics" of the Bwiti chapel in his study of religion among the Fang in equatorial Africa. James W. Fernandez, *Bwiti: An Ethnography of the Religious Imagination in Africa* (Princeton: Princeton University Press, 1982), 377, 408–12. Lindsay Jones makes a similar point, introducing the phrase "ritual-architectural event" to emphasize that a building's meanings are related to the architecture, the human users, and the ceremonial occasion. See Lindsay Jones, *Twin City Tales: A Hermeneutical Reassessment of Tula and Chichén Itzá* (Niwot, Colo.: University Press of Colorado, 1995), 186–210.

CHAPTER SIX

1. Fieldnotes, 8 September 1993, Dinner Key Auditorium, Miami. The quotation from the woman in the crowd was printed in Ana Santiago, "Thousands of Cuban Exiles Gather to Pay Tribute to Island's Patron Saint," *Miami Herald*, 9 September 1993, 8B.

2. It might be helpful to say a word or two about how I use the term "ritual." Some scholars, like Jack Goody, have proposed that we abandon the term; others, like Fritz Staal, have claimed that rituals are "meaningless." I obviously think we can use the term, and I believe that although they are multivocal and ambivalent, they are social spaces in which meaning (and power) are negotiated. Rituals, as I view them, are embodied social practices that place participants temporally and spatially and thus negotiate meaning and power. Interpreters have traded on several analogies to understand ritual—ludic, dramaturgical, and textual, to mention just three. For my purposes, I have found the term "practice" most helpful. Rituals, then, are practices. I have learned from Pierre Bourdieu in this regard, although he does not say all that I want to about ritual. Catherine Bell comes closest to my own view in many ways, and I use the term "practice" with her warnings in mind about the ways in which it can reproduce the usual dichotomies, such as the false distinctions between "thought" and "action." As I use the term, "practices" involve both. Ritual practices also usually involve formality, fixity, and repetition; but these are not inherent or universal qualities, as Bell notes (92). I owe a debt to Jonathan Z. Smith for my emphasis on the significance of place in ritual. Several theorists have drawn attention to the significance of the body in ritual. Although I believe that Ron Grimes's criticisms of Paul Connerton's use of the term "bodily practices" are persuasive, I still find Connerton's analysis helpful in many ways in this regard (72–104). To interpret ritual practices is *not*, as Clifford Geertz has suggested of the interpretation of symbols, "more like grasping a proverb, catching an allusion, or seeing a joke" (70). Rather, I think it is more like making sense of gestures, as Ruel Tyson argues, or like interpreting the evocations of smells, as Dan Sperber has claimed. Their meaning never can be reduced to their cognitive content or social function, although those are important in understanding rituals. To interpret the meaning of rituals, then, is to attend to the multiple and ambiguous significations of bodily practices like waving, kneeling, and singing. Since this study focuses on religion and displacement, I am most interested in the ways in which rituals position participants in time and space. The social space of ritual does not "reflect" beliefs or social relations related to diasporic life, however. Rather, ritual is the arena in which those beliefs and relations are continually *constituted*. They must be continually negotiated because the work accomplished in most rituals never is complete or finished. The identity and power negotiated ritually always are precarious. Jack Goody, "Religion and Ritual," *British Journal of Sociology* 12 (1961): 142–64; Fritz Staal, "The Meaninglessness of Ritual," *Numen* 26 (1975): 2–22; Pierre Bourdieu, *Outline of a Theory of Practice*, trans. Richard Nice (Cambridge: Cambridge University Press, 1977); Catherine Bell, *Ritual Theory, Ritual Practice*

(New York: Oxford University Press, 1992); Jonathan Z. Smith, *To Take Place: Toward Theory in Ritual* (Chicago: University of Chicago Press, 1987); Paul Connerton, *How Societies Remember* (Cambridge: Cambridge University Press, 1975); Ronald L. Grimes, "Reinventing Ritual," *Soundings* 75 (Spring 1992): 21–41; Clifford Geertz, *Local Knowledge* (New York: Basic Books, 1983), 70; Dan Sperber, *Rethinking Symbolism*, trans. Alice L. Morton (Cambridge: Cambridge University Press, 1975); Ruel W. Tyson Jr., introduction to *Diversities of Gifts: Field Studies in Southern Religion*, ed. Ruel W. Tyson Jr., James L. Peacock, and Daniel W. Patterson (Urbana: University of Illinois Press, 1988), 3–20.

3. In several years of regular visits to the shrine, only *one* Cuban exile suggested to me that ritual practices had no nationalistic significance: "My devotion is only between me and the Virgin," an elderly woman confided one Saturday afternoon on the steps of the shrine in Miami. Interview #264, 11 June 1994, female, age 70, born Havana, arrived 1965. The quotation is from Interview #222, 5 June 1994, male, age 77, born Sagua la Grande, arrived 1961.

4. For an overview of the annual ritual cycle at the shrine, which has changed very little since 1967, when the "provisional chapel" was built, see the schedules of events printed by the shrine each year. The shrine's records were lost in Hurricane Andrew in 1992, but most of those schedules survive in a file marked "Ermita de la Caridad," Cuban Archives, Richter Library, University of Miami, Coral Gables.

5. "Prayer to Our Lady of Charity," prayer card, printed by Ermita de La Caridad, Miami. Interview #284, 7 September 1994, female, age 40, born Havana, arrived 1969, resides Hollywood, Florida. One classic work on rituals associated with the life cycle is Arnold Van Gennep, *The Rites of Passage*, trans. M. B. Vizedom and G. L. Caffee (1909; reprint Chicago: University of Chicago Press, 1960). Pierre Bourdieu added an interesting insight to the analysis of these rites by emphasizing how they legitimate social boundaries. He suggested that we relabel them "rites of legitimization" or "rites of institution." See Pierre Bourdieu, "Rites as Acts of Institution," in *Honor and Grace in Anthropology*, ed. J. G. Peristiany and Julian Pitt-Rivers (Cambridge and New York: Cambridge University Press, 1992), 79–89.

6. Interview #20, 3 February 1992, male, age 34, born Havana, arrived 1967; Fieldnotes, 3 February 1992, Shrine of Our Lady of Charity; Interview #233, 9 June 1994, male, age 32, born Holguín, arrived 1964, resides New Jersey.

7. Fieldnotes, 29 January 1992, municipal mass, Shrine of Our Lady of Charity; Interviews #10–14, 29 January 1992, especially the daughter: Interview #14, 29 January 1992, female, age ?, born Cabaiguán. (She did not want to tell me her age or date of arrival.)

8. "Alejandro" (from Havana) to Agustín Román, 12 June 1994, the author's files, previously in Bishop Roman's files at the Pastoral Center, Miami Shores. Other Cuban letter-writers say the same—that they listen to the mass on Radio Martí. For example, a twenty-four-year-old male from Las Villas (J.M., 1 May 1994) and a fifty-two-year-old female from Camagüey (A.V., 20 September 1994), both in the author's files. Fieldnotes, Shrine of Our Lady of Charity, 11 June 1994. Before the mass that night I also conducted an unstructured interview with the layman who organizes the radio broadcasts and reads from the Scriptures at the mass. He estimated the number of Cuban listeners at 3,000,000. Interview, O.R., Shrine of Our Lady of Charity, 12 June 1994. There is no way of knowing for certain how many Cubans listen, but the correspondence from Cuba sent to the shrine indicates that many certainly do. On correspondence to shrines as pilgrimage, or "writing as going," see the insightful analysis in Robert A. Orsi, "The Center Out There, In Here, and Everywhere Else: The Nature of Pilgrimage to the Shrine of Saint Jude, 1929–1965," *Journal of Social History* 25 (Winter 1991): 213–32.

9. Interview, O.R., 12 June 1994, Shrine of Our Lady of Charity.

10. Jay P. Dolan, *The Immigrant Church: New York's Irish and German Catholics, 1815–1865* (Baltimore: Johns Hopkins University Press, 1975), 71–72; Robert A. Orsi, *The*

Madonna of 115th Street: Faith and Community in Italian Harlem, 1880–1950 (New Haven: Yale University Press, 1985), 51. The tendency to form religious organizations according to premigrational regional associations has been common to most immigrants in the United States, not just Catholics. As John Bodnar points out, "East European Jews repeatedly established orthodox congregations along regional lines." Bodnar mentions twenty-four such communities in Providence, Rhode Island, between 1874 and 1914. John Bodnar, *The Transplanted: A History of Immigrants in Urban America* (Bloomington: Indiana University Press, 1985), 147–48.

11. Interview, Agustín Román, 7 July 1993, Shrine of Our Lady of Charity, Miami. The number of names on the list (42,000) has been confirmed by a number of clergy and confraternity members. The estimate that "about 20,000" are "active" members of the confraternity was offered by the layperson who has primary responsibility for its maintenance: Interview, S.A., 8 September 1994, Annual Festival, Hialeah, Florida. For an example of how Román exhorted devotees to attend the municipal masses, see his messages to the confraternity. One typical message, reminding members "not to forget the pilgrimages of your municipality," was included in *Caridad* 1, no. 3 (November–December 1969), Cuban Archives, Richter Library, University of Miami, Coral Gables.

12. Fieldnotes, 24 May 1993, municipal mass for Fomento, Shrine of Our Lady of Charity; Interview #301, 8 September 1994, female, age 70, born Havana, arrived 1959. About 140 attended one municipal mass for Jagüey Grande: Fieldnotes, 9 July 1993, municipal mass for Jagüey Grande, Shrine of Our Lady of Charity.

13. Fieldnotes, 7 February 1992, municipal mass, Holguín, Shrine of Our Lady of Charity.

14. Interview #162, 6 June 1993, female, age 73, born Matanzas, arrived 1980.

15. Quoted in Linda Bryon, "Una tarde de fe y romería," *La Voz*, 24 February 1989; Interview #66, 1 March 1992, female, age 51, born Manzanillo, arrived 1967.

16. Gloria Estefan, *Mi Tierra*, sound recording, Sony Music Entertainment, manufactured by Epic, 1993. They played the tape of Gloria Estephan's "Mi Tierra" at a romería in 1994: Fieldnotes, 5 June 1994, romería for Western Provinces, Shrine of Our Lady of Charity.

17. It is interesting to note that this poem by Julio Estorino ("Mi Tierra"), vice president of "La Junta Patriótica Cubana," was reprinted in the opening pages of a locally published history of the Cuban municipalities: Joaquín Freire Díaz, *Historia de los municipios de Cuba* (Miami: La Moderna Poesía, 1985), 7–10. Fieldnotes, 1 March 1992, romería for Eastern Provinces, Shrine of Our Lady of Charity.

18. Interview #215, 5 June 1994, male, age 45, born San Luis, arrived 1992. Fieldnotes, 5 June 1994, romería for Western Provinces, Shrine of Our Lady of Charity.

19. Fieldnotes, 1 March 1992, romería for Eastern Provinces and Fieldnotes, 6 June 1993, romería for Western Provinces, Shrine of Our Lady of Charity.

20. Interview, Agustín Román, 9 June 1994, Pastoral Center, Miami Shores. A number of anthropologists have analyzed religious drama in various cultures. Victor Turner is among them. For example, see Victor Turner, *From Ritual to Theater*, Performance Studies Series (New York: PAJ Publications, 1982). For a helpful overview of the use of *tableaux vivants* in Catholic "sacramental plays," see s.v. "Auto Sacramentales," *New Catholic Encyclopedia*, vol. 1 (Washington, D.C.: Catholic University of America, 1967).

21. Fieldnotes, 1 March 1992, romería for Eastern Provinces, Shrine of Our Lady of Charity. The four teenagers included a male, age 16, who was born in exile in Colombia and has lived in Miami since he was four years old. The other three were young women, ages 14, 15, and 17. Two of them confessed to intense devotion to Our Lady of Charity.

22. Quoted in "Miles aclaman a la Caridad del Cobre," *El Nuevo Herald*, 9 September 1991, 1B. The second quotation is from Interview #109, 11 February 1992, female, age 57, born Guanajay, arrived 1966. Sixty-five percent of those who participated in my structured

interviews at the shrine indicated that the festival mass was very important personally to them. Even some who did not attend regularly said that.

23. "800 Assist at Mass for Cuba," *The Voice*, 16 September 1960, 10; "Exiles from Communism Pray to Cuba's Patron," *The Voice*, 15 September 1961. See also Cecilio J. Morales Jr., *Hispanic Portrait of Evangelization: The Shrine of Our Lady of Charity*, no. 5 (Washington, D.C.: Committee on Evangelization, National Conference of Catholic Bishops, 1981), 13, and Michael J. McNally, *Catholicism in South Florida, 1868–1968*, (Gainesville: University Press of Florida, 1982), 160.

24. John Underwood, "Exiles Pray for End of Tyranny," *Miami Herald*, 9 September 1961, 1A, 2A. Cuban woman quoted in Ligia Guillén, "Jubileo de la Virgen en el exilio," *La Voz Católica*, 29 August 1986, 1, 5. Clerical estimates of the crowd put it at 30,000. For instance, see Morales, *Hispanic Portrait*, 13.

25. The largest crowds, 25,000 or more, came to Miami Stadium for the first masses in the early 1960s. The smallest were in 1992, just fifteen days after Hurricane Andrew had struck the area and the clergy were unable to announce the new location until days before, and in 1993, when the event was held indoors at Dinner Key Auditorium, which held only 6,000. The attendance in 1994, when it was held at the racetrack, returned to the usual size. About 12,000 attended. My estimates are based on those reported by the local press. I relied especially on estimates from the *Miami Herald*, rather than *La Voz Católica*, the local Catholic periodical. For 1993, I calculated the size of the crowd myself by asking the facilities manager of the Dinner Key Auditorium how many folding chairs they had put out and then adding some for those who were forced to stand that evening. Telephone interview with author, 9 September 1993, facilities manager, Dinner Key Auditorium, Miami.

26. Interview, Father Juan Sosa, 9 June 1993, St. Catherine of Siena Parish, Miami.

27. Fieldnotes, 7 September 1993, feast-day vigil, Shrine of Our Lady of Charity. Among the local singers who performed that evening were Aleida Leal, Irene Farrach, and Rolando Ochoa. The Mexican band is Mora Arriaga, and they have performed at the vigil each year since 1983.

28. My account in the next paragraphs follows my fieldnotes: Fieldnotes, 8 September 1993, Dinner Key Auditorium, Miami.

29. "Virgen de la Caridad, Reúne a tus hijos en el amor," Program for Festival Mass, Office of Liturgy and Spiritual Life, Archdiocese of Miami, 1993, in the author's files; Fieldnotes, 8 September 1992, feast-day mass, Bayfront Park, Miami. During the rosary in 1992, I had wandered outside the outdoor arena, which borders the waterfront mall that attracts tourists, in order to observe the Virgin's arrival by boat. I noticed that a couple, dressed like tourists, with cameras dangling from their necks, walked into the amphitheater. I waited for them to emerge again, since I was sure that they would discover that the Spanish-language celebration was not for them. When they came out two minutes later, as expected, I interviewed the German tourists for a few minutes. They had wandered in because they saw a large crowd and assumed it was entertainment. They seemed baffled by the ritual, despite my attempts to explain it to them. They left after we talked, to return to the adjoining outdoor mall where they might be more comfortable. Fieldnotes, 8 September 1993, feast-day mass, Dinner Key Auditorium, Miami; Interview, Father Luís Pérez, 9 March 1994, San Lázaro Catholic Church, Hialeah. Pérez also offered the sermon one year, in 1964. See "20,000 at Stadium Mass in Honor of Blessed Virgin," *The Voice*, 11 September 1964, 15.

30. Fieldnotes, 8 September 1994, feast-day mass, Hialeah Racetrack, Hialeah. The private group which brought the Virgin by helicopter was Hermanos al Rescate (Brothers to the Rescue). They are beloved by local Cubans for their efforts to locate and rescue Cuban rafters in the waters off South Florida's coast.

31. Fieldnotes, 8 September 1993, feast-day mass, Dinner Key Auditorium, Miami.

32. Fieldnotes, 8 September 1993, return of the Virgin after the feastday mass, Shrine of Our Lady of Charity.

33. Quoted in Maydel Santana, "'Salva a Cuba,' piden cubanos a Virgen," *El Nuevo Herald*, 9 September 1993, 1A, 9A.

34. Catherine Bell makes a similar point about belief and ritual, when she discusses the "minimal consent" that ritual requires: "Ritualized practices afford a great diversity of interpretation in exchange for little more than consent to the form of the activities." Bell, *Ritual Theory*, 186.

35. Connerton, *How Societies Remember*, 6. My analysis of collective memory here also has been shaped by other works, including Maurice Halbwachs, *The Collective Memory*, trans. Francis J. Ditter Jr. and Vida Yazdi Ditter (1950; reprint, New York: Harper amd Row, 1980), and Eric Hobsbawm and Terrance Ranger, eds., *The Invention of Tradition* (Cambridge: Cambridge University Press, 1983).

POSTSCRIPT

1. Interview, Agustín Román, 7 July 1993, Shrine of Our Lady of Charity.

2. Both Nicaraguans and Haitians also have their national patronesses, and those play an important role in their diasporic religions. For instance, see Katherine Borland, "The Gritería in Miami: A Nicaraguan Home-Based Festival," *Folklore Forum* 25, no. 1 (1992): 19–27. Reform Jews in Europe and America traditionally did not see themselves as in exile. On this see Nathan Glazer, *American Judaism*, 2nd ed. (Chicago: University of Chicago Press, 1989), 9, 40. For a helpful analysis of the concept of exile in Judaism, see Arnold M. Eisen, *Galut: Modern Jewish Reflection on Homelessness and Homecoming* (Bloomington: Indiana University Press, 1986). The quotation about Jews as models for Cubans is from Eduardo Boza Masvidal, Agustín A. Román, and Enrique San Pedro, S.J., *CRECED: Documento final* (Miami: Comunidades de reflexión eclesial Cubana en la diáspora [CRECED], 1993), 102–6. Interview, "Ricardo," 11 March 1994, Miami.

3. I take up the issues concerning historical narratives in greater detail in Thomas A. Tweed, ed., *Retelling U.S. Religious History* (Berkeley: University of California Press, 1997), 1–23. The contributors to that volume explored how other motifs—especially contact, boundary, and exchange—might open the way to compose other stories about United States religion. I have argued for the importance of place as a theme for narrating United States religious history in "Asian Religions in America: Reflections on an Emerging Subfield," in *Religious Diversity and American Religious History: Studies in Traditions and Cultures*, ed. Walter Conser and Sumner Twiss (Athens: University of Georgia Press, forthcoming). On the Vietnamese as "forced migrants" see Paul James Rutledge, *The Vietnamese Experience in America* (Bloomington: Indiana University Press, 1992), 8–11. On Vietnamese American religion see Paul James Rutledge, *The Role of Religion in Ethnic Self-Identity: A Vietnamese Community* (Lanham, Md.: University Press of America, 1985), and Rutledge, *Vietnamese Experience*, 47–54.

4. I borrow the term "contact zones" from Mary Louise Pratt, *Imperial Eyes: Travel Writing and Transculturation* (London and New York: Routledge, 1992), 6–7, but I use it slightly differently here. Meeting or contact has been an important theme in many monographs that have traced native-colonist encounters or African-European interactions in the Americas. For example, see the ethnohistorical study by James Axtell: *The Invasion Within: The Contest of Cultures in Colonial North America* (New York: Oxford University Press, 1985).

5. Robert Tames, "The Americans on Their Travels," *Harper's New Monthly Magazine* 31 (June 1865): 57–63. For a provocative account of Mexican circulatory migrations, which

challenges the usual notions, see Roger Rouse, "Mexican Migration and the Social Space of Postmodernism," *Diaspora* 1 (Spring 1991): 8–23. Rouse's account does not deal with religion, however.

6. Jay P. Dolan argued for the usefulness of "migration" as a theme, although that call has been neglected. Jay P. Dolan, "The Immigrants and Their Gods: A New Perspective in American Religious History," *Church History* 57 (March 1988): 61–72. Even earlier, other scholars noted the importance of the movements of people across space for United States religious history. "Americans during their formative years were a people in movement through space," Sidney E. Mead reminded readers in his 1963 collection of essays. Sidney E. Mead, *The Lively Experiment: The Shaping of Christianity in America* (New York: Harper and Row, 1963), 7. So, too, Martin Marty used a related theme—pilgrimage or travel—to tell a wide-ranging story of religion in the United States: *Pilgrims in Their Own Land: 500 Years of Religion in America* (Boston: Little, Brown, 1984).

7. Herbert E. Bolton, *The Wider Horizons of American History* (1939; reprint, Notre Dame: University of Notre Dame Press, 1967), 1–3.

8. I am indebted to Anna L. Peterson for the insight about religious utopias in the United States and Nicaragua. A number of scholars have begun to place the study of religion in the United States in wider geographical contexts. Scholars of the United States always have noted, to some extent, the connections to the nations across the Atlantic, especially Great Britain. There could be more of that kind of comparative work still. Jon Butler has called for a "transatlantic" perspective: "The Future of American Religious History: Prospectus, Agenda, and Transatlantic Problematique," *William and Mary Quarterly* 42 (1985): 167–83. Winthrop Hudson raised the issue in a different way in "How American Is Religion in America?," in *Reinterpretation in American Church History*, ed. Jerald C. Brauer (Chicago: University of Chicago Press, 1968), 153–68. So did William R. Hutchison: "The Americanness of the Social Gospel: An Inquiry in Comparative History," *Church History* 44 (September 1975): 367–81. Scholars who have studied Africans in the "New World" have been doing comparative history of sorts from the start. A documentary history project that is under way promises to extend the frame of reference for U.S. religious history even farther across the Atlantic, to the coast of Africa. See David W. Wills and Albert J. Raboteau, "Rethinking American Religious History: A Progress Report on 'Afro-American Religious History: A Documentary Project,'" *Council of Societies for the Study of Religion Bulletin* 20 (September 1991): 57–61. Turning to the Pacific world, Laurie Maffly-Kipp has offered a revisionist view of United States religious history in "Eastward Ho!: American Religion from the Perspective of the Pacific Rim," in Tweed, *Retelling U.S. Religious History*, 127–48. Even though much remains to be done, the most careful comparative study has been focused on the United States and Canada. See Robert T. Handy, *A History of the Churches in the United States and Canada* (New York: Oxford University Press, 1976), and Mark A. Noll, *A History of Christianity in the United States and Canada* (Grand Rapids, Mich.: Eerdmans, 1992). Handy also offered an insightful, and succinct, comparison in "Protestant Patterns in Canada and the United States: Similarities and Differences," in *In the Great Tradition: Essays on Pluralism, Voluntarism, and Revivalism*, ed. Joseph D. Ban and Paul R. Dekar (Valley Forge, Pa.: Judson Press, 1982), 33–51. I do not know of comparable articles or books on U.S. and Latin American religion, but such analysis is needed. Students of U.S. religion who might want to consider Latin America more fully could begin with a historical overview of the region. One of the most influential has been translated into English recently: Tulio Halperín Donghi, The *Contemporary History of Latin America*, ed./ trans. John Charles Chasteen (Durham: Duke University Press, 1993). For brief and accessible overviews of religion in Latin America, see Thomas G. Sanders, "Religion in Latin America," in *Latin America: Perspectives on a Region*, ed. Jack W. Hopkins (New York and London: Holmes and Meier, 1987), 103–16, and Mar-

garet E. Crahan, "Religion: Reconstituting Church and Pursuing Change," in *Americas: New Interpretive Essays*, ed. Alfred Stepan (New York: Oxford University Press, 1992), 152–71. For a collaborative effort to survey Latin American religious (especially Christian) history see Enrique Dussel, ed., *The Church in Latin America, 1492–1992* (Maryknoll, N.Y.: Orbis Books; Kent: Burns and Oats, 1992). For a helpful review of six recent works on Latin American religion, see Anna L. Peterson, "Religion in Latin America: New Methods and Approaches," *Religious Studies Review* 21 (January 1995): 3–8. For a collaborative attempt to narrate the religious history of the Americas until 1776 by focusing on, in turn, Iberian, French, and British Christianity, see Charles H. Lippy, Robert Choquette, and Stafford Poole, *Christianity Comes to the Americas, 1492–1776* (New York: Paragon House, 1992).

9. The location of Miami near the geographical center of the hemisphere was emphasized, for instance, in a volume celebrating the golden anniversary of the city. On the opening page a map of the hemisphere placed Miami in the center. Concentric circles extended outward from there, measuring the distances in miles from that urban area. Below that the heading read, "Centering the Hemisphere." The local boosters of the Public Relations Committee boasted: "Situated virtually at the center of the Western Hemisphere, Miami is near more important cities than any other metropolis in the New World." City of Miami, *City of Miami, Florida, Golden Anniversary, 1896–1946: Reviewing the Past and Forecasting the Future* (Miami: City of Miami, 1946). Since then many others have made similar claims, including journalists. See Cathy Booth, "Miami: The Capital of Latin America," *Time*, special issue, Fall 1993, 82–85.

10. For further references to the secondary literature about diasporas, see the bibliography and the notes to chapter 4. James Clifford, "Diasporas," *Cultural Anthropology* 9 (August 1994) 306–7. Eisen, *Galut. Galut* is the Hebrew term used in the Bible to refer to "exile" or, more precisely, Jewish exile in Babylon (II Kings 25:27; Jer. 29:22; Ezek. 33:21). *Diaspora* is a Greek term meaning "dispersion" that refers to any land outside of Erets Israel where Jews live. On this see s.v. "Galut" in *The Encyclopedia of Judaism*, ed. Geoffrey Wigader (New York: Macmillan, 1989).

11. Anny Bakalian, *Armenian-Americans: From Being to Feeling Armenian* (New Brunswick, N.J.: Transaction Publishers, 1993). See also Susan Pattie, "At Home in Diaspora: Armenians in America," *Diaspora* 3 (Fall 1994): 185–98; Smith, "Map Is Not Territory," in his *Map Is not Territory: Studies in the History of Religions* (Chicago: University of Chicago Press, 1978); Smith, *To Take Place: Toward Theory in Ritual* (Chicago: University of Chicago Press, 1987).

12. My analysis of the vertical and horizontal dimensions of religion has been informed, in part, by James W. Fernandez's interpretation of the Bwiti chapel in *Bwiti: An Ethnography of the Religious Imagination in Africa* (Princeton: Princeton University Press, 1982), 377, 408–12. Catherine Bell's treatment of the spatial dimensions of ritualization also helped in this regard. Bell, *Ritual Theory, Ritual Practice* (New York: Oxford Unversity Press, 1992) 125.

13. Diana L. Eck, *Banaras: City of Light* (Princeton: Princeton University Press, 1982), 6, 34–42. On Hindu temples as *tirthas* see George Michell, *The Hindu Temple: An Introduction to Its Meanings and Forms* (1977; reprint, Chicago: University of Chicago Press, 1988), 66.

14. On the distinction between forced and impelled migration, see s.v. "Migration" in *The Social Science Encyclopedia* (London: Routledge and Kegan Paul, 1985). For a helpful introduction to the Cherokee "removal" see Michael D. Green and Theda Perdue, *The Cherokee Removal: A Brief History with Documents* (Boston: Bedford Books, St. Martin's Press, 1995).

15. For a useful introduction to Creek culture before and after removal, in the wider context of the history of other natives of the Southeast, see Charles Hudson, *The Southeastern Indians* (Knoxville: University of Tennessee Press, 1976). See also James W. Covington, *The*

Seminoles of Florida (Gainesville: University Press of Florida, 1993). On the Vietnamese see the works by Paul James Rutledge cited earlier: *The Vietnamese Experience* and *The Role of Religion in Ethnic Self-Identity.* On Armenian American Christians see Bakalian, *Armenian-Americans,* 89–125.

16. Gisbert Rinschede claimed that the National Shrine of Our Lady of Czestochowa was the fourth most visited Catholic pilgrimage site in the United States. (The Shrine of Our Lady of Charity in Miami was sixth.) See Rinschede, "Catholic Pilgrimage Places in the United States." For the official history of the Polish American shrine, written by a priest, see Gabriel Lorenc, *American Czestochowa* (Doylestown, Pa.: National Shrine of Our Lady of Czestochowa, 1989). That volume also includes an interesting narrative of Polish political and religious history.

Select Bibliography

The following bibliography contains only the published and unpublished sources that were most relevant for this study. It is not a complete record of all of the materials I have consulted or cited in the notes.

MANUSCRIPT SOURCES

Archives, *La Voz Católica*, Archdiocese of Miami, Pastoral Center, Miami Springs, Florida.
"Ermita de la Caridad," File, Cuban Archives, Special Collections, Richter Library, University of Miami, Coral Gables, Florida.
Historical Association of Southern Florida, Archives, Miami, Florida.
Letters (76) to the Shrine of Our Lady of Charity in Miami from devotees in Cuba and the United States (1994–96), originally in the office of Bishop Agustín Román, Archdiocese of Miami, Pastoral Center, Miami Springs, Florida, now in the author's files.
"Scrapbook." Records. Myers Construction Group, Inc. Miami, Florida.
"Shrine of Our Lady of Charity (1966–1973)," File, Archdiocese of Miami Archives, Pastoral Center, Miami Springs, Florida.
"Virgen del Cobre," Vertical File, Library, St. Vincent dePaul Regional Seminary, Boynton Beach, Florida.

PERIODICALS

Bohemia
Cuba diáspora: Anuario de la iglesia cubano
Diario Las Américas
The Florida Catholic
Ideal
Miami Herald

El Nuevo Herald
Patria
Radio Peace
The Voice
La Voz Católica

BOOKS, ARTICLES, AND PAMPHLETS

Abbot, Abiel. *Letters Written in the Interior of Cuba.* Boston: Bowles and Dearborn, 1829.
Aguilar, Alberto. "Illescas: Hospital de la Caridad." *Boletín de la Sociedad Española de Excursiones* 35 (1927): 120–37.
Alexander, James Edward C. B. *Transatlantic Sketches.* 2 vols. London: Richard Bentley, 1833.
Allman, T. D. *Miami: City of the Future.* New York: Atlantic Monthly Press, 1987.
"El alto clero no descansa en su actividad por difundir y confundir al pueblo cubano." *Bohemia* 53, no. 38 (17 September 1961): 68.
Álvarez, P. Fr. Paulino. *Breve historia de la Virgen de la Caridad del Cobre seguida de un triduo y novena.* Vergara: El santísimo Rosario, 1902.
Anderson, Benedict. *Imagined Communities: Reflections on the Origin and Spread of Nationalism.* Rev. ed. New York and London: Verso, 1991.
Artes de Lagueruela, Asela. *La Guerra Chiquita.* 1953. Reprint, Havana: Editorial Letras Cubanas; New York: Distribuido por Ediciones Vitral, 1982.
Arzobispado de la Habana. *Novena a la Santísima Virgen de la Caridad del Cobre patrona de Cuba.* Havana: La Universal, 1926.
Badone, Ellen, ed. *Religious Orthodoxy and Popular Faith in European Society.* Princeton: Princeton University Press, 1990.
Bakalian, Anny. *Armenian-Americans: From Being to Feeling Armenian.* New Brunswick, N.J.: Transaction Publishers, 1993.
Baquero, Gastón. "El negro en Cuba." *La enciclopedia de Cuba,* vol. 5, 415–53. San Juan and Madrid: Enciclopedia y Clásicos Cubanos, 1974.
Basch, Linda, Christina Blanc-Szanton, and Nina Glick Schiller. "Towards a Transnational Perspective on Migration." Annals of the New York Academy of the Sciences, no. 645. New York: New York Academy of the Sciences, 1992.
Behar, Ruth, ed. *Bridges to Cuba/Puentes a Cuba.* Ann Arbor: University of Michigan Press, 1995.
———. *Santa María del Monte: The Presence of the Past in a Spanish Village.* Princeton: Princeton University Press, 1986.
Bell, Catherine. *Ritual Theory, Ritual Practice.* New York: Oxford University Press, 1992.
Bethell, Leslie, ed. *Cuba: A Short History.* Cambridge: Cambridge University Press, 1993.
Betto, Frei. *Fidel and Religion: Conversations with Frei Betto.* Melbourne, Australia: Ocean Press, 1990.
Bischoff, Henry. "Caribbean Peoples in New Jersey: An Overview." *New Jersey History* 113 (Spring/Summer 1995): 1–32.
Bodnar, John. *The Transplanted: A History of Immigrants in Urban America.* Bloomington: Indiana University Press, 1985.
Bolton, Herbert E. *The Wider Horizons of American History.* 1939. Reprint, Notre Dame: University of Notre Dame Press, 1967.
Booth, Cathy. "Miami: The Capital of Latin America." *Time,* special issue, Fall 1993, 82–85.

Borland, Katherine. "The Gritería in Miami: A Nicaraguan Home–Based Festival." *Folklore Forum* 25, no. 1 (1992): 19–27.

Boswell, Thomas D., and James R. Curtis. *The Cuban-American Experience: Culture, Images, and Perspectives*. Totowa, N.J.: Rowman and Allanheld, 1983.

———. "The Hispanization of Metropolitan Miami." In *South Florida: Winds of Change*, ed. Thomas D. Boswell, 140–61. Prepared for the Annual Conference of the Association of American Geographers. Miami, 1991.

Boswell, Thomas D., and Manuel Rivero. *Demographic Characteristics of Pre-Mariel Cubans Living in the United States: 1980*. Miami: Research Institute for Cuban Studies, University of Miami, [1985].

Bourdieu, Pierre. *Outline of a Theory of Practice*. Trans. Richard Nice. Cambridge: Cambridge University Press, 1977.

Bourguet, Marie-Noëlle, Lucette Valensi, and Nathan Wachtel, eds. *Between Memory and History*. Chur, Switzerland: Harwood Academic Publishers, 1990.

Boyarin, Daniel, and Jonathan Boyarin. "Diaspora: Generational Ground of Jewish Identity." *Critical Inquiry* 19 (1993): 693–725.

Boza Masvidal, Eduardo. "Conservemos la pureza de nuestra fe." *Cuba diáspora* (1978).

———. "Una imagen que es un símbolo." In *Ermita de la Caridad*. Miami: Ermita de la Caridad, 1986.

Boza Masvidal, Eduardo, Agustín A. Román, and Enrique San Pedro, S.J. *CRECED: Documento final*. Miami: Comunidades de reflexión eclesial Cubana en la diáspora (CRECED), 1993.

Bradley, Martin B., et al. *Churches and Church Membership in the United States, 1990*. Atlanta: Glenmary Research Center, 1992.

Branch, Karen. "A Symbol of Faith Desecrated." *Miami Herald*, 24 November 1994, 1A.

Brandon, George. *Santería from Africa to the New World: The Dead Sell Memories*. Bloomington: Indiana University Press, 1993.

Breckenridge, Carol, and Arjun Appadurai. "On Moving Targets." *Public Culture* 2 (1989): i.

Brereton, Joel. "Sacred Space." In *Encyclopedia of Religion*, ed. Mircea Eliade. New York: Macmillan, 1987.

Bretos, Miguel A. *Cuba and Florida: Exploration of an Historic Connection, 1539–1991*. Miami: Historical Association of Southern Florida, 1991.

Brown, David Hilary. "Garden in the Machine: Afro-Cuban Sacred Art and Performance in Urban New Jersey and New York." 2 vols. Ph.D. diss., Yale University, 1989.

Brown, Karen McCarthy. *Mama Lola: A Vodou Priestess in Brooklyn*. Berkeley: University of California Press, 1991.

Brown, Richard Harvey, and George V. Coelho, eds. *Migration and Modernization: The Indian Diaspora in Comparative Perspective*. Studies in Third World Societies. Williamsburg, Va.: Department of Anthropology, William and Mary College, 1987.

Bryan, Lina. "Una tarde de fe y romería." *La Voz Católica*, 24 February 1989, 11.

Bucuvalas, Tina, Peggy A. Bulger, and Stetson Kennedy. *South Florida Folklife*. Jackson: University Press of Mississippi, 1994.

Burawoy, Michael. *Ethnography Unbound: Power and Resistance in the Modern Metropolis*. Berkeley: University of California Press, 1991.

Burunat, Silvia, and Ofelia García, eds. *Veinte años de literatura cubanoamericana: Antología 1962–1982*. Tempe: Bilingual Press/Editorial Bilingüe, 1988.

Burwell, Ronald J., Peter Hill, and John F. Van Wicklin. "Religion and Refugee Resettlement in the United States: A Research Note." *Review of Religious Research* 27 (June 1986): 356–66.

Bynum, Caroline Walker, Steven Harrell, and Paula Richman, eds. *Gender and Religion: On the Complexity of Symbols.* Boston: Beacon, 1986.

Cabrera, Lydia. "Babalú Ayé–San Lázaro." In *La enciclopedia de Cuba*, Vol. 6: 268–82. San Juan and Madrid: Enciclopedia y Clásicos Cubanos, 1974.

———. *El monte.* Miami: Ediciones Universal, 1992.

———. *Yemayá y Ochún.* 2nd ed. New York: C.R., 1980.

Calzadilla, Jorge Ramírez, et al. *La religión en la cultura: Estudios realizados por científicos cubanos.* Department of Socioreligious Studies, Psychological and Sociological Studies Center. Havana: Editorial Academia, 1990.

Cañizares, Raúl J. "Cuban Racism and the Myth of the Racial Paradise." *Ethnic Studies Report* 8, no. 2 (July 1990): 27–32.

———. *Walking with the Night: The Afro-Cuban World of Santería.* Rochester, Vt.: Destiny Books, 1993.

Cantero, Araceli M. "Un manto que refleje su blancura." *La Voz Católica*, 24 February 1989, 4.

———. "Surge 'Cachita' barroca y guajira." *La Voz Católica*, 30 August 1991, 9, 16.

———. "También pintó para la Virgen." *La Voz Católica*, 21 January 1994, 16.

"Capellán de una peregrinación nacional." *Cuba diáspora* (1981): 92.

Carrasco, Davíd. *Religions of Mesoamerica: Cosmovisions and Ceremonial Centers.* San Francisco: Harper and Row, 1990.

Carrasco, Teok. "Descripción del mural." In *Ermita de la Caridad*, 38–41. Miami: Ermita de la Caridad, 1986.

Carter, Thomas, and Bernard L. Herman, eds. *Perspectives in Vernacular Architecture, III.* Columbia: University of Missouri Press, 1989.

Castellanos, Jorge, and Isabel Castellanos. *Cultura afrocubana 3: Las religiones y las lenguas.* Miami: Ediciones Universal, 1992.

Castro Ruz, Fidel. *Fidel y la religión: Conversaciones con Frei Betto.* Havana: Oficina de Publicaciones del Consejo de Estado, 1985.

Cattel, Alexander Gilmore. *To Cuba and Back in 22 Days.* Philadelphia: Times Printing House, 1874.

Cavendish, James C., and Mark Chaves. "More Evidence on U.S. Catholic Church Attendance." *Journal for the Scientific Study of Religion* 33, no. 4 (1994): 376–81.

El Centro Cristiano de Medios de Comunicación, Juan Clark, Roberto Eduardo Hernández. *Manual de orientación para refugiados.* Miami: Archdiocese of Miami, 1980.

Chidester, David, and Edward T. Linenthal, eds. *American Sacred Space.* Bloomington: Indiana University Press, 1995.

Chow, Rey. *Writing Diaspora: Tactics of Intervention in Contemporary Cultural Studies.* Bloomington: Indiana University Press, 1993.

Christian, William A., Jr. *Local Religion in Sixteenth-Century Spain.* Princeton: Princeton University Press, 1981.

———. *Person and God in a Spanish Valley.* Rev. ed. Princeton: Princeton University Press, 1989.

City of Miami. *City of Miami, Florida, Golden Anniversary, 1896–1946: Reviewing the Past and Forecasting the Future.* Miami: City of Miami, 1946.

City of Miami. Planning, Building, and Zoning Department. *La Pequeña Habana: Community Development Target Area.* Neighborhood Planning Program, 1994–96. Miami: City of Miami, n.d.

City of Miami. Planning Department. "Design Guidelines and Standards: Latin Quarter District." Miami: City of Miami, 1988.

Clark, Juan. "Una encuesta sobre la diáspora cubana." *Ideal* 21, no. 262 (1993): 9–11.

———. *Mito y realidad: Testimonios de un pueblo*. 2nd ed. Miami and Caracas: Saeta Ediciones, 1992.

———. *Religious Repression in Cuba*. Coral Gables, Fla.: North-South Center, University of Miami, 1986.

Clark, Sydney A. *Cuban Tapestry*. New York: Robert M. McBride and Company, 1936.

Clavijo, Uva de Aragón. *El caimán ante el espejo: Un ensayo de interpretación de lo cubano*. Miami: Ediciones Universal, 1993.

Clifford, James. "Diasporas." *Cultural Anthropology* 9 (August 1994): 302–38.

"El Cobre: Basílica Menor." *Cuba diáspora* (1981): 50–51.

"Cofradía de la Caridad del Cobre." *Boletín Mensual* (Santuario de Nuestra Señora de la Caridad del Cobre [Hialeah]) 2, no. 3 (March 1994): 3.

Coleman, Simon, and John Elsner. *Pilgrimage: Past and Present in the World Religions*. Cambridge: Harvard University Press, 1995.

Comaroff, John, and Jean Comaroff. *Ethnography and the Historical Imagination*. Boulder; Colo.: Westview, 1992.

Conferencia Episcopal Cubana. *Encuentro nacional eclesial cubano*. Havana: Conferencia Episcopal Cubana, 1987.

Connerton, Paul. *How Societies Remember*. Cambridge: Cambridge University Press, 1989.

Conzen, Michael P. "Ethnicity on the Land." In *The Making of the American Landscape*, ed. Michael P. Conzen, 221–48. Boston and London: Unwin Hyman, 1990.

———, ed. *The Making of the American Landscape*. Boston and London: Unwin Hyman, 1990.

Cortina, Betty. "12,000 Attend Special Mass." *Miami Herald*, 9 September 1994, 19A.

Courtright, Paul B. "Shrines." In *Encyclopedia of Religion*, ed. Mircea Eliade. New York: Macmillan, 1987.

Covington, James W. *The Seminoles of Florida*. Gainesville: University Press of Florida, 1993.

Crahan, Margaret E. "Cuba: Religion and Revolutionary Institutionalization." *Journal of Latin American Studies* 17 (November 1985): 319–40.

———. "Religion: Reconstituting Church and Pursuing Change." In *Americas: New Interpretive Essays*, ed. Alfred Stepan, 152–71. New York: Oxford University Press, 1992.

———. *Religion and Revolution: Cuba and Nicaragua*. Working Paper No. 174, Latin American Program, Wilson Center. Washington, D.C.: Smithsonian Institution, 1987.

Crumrine, N. Ross, and Alan Morinis, eds. *Pilgrimage in Latin America*. Contributions to the Study of Anthropology, no. 4. Westport, Conn.: Greenwood, 1991.

Curtis, James R. "Miami's Little Havana: Yard Shrines, Cult Religion, and Landscape." *Journal of Cultural Geography* 1 (Fall/Winter 1980): 1–15.

Dana, Richard Henry, Jr. *To Cuba and Back*. 1859. Reprint, Carbondale: Southern Illinois University Press, 1966.

Davies, J.G. "Architecture." In *Encyclopedia of Religion*, ed. Mircea Eliade. New York: Macmillan, 1987.

Dávila Miguel, Jorge. "Intentan robar estatua de la Virgen." *El Nuevo Herald*, 24 November 1994, 1A.

De Certeau, Michel. *The Practice of Everyday Life*. Trans. Steven F. Rendell. Berkeley: University of California Press, 1984.

Deck, Allan Figueroa. "The Spirituality of the United States Hispanics: An Introductory Essay." *U.S. Catholic Historian* 9 (Spring 1990): 137–46.

Desmangles, Leslie G. *The Faces of the Gods: Vodou and Roman Catholicism in Haiti.* Chapel Hill: University of North Carolina Press, 1992.

Devocionario a Nuestra Señora de la Caridad del Cobre: Historia, misterios, rosario, novena, oraciónes, y fotografías. Preface by Evelio Díaz Cía, Auxiliary Bishop of Havana. Miami Springs: Language Research Press, n.d. [after 10 September 1987].

Dewhurst, C. Kurt, Betty MacDowell, and Marsha MacDowell. *Religious Folk Art in America: Reflections of Faith.* New York: E. P. Dutton, 1983.

Díaz de Villar, Delia. "Historia de la devoción a la Virgen de la Caridad." In *Ermita de la Caridad*, 12–18. Miami: Ermita de la Caridad, 1986.

———. "Historia de la Virgen de la Caridad." In *La enciclopedia de Cuba*, vol. 6, 259–67. San Juan and Madrid: Enciclopedia y Clásicos Cubanos, 1974.

Díaz-Stevens, Ana María. *Oxcart Catholicism on Fifth Avenue: The Impact of the Puerto Rican Migration upon the Archdiocese of New York.* Notre Dame: University of Notre Dame Press, 1993.

———. "Postwar Migrants and Immigrants from the Spanish-Speaking Caribbean: Their Impact upon New Jersey Catholic History." *New Jersey History* 113 (Spring/Summer 1995): 61–81.

Didion, Joan. *Miami.* New York: Pocket Books, 1987.

Dillenberger, John. *The Visual Arts and Christianity in America.* New York: Crossroad, 1988.

Dixon, Heriberto. "The Cuban-American Counterpoint: Black Cubans in the United States." *Dialectical Anthropology* 13 (1988): 227–39.

Dolan, Jay P. *The American Catholic Experience.* 1985. Reprint, Notre Dame: University of Notre Dame Press, 1992.

———. *The Immigrant Church: New York's Irish and German Catholics, 1815–1865.* Baltimore: Johns Hopkins University Press, 1975.

———. "The Immigrants and Their Gods: A New Perspective in American Religious History." *Church History* 57 (March 1988): 61–72.

Dolan, Jay P., and Allan Figueroa Deck, S.J., eds. *Hispanic Catholic Culture in the U.S.: Issues and Concerns.* Notre Dame History of Hispanic Catholics in the U.S. Series, no. 3. Notre Dame: University of Notre Dame Press, 1994.

Dolan, Jay P., and Jaime R. Vidal, eds. *Puerto Rican and Cuban Catholics in the U.S., 1900–1965.* Notre Dame History of Hispanic Catholics in the U.S. Series no. 2. Notre Dame: University of Notre Dame Press, 1994.

Dossick, Jesse J. *Cuba, Cubans, and Cuban-Americans, 1902–1991: A Bibliography.* Coral Gables, Fla. North-South Center, University of Miami, 1992.

Drake, John Gibbs St. Clair. "African Diaspora and Jewish Diaspora: Convergence and Divergence." In *Jews in Black Perspectives: A Dialogue*, ed. Joseph R. Washington Jr., 19–41. Rutherford, N.J.: Fairleigh Dickinson University Press, 1984.

Duany, Jorge. "Neither Golden Exile nor Dirty Worms: Ethnic Identity in Recent Cuban-American Novels." In *Cuban Studies 23*, ed. Jorge Pérez-López, 167–83. Pittsburgh: University of Pittsburgh Press, 1993.

Dussel, Enrique, ed. *The Church in Latin America, 1492–1992.* Marynoll, N.Y.: Orbis Books; Kent: Burns and Oats, 1992.

Eade, John, and Michael J. Sallnow, eds. *Contesting the Sacred: The Anthropology of Christian Pilgrimage.* London and New York: Routledge, 1991.

Eck, Diana L. *Banaras: City of Light.* Princeton: Princeton University Press, 1982.

Ecos de Santa Cruz del Sur: Boletín oficial del Municipio de Santa Cruz del Sur en el exilio. Vol. 2, no. 2 (March/April, 1994).

Editors of *Architectural Record. Religious Buildings.* New York: McGraw-Hill, 1979.

Eisen, Arnold M. *Galut: Modern Jewish Reflection on Homelessness and Homecoming.* Bloomington: Indiana University Press, 1986.

Eliade, Mircea. *The Sacred and the Profane.* Trans. Willard R. Trask. New York and London: Harcourt Brace Jovanovich, 1959.

Eriksen, Thomas Hylland. *Ethnicity and Nationalism: Anthropological Perspectives.* London and Boulder: Pluto Press, 1993.

Ermita de la Caridad. *La Virgen de la Caridad: Historia y presencia en el pueblo cubano.* Sound recording. Miami: Ermita de la Caridad, 1993.

Ermita de la Caridad. Miami: Ermita de la Caridad, 1986.

Estefan, Gloria. *Mi Tierra.* Sound Recording. Sony Music Entertainment, manufactured by Epic, 1993.

Estévez, Felipe J., ed. *Félix Varela: Letters to Elpidio.* New York: Paulist Press, 1989.

Estorino, Julio. "Arnaldo Socorro: El mártir de la Virgen Mambisa." *Ideal* 9, no. 107 (1 October 1979): 39–40.

Featherstone, Mike, ed. *Global Culture: Nationalism, Globalization, and Modernity.* London: Sage Publications, 1990.

Fenton, John Y. *Transplanting Religious Traditions: Asian Indians in America.* Westport, Conn.: Praeger, 1988.

Fernández, Damián J., ed. *Cuban Studies since the Revolution.* Gainesville: University Press of Florida, 1992.

Fernandez, James W. *Bwiti: An Ethnography of the Religious Imagination in Africa.* Princeton: Princeton University Press, 1982.

Fernández, Manuel. *Religión y revolución en Cuba: Veinticinco años de lucha ateísta.* Miami: Saeta Ediciones, 1984.

Fernández, Roberto G. *Raining Backwards.* Houston: Arte Publico Press, 1988.

"Fidel Castro y la revolución: Frases para la historia." *Bohemia*, Edición de la libertad, part 3, vol. 51, no. 5 (1 February 1959): 50–51.

Fields, Barbara Jeanne. "Slavery, Race, and Ideology in the United States of America." *New Left Review*, no. 181 (May/June 1990): 95–118.

Flores-Peña, Ysamur, and Roberta J. Evanchuk. *Santería Garments and Altars.* Jackson: University Press of Mississippi, 1994.

Fonseca, Onofre de. *Historia de la aparición milagrosa de Nuestra Señora de la Caridad del Cobre sacada de un manuscrito que el primer capellán que fué de ella componía el año de 1703. . . .* Santiago de Cuba: Impr. del Real Consuldado de Santiago de Cuba por Loreto Espinel, 1830.

Foucault, Michel. *Power/Knowledge: Selected Interviews and Other Writings, 1972–1977*, ed. Colin Gordon. New York: Pantheon Books, 1980.

Freedberg, David. *The Power of Images: Studies in the History and Theory of Response.* Chicago: University of Chicago Press, 1989.

Freire Díaz, Joaquín. *Historia de los municipios de Cuba.* Miami: La Moderna Poesía, 1985.

"Galut." In *The Encyclopedia of Judaism*, ed. Geoffrey Wigader. New York: Macmillan, 1989.

Gannon, Michael V. *The Cross in the Sand: The Early Catholic Church in Florida, 1513–1870.* 1965. Reprint, Gainesville: University Press of Florida, 1989.

———. *Florida: A Short History.* Gainesville: University Press of Florida, 1993.

García, Concepción. "El mural de la Ermita." *Cuba diáspora* 7 (1979): 73–78.

García, Cristina. *Dreaming in Cuban.* New York: Knopf, 1992.

García, María Cristina. *Havana USA: Cuban Exiles and Cuban Americans in South Florida, 1959–1994.* Berkeley: University of California Press, 1996.

García Enseñat, Ezequiel. "La media luna de la imagen de la Virgen del Cobre." *Archivos del Folklore Cubano* 5, no. 1 (1930): 30–33.

García Tudurí, Mercedes. "La educación de Cuba." In *La enciclopedia de Cuba*, ed. Vincente Báez, vol. 6. San Juan and Madrid: Enciclopedia y Clásicos Cubanos, 1974.

Gellner, Ernest. *Nations and Nationalism*. Ithaca: Cornell University Press, 1983.

Gibson, Olive G. *The Isle of a Hundred Harbors*. Boston: Bruce Humphries, Inc., 1940.

Gilroy, Paul. *The Black Atlantic: Modernity and Double Consciousness*. Cambridge: Harvard University Press, 1993.

Glazer, Nathan. *American Judaism*. 2nd ed. Chicago: University of Chicago Press, 1989.

Gómez, Chuck, and Miguel Pérez. "Cubans Flock to Dedication of Shrine." *Miami Herald*, 3 December 1973, 1B, 2B.

Gómez, Máximo. "Diario de campaña." In *La enciclopedia de Cuba*, ed. Vincente Báez, vol. 4, document 6. San Juan and Madrid: Enciclopedia y Clásicos Cubanos, 1974.

González Kirby, Diana, and Sara María Sánchez. "Santería: From Africa to Miami via Cuba: Five Hundred Years of Worship." *Tequesta* 48 (1988): 36–48.

González y Arocha, Guillermo. *Estudio del escrito de Miss Irene Aloha Wright Nuestra Sra. de la Caridad del Cobre, Santiago de Cuba, Nuestra Sra. de la Caridad Illescas, Castilla, España*. Havana: Seoane y Fernández, 1928.

———. "La piadosa tradición de la Virgen de la Caridad del Cobre." *Archivos del Folklore Cubano* 3, no. 2 (April–June 1928): 97–114.

Gowans, Alan. *Styles and Types of North American Architecture: Social Function and Cultural Expression*. New York: Icon Editions, HarperCollins, 1992.

Gralnick, William A. "'Our Lady of Charity': You Don't Have to Be Cuban to Love Ermita." *Miami Today*, 1 December 1983, 16.

Gravette, A. G. *Cuba: Official Guide*. National Institute of Tourism, Cuba. London and Basingstoke: Macmillan, 1988.

Green, Charles, and Arnold Markowitz. "One Nation, Many Languages." *Miami Herald*, 28 April 1993, 1A, 4A.

Green, Michael D., and Theda Perdue. *The Cherokee Removal: A Brief History with Documents*. Boston: Bedford Books, St. Martin's, 1995.

Green, Nancy L. "The Comparative Method and Poststructural Structuralism—New Perspectives for Migration Studies." *Journal of American Ethnic History* 13 (Summer 1994): 3–22.

Grimes, Ronald L. "Reinventing Ritual." *Soundings* 75 (Spring 1992): 21–41.

Guillén, Ligia. "Jubileo de la Virgen en el exilio." *La Voz Católica*, 29 August 1986, 1, 5.

Gupta, Akhil, and James Ferguson. "Beyond 'Culture': Space, Identity, and the Politics of Difference." *Cultural Anthropology* 7 (February 1992): 6–22.

Gutiérrez, Ramón A. "El Santuario de Chimayó: A Syncretic Shrine in New Mexico." In *Feasts and Celebrations in North American Ethnic Communities*, ed. Ramón A. Gutiérrez and Geneviève Fabre, 71–86. Albuquerque: University of New Mexico Press, 1995.

Hageman, Alice L., and Philip E. Wheaton, eds. *Religion in Cuba Today*. New York: Association Press, 1971.

Halbwachs, Maurice. *The Collective Memory*. Trans. Francis J. Ditter Jr. and Vida Yazdi Ditter. 1950. Reprint, New York: Harper and Row, 1980.

Hall, Stuart. "Cultural Identity and Diaspora." In *Identity: Community, Culture, Difference*, ed. Jonathan Rutherford, 222–37. London: Lawrence and Wishart, 1990.

Halperín Donghi, Tulio. *The Contemporary History of Latin America*. Ed. and Trans. John Charles Chasteen. Durham: Duke University Press, 1993.

Hancock, David. "Judge: City Can Ban Sacrifices." *Miami Herald*, 6 October 1989, 1B, 2B.

Handy, Robert T. *A History of the Churches in the United States and Canada.* New York: Oxford University Press, 1976.

———. "Protestant Patterns in Canada and the United States: Similarities and Differences." In *In the Great Tradition: Essays on Pluralism, Voluntarism, and Revivalism*, ed. Joseph D. Ban and Paul R. Dekar, 33–51. Valley Forge, Pa.: Judson Press, 1982.

Haraway, Donna. *Simians, Cyborgs, and Women: The Reinvention of Nature.* New York: Routledge, 1991.

Hayes, Bartlett H. *Tradition Becomes Innovation: Modern Religious Architecture in America.* New York: Pilgrim Press, 1983.

Heer, David M. "Migration." In *The Social Science Encyclopedia*, ed. Adam Kuper and Jessica Kuper, 524–26. London: Routledge and Kegan Paul, 1985.

Helg, Aline. *Our Rightful Share: The Afro-Cuban Struggle for Equality, 1886–1912.* Chapel Hill: University of North Carolina Press, 1995.

Hendricks, Glenn. *The Dominican Diaspora: From the Dominican Republic to New York City.* New York and London: Teachers College Press, 1974.

Hernández, M. *Historia de la Virgen de la Caridad del Cobre: Patrona de los cubanos.* Havana: M. Comas, 1915.

Hernando, Father José Luis. "La Virgen es Nuestra Señora de los Mandados." *La Voz Católica*, 13 September 1985, 15.

Herrera, María Christina. "The Cuban Ecclesial Enclave in Miami: A Critical Profile." *U.S. Catholic Historian* 9 (Spring 1990): 209–21.

Herskovits, Melville J. "African Gods and Catholic Saints in New World Negro Belief." *American Anthropologist* 39 (1937): 635–43.

Hobsbawm, Eric, and Terrance Ranger, eds. *The Invention of Tradition.* Cambridge: Cambridge University Press, 1983.

Hooson, David, ed. *Geography and National Identity.* Institute of British Geographers Special Publication Series. Oxford: Blackwell, 1994.

Howe, Julia Ward. *A Trip to Cuba.* Boston: Ticknor and Fields, 1860.

Hudson, Charles. *The Southeastern Indians.* Knoxville: University of Tennessee Press, 1976.

Isasi-Díaz, Ada María, and Yolanda Tarango. *Hispanic Women: Prophetic Voice in the Church.* San Francisco: Harper and Row, 1988.

Jackson, Michael. *Paths toward a Clearing: Radical Empiricism and Ethnographic Enquiry.* Bloomington: Indiana University Press, 1989.

Jacobson, Matthew Frye. *Special Sorrows: The Diasporic Imagination of Irish, Polish, and Jewish Immigrants in the United States.* Cambridge: Harvard University Press, 1995.

Joe, Barbara E. "The Church in Cuba—A Dawn?" *America*, 7 December 1991, 428–31.

Jones, Lindsay. *Twin City Tales: A Hermeneutical Reassessment of Tula and Chichén Itzá.* Niwot, Colo.: University Press of Colorado, 1995.

Jorge, Antonio, Jaime Suchliki, and Adolfo Leyva de Varona, eds. *Cuban Exiles in Florida.* Coral Gables: North-South Center, University of Miami, 1991.

Judson, Lyman, and Ellen Judson. *Your Holiday in Cuba.* New York: Harper and Brothers, 1952.

Kammen, Michael G. *Mystic Chords of Memory: The Transformation of Tradition in American Culture.* New York: Knopf, 1991.

Kane, Paula M. *Separatism and Subculture: Boston Catholicism, 1900-1920.* Chapel Hill: University of North Carolina Press, 1994.

Kenneally, James J. *The History of American Catholic Women.* New York: Crossroad, 1990.

Kennelly, Karen, ed. *American Catholic Women: A Historical Exploration.* New York: Macmillan, 1989.

Kilson, Martin L., and Robert I. Rotberg, eds. *The African Diaspora*. Cambridge: Harvard University Press, 1976.

Kimball, Richard Burleigh. *Cuba and the Cubans*. New York: Samuel Hueston, 1850.

King, Geoff. *Mapping Reality: An Exploration of Cultural Cartographies*. New York: St. Martin's, 1996.

Kirk, John. *Between God and the Party: Religion and Politics in Revolutionary Cuba*. Tampa: University Press of South Florida, 1989.

———. *José Martí: Mentor of the Cuban Nation*. Tampa: University Presses of Florida, 1983.

Kivisto, Peter. "Religion and the New Immigrants." In *A Future for Religion?: New Paradigms for Social Analysis*, ed. William H. Swatos Jr., 92–108. Newbury Park, Calif.: Sage Publications, 1993.

Larrubia, Evelyn. "Pasaje a la libertad tiene alto precio para balseros." *El Nuevo Herald*, 6 September 1994, 1A, 4A.

Las Casas, Bartolemé de. "Historia de las Indias." In *Obras escogidas*, ed. J. Pérez de Tudela, vols. 1–2. Madrid: Biblioteca de Autores Españoles, 1957–58.

———. *Short Account of the Destruction of the Indies*. Trans. by Nigel Griffin. London: Penguin Books, 1992.

Lefebvre, Henri. *The Production of Space*. Trans. Donald Nicholson-Smith. Oxford: Blackwell, 1991.

Leiseca, Juan Martín. *Apuntes para la historia eclesiástica de Cuba*. Havana: Carasa y Cía, 1938.

Levine, Robert M. *Tropical Diaspora: The Jewish Experience in Cuba*. Gainesville: University Press of Florida, 1993.

Liga de Damas de Acción Católica Cubana. *Nuestra Señora de la Caridad del Cobre, patrona de Cuba: Historia, devoción, novena*. Havana: Liga de Damas de Acción Católica Cubana, 1950.

Lippy, Charles H., Robert Choquette, and Stafford Poole. *Christianity Comes to the Americas, 1492–1776*. New York: Paragon House, 1992.

Lorenc, Gabriel. *American Czestochowa*. Doylestown, Pa.: National Shrine of Our Lady of Czestochowa, 1989.

Loret de Mola, Florinda Alzaga. "La Virgen de la Caridad en la historia de Cuba." *Ideal* (1992): 5–6.

Lowenthal, David, and Martyn J. Bowden, eds. *Geographies of the Mind: Essays in Historical Geosophy*. New York: Oxford University Press, 1976.

Lubar, Steven, and W. David Kingery, eds. *History from Things: Essays on Material Culture*. Washington and London: Smithsonian Institution Press, 1993.

MacCorkle, Lyn. *Cubans in the United States: A Bibliography for Research in the Social and Behavioral Sciences, 1960–1983*. Westport, Conn.: Greenwood, 1984.

Mach, Zdzislaw. *Symbols, Conflict, and Identity: Essays in Political Anthropology*. Albany: State University of New York Press, 1993.

Madden, Richard Robert. *The Island of Cuba*. London: C. Gilpin, 1849.

Mahmood, Cynthia K., and Sharon L. Armstrong. "Do Ethnic Groups Exist?: A Cognitive Perspective on the Concept of Cultures." *Ethnology* 31 (January 1992): 1–14.

Malkki, Liisa H. "National Geographic: The Rooting of Peoples and the Territorialization of National Identity among Scholars and Refugees." *Cultural Anthropology* 7 (February 1992): 24–44.

———. *Purity and Exile: Violence, Memory, and National Cosmology among Hutu Refugees in Tanzania*. Chicago: University of Chicago Press, 1995.

Marks, Henry S. "Jewish Pioneers in Miami, 1896–1906." M.A. thesis, University of Miami, 1956.

Markus, Thomas A. *Buildings and Power*. London and New York: Routledge, 1993.

Marrero, Leví. *Cuba: Economía y sociedad: El Siglo XVII (III)*. Vol. 5. Madrid: Editorial Playor, 1976.

———. *Los esclavos y la Virgen del Cobre: Dos siglos de lucha por la libertad de Cuba*. Miami: Ediciones Universal, 1980.

Martí, José. "Un Poema de Martí a la Virgen." *Cuba diáspora* (1978): 77–78.

Martin, Lydia, and Tananarive Due. "Does Pluto's Presence Signal Castro's End?" *Miami Herald*, 28 August 1994, 1J, 5J.

Marty, Martin. *Pilgrims in Their Own Land: 500 Years of Religion in America*. Boston: Little, Brown, 1984.

Marzal, Manuel María, S.J. "Daily Life in the Indies (Seventeenth and Early Eighteenth Centuries)." In *The Church in Latin America, 1492–1992*, ed. Enrique Dussel, Marynoll, N.Y.: Orbis Books; Kent: Burns and Oats, 1992.

Matovina, Timothy M. "Our Lady of Guadalupe Celebrations in San Antonio, Texas, 1840–41." *Journal of Hispanic/Latino Theology* 1 (November 1993): 77–96.

Maza Miguel, Manuel, S.J. *El clero cubano y la independencia: Las investigaciónes de Francisco González del Valle (1881–1942)*. Santa Domingo: República Dominicana for the Centro de Estudios Sociales Padre Juan Montalvo, S.J., y Centro Pedro Francisco Bonó, 1993.

McBrien, Richard P, ed.. *The HarperCollins Encyclopedia of Catholicism*. San Francisco: Harper San Francisco, 1995.

McCaffrey, Lawrence J. *The Irish Diaspora in America*. Bloomington: Indiana University Press, 1976.

McDannell, Colleen. "Interpreting Things: Material Culture Studies and American Religion." *Religion* 21 (1991): 371–87.

———. *Material Christianity: Religion and Popular Culture in America*. New Haven: Yale University Press, 1995.

McNally, Michael J. *Catholicism in South Florida, 1868–1968*. Gainesville: University Press of Florida, 1982.

———. "Presence and Persistence: Catholicism among Latins in Tampa's Ybor City, 1885–1985." *U.S. Catholic Historian* 14 (Spring 1996): 73–91.

Mead, Sidney E. "The American People: Their Space, Time, and Religion." In *The Lively Experiment: The Shaping of Christianity in America*, 1–15. New York: Harper and Row, 1963.

Meinig, D. W., ed. *The Interpretation of Ordinary Landscapes: Geographical Essays*. New York: Oxford University Press, 1979.

Mesa-Lago, Carmelo. "Three Decades of Studies on the Cuban Revolution." In *Cuban Studies since the Revolution*, ed. Damián J. Fernández, 9–44. Gainesville: University Press of Florida, 1992.

"Miami: America's Casablanca." *Newsweek*, 25 January 1988, 22–29.

Michell, George. *The Hindu Temple: An Introduction to Its Meanings and Forms*. 1977. Reprint, Chicago: University of Chicago Press, 1988.

"Miles aclaman a la Caridad del Cobre." *El Nuevo Herald*, 9 September 1991, 1B.

Mohl, Raymond A. "Black Immigrants: Bahamians in Early Twentieth-Century Miami." *Florida Historical Quarterly* 65 (January 1987): 271–97.

Mol, Hans, ed. *Identity and Religion: International, Cross-Cultural Approaches*. London: Sage Publications, 1978.

Moore, Deborah Dash. *To the Golden Cities: Pursuing the American Jewish Dream in Miami and L.A.* New York: Free Press, 1994.

Morales, Cecilio J., Jr. *Hispanic Portrait of Evangelization: The Shrine of Our Lady of*

Charity. No. 5. Washington, D.C.: Committee on Evangelization, National Conference of Catholic Bishops, 1981.

Moran, J. Anthony. *Pilgrims' Guide to America: U.S. Catholic Shrines and Centers of Devotion.* Huntington, Ind.: Our Sunday Visitor Publishing Division, 1992.

Morinis, Alan, ed. *Sacred Journeys: The Anthropology of Pilgrimage.* Contributions to the Study of Anthropology, no. 7. Westport, Conn.: Greenwood, 1992.

Mudimbe, V. Y., ed. "Nations, Identities, and Cultures." *South Atlantic Quarterly,* special issue, 94, no. 4 (Fall 1995).

"El mural de la Ermita." Pamphlet. Miami: Ermita de la Caridad, n.d.

Murphy, Joseph M. *Santería: An African Religion in America.* Boston: Beacon, 1988.

———. *Working the Spirit: Ceremonies of the African Diaspora.* Boston: Beacon, 1994.

Nolan, Mary Lee, and Sidney Nolan. *Christian Pilgrimage in Modern Western Europe.* Studies in Religion. Chapel Hill: University of North Carolina Press, 1989.

Noll, Mark A. *A History of Christianity in the United States and Canada.* Grand Rapids, Mich.: Eerdmans, 1992.

Novena a la Santísima Virgen de la Caridad del Cobre, patrona de Cuba: Invocación por la liberación de Cuba. Miami: Majestic Printing, 1972.

Novena a la Virgen Santísima de la Caridad del Cobre. Havana: Pedro Martínez, 1880.

Novena a Nuestra Señora de la Caridad. Havana: Departmento de Medios de Comunicación Social, Archidiócesis de La Habana, 1994.

Nuestra Señora de la Caridad del Cobre, patrona de Cuba: Historia, devoción, novena. Havana: Liga de Damas de Acción Católica Cubana Consejo Nacional, 1950.

Olson, James S. *Catholic Immigrants in America.* Chicago: Nelson-Hall, 1987.

Olson, James S., and Judith E. Olson. *Cuban Americans: From Trauma to Triumph.* New York: Twayne, 1995.

Orsi, Robert A. "The Center Out There, In Here, and Everywhere Else: The Nature of Pilgrimage to the Shrine of Saint Jude, 1929–1965." *Journal of Social History* 25 (Winter 1991): 213–32.

———. " 'Have You Ever Prayed to Saint Jude?': Reflections on Fieldwork in Catholic Chicago." In *Reimagining Denominationalism: Interpretive Essays,* ed. Robert Bruce Mullin and Russell E. Richey, 134–61. New York: Oxford University Press, 1994.

———. " 'He Keeps Me Going': Women's Devotion to Saint Jude Thadeus and the Dialectics of Gender in American Catholicism, 1929–1965." In *Belief in History: Innovative Approaches to European and American Religion,* ed. Thomas Kselman. Notre Dame: Notre Dame University Press, 1991.

———. *The Madonna of 115th Street: Faith and Community in Italian Harlem, 1880–1950.* New Haven: Yale University Press, 1985.

———. *Thank You, St. Jude: Women's Devotion to the Patron Saint of Hopeless Causes.* New Haven: Yale University Press, 1996.

Ortiz, Fernando. "Los cabildos afro-cubana." *Revista Bimestre Cubana* 16, no. 1 (January–February 1921): 5–39.

———. "La semi luna de la Virgen de la Caridad del Cobre." *Archivos del Folklore Cubano* 4, no. 2 (April–July 1929): 161–63.

———. "Virgen de la Caridad." Notes and outline for an unpublished manuscript. Archivo Literario de la Biblioteca del Instituto de Literatura y Linguística, Havana, Cuba.

O'Steen, Bob. "Young and Old Showed Emotion: Flags Waved in 'Silent Applause.' " *The Voice,* 7 December 1973, 13.

"Our Lady of Charity Shrine." Pamphlet. Miami: Ermita de la Caridad, n.d.

Palmié, Stephan. "Afro-Cuban Religion in Exile: Santería in South Florida." *Journal of Caribbean Studies* 5 (Fall 1986): 171–79.

Park, Chris C. *Sacred Worlds: An Introduction to Geography and Religion*. London and
    New York: Routledge, 1994.
Pattie, Susan. "At Home in Diaspora: Armenians in America." *Diaspora* 3 (Fall 1994):
    185–98.
Paul VI. "Evangelii Nuntiandi." In *On Evangelization in the Modern World*, 7. Washington,
    D.C.: USCC Office for Publishing and Promotion Services, 1975.
Pau-Llosa, Ricardo. *Cuba*. Pittsburgh: Carnegie Mellon University Press, 1993.
Payne, Stanley G. *Spanish Catholicism: An Historical Overview*. Madison: University of
    Wisconsin Press, 1984.
Pedraza, Silvia. "Cubans in Exile, 1959–1989: The State of the Research." In *Cuban
    Studies since the Revolution*, ed. Damián J. Fernández. Gainesville: University Press
    of Florida, 1992.
Pena Monte, Gustavo. "Miles de cubanos en la dedicación de la Ermita." *La Voz Católica*
    (Spanish suppl.), 7 December 1973, 16.
Pérez, Lisandro. "Cuban Catholics in the United States." In *Puerto Rican and Cuban
    Catholics in the U.S., 1900–1965*, ed. Jay P. Dolan and Jaime R. Vidal. Notre Dame
    History of Hispanic Catholics in the U.S. Series, no. 2. 158–88. Notre Dame:
    University of Notre Dame Press, 1994.
———. "Cubans in the United States." *Annals of the American Academy of Political and
    Social Science* 487 (September 1986): 126–37.
Pérez, Louis A., Jr. "Between Baseball and Bullfighting: the Quest for Nationality in Cuba,
    1868–1898." *Journal of American History* 81 (September 1994): 493–517.
———. *Cuba and the United States: Ties of Singular Intimacy*. Athens: University of
    Georgia Press, 1990.
———. *Cuba before Reform and Revolution*. New York: Oxford University Press, 1988.
———. *Cuba between Empires, 1878–1902*. Pittsburgh: University of Pittsburgh Press,
    1983.
———. *A Guide to Cuban Collections in the United States*. Westport, Conn.: Greenwood,
    1991.
———. "History, Historiography, and Cuban Studies: Thirty Years Later." In *Cuban
    Studies since the Revolution*, ed. Damián J. Fernández. Gainesville: University Press
    of Florida, 1992.
———, ed. *Slaves, Sugar, and Colonial Society: Travel Accounts of Cuba, 1801–1899*.
    Wilmington, Del.: Scholarly Resources Books, 1992.
Pérez, Pedro Luís. "Vida de San Lázaro, amigo de Jesucristo." Pamphlet. N.p., n.d.
Pérez-López, Jorge, ed. *Cuban Studies 23*. Pittsburgh: University of Pittsburgh Press, 1993.
Petersen, Anna L. "Religion in Latin America: New Methods and Approaches." *Religious
    Studies Review* 21 (January 1995): 3–8.
Petersen, William. "A General Typology of Migration." *American Sociological Review* 23
    (June 1958): 256–66.
Philalethes, Demoticus. *Yankee Travels through the Island of Cuba*. New York: Appleton,
    1856.
Pichardo, Hortensia, ed. *Documentos para la historia de Cuba*. Havana: Editorial de
    Ciencias Sociales, 1977.
"Un poema de Martí a la Virgen." *Cuba diáspora* (1978): 77–78.
"Poll: Optimism Dips over Quick Castro Fall." *Miami Herald*, 5 May 1992, 1B, 2B.
Ponte Domínguez, Francísco. *Historia de la Guerra de los Diez Años*. Havana: El Siglo
    XX, 1972.
Poole, Stafford, C.M. *Our Lady of Guadalupe: The Origins and Sources of a Mexican Na-
    tional Symbol, 1531–1797*. Tucson and London: University of Arizona Press, 1995.

Portes, Alejandro, and Alex Stepick. *City on the Edge: The Transformation of Miami.* Berkeley: University of California Press, 1993.

Portuondo Zúñiga, Olga. *La Virgen de la Caridad del Cobre: Símbolo de cubanía.* Santiago de Cuba: Editorial Oriente, 1995.

Poyo, Gerald E. "Cuban Communities in the United States: Toward an Overview of the Ninteenth-Century Experience." In *Cubans in the United States,* ed. Miren Uriarte-Gastón and Jorge Cañas Martínez. Boston: Center for the Study of the Cuban Community, 1984.

Pratt, Mary Louise. *Imperial Eyes: Travel Writing and Transculturation.* London and New York: Routledge, 1992.

Primiano, Leonard Norman. "Vernacular Religion and the Search for Method in Religious Folklife." *Western Folklore* 54 (January 1995): 37–56.

"Que la Virgen de la Caridad una al exilio y lo conduzca a la liberación . . ." *La Voz Católica* (Spanish suppl.), 7 December 1973, 16.

Quintana, Nicolás. "Evolución histórica de la arquitectura en Cuba." In *La enciclopedia de Cuba,* ed. Vincente Báez, vol. 5. San Juan and Madrid: Enciclopedia y Clásicos Cubanos, 1974.

Ramirez, D. Bernardino. *Novena a la Virgen Santísima de la Caridad del Cobre.* Havana: Imprenta de D. Pedro Martinez, 1880.

Ramirez, Ricardo. "The Hispanic Peoples of the United States and the Church from 1865–1985." *U.S. Catholic Historian* 9 (Spring 1990): 165–77.

Rieff, David. *The Exile: Cuba in the Heart of Miami.* New York: Simon and Schuster, 1993.
———. *Going to Miami: Exiles, Tourists, and Refugees in the New America.* Boston: Little, Brown, 1987.

Rinschede, Gisbert. "Catholic Pilgrimage Places in the United States." In *Pilgrimage in the United States, Geographia Religionum,* ed. Gisbert Rinschede and S. M. Bhardwaj, vol. 5. Berlin: Dietrich Reimer Verlag, 1990.

Robertson, George, et al. *Travellers' Tales: Narratives of Home and Displacement.* London and New York: Routledge, 1994.

Rodríguez, José Ignacio. *Vida del presbítero Don Félix Varela.* Havana: O Novo Mundo, 1878.

Rodríguez Adet, Manuel. "Cuba y la Virgen de la Caridad." In *La Virgen de la Caridad: Patrona de Cuba,* ed. Mario Vizcaíno. Colección: Cultura Cubano; Miami: Instituto pastoral del sureste, 1981.

Román, Agustín A., "La patrona de la diáspora cubana." *El Nuevo Herald,* November 1994.
———. "The Popular Piety of the Cuban People." M.A. thesis, Barry University, 1976.
———. "La Virgen de la Caridad en Miami." In *Ermita de la Caridad,* 6–8. Miami: Ermita de la Caridad, 1986.

Román, Agustín A., and Marcos Antonio Ramos. "The Cubans, Religion, and South Florida." In *Cuban Exiles in Florida,* ed. Antonio Jorge, Jaime Suchliki, and Adolfo Leyva de Varona, 111–43. Miami: North-South Center, University of Miami, 1991.

Rouse, Irving. *The Taínos: Rise and Decline of the People Who Greeted Columbus.* New Haven: Yale University Press, 1992.

Rouse, Roger. "Mexican Migration and the Social Space of Postmodernism." *Diaspora* 1 (Spring 1991): 8–23.

Rutledge, Paul James. *The Role of Religion in Ethnic Self-Identity: A Vietnamese Community.* Lanham, Md.: University Press of America, 1985.
———. *The Vietnamese Experience in America.* Bloomington: Indiana University Press, 1992.

Safran, William. "Diasporas in Modern Societies: Myths of Homeland and Return." *Diaspora* 1, no. 1 (1991): 83–99.

Said, Edward. "The Mind of Winter: Reflections on Life in Exile." *Harper's* 269
(September 1984): 49–55.
———. "Reflections of Exile." *Granta* 13 (1984): 159–72.
Sanders, Thomas G. "Religion in Latin America." In *Latin America: Perspectives on a
Region*, ed. Jack W. Hopkins, 103–16. New York and London: Holmes and Meier,
1987.
Sandoval, Mercedes Cros. *Mariel and Cuban National Identity*. Miami: Editorial SIBI, 1986.
———. *La religión Afro-Cubana*. Madrid: Playor, 1975.
Sandoval, Moisés, *On the Move: A History of the Hispanic Church in the United States*.
Maryknoll, N.Y.: Orbis, 1990.
———. ed. *Fronteras: A History of the Latin American Church in the USA since 1513*. San
Antonio: Mexican American Cultural Center, 1983.
———. "Hispanic Catholics: Historical and Cultural Analysis." *U.S. Catholic Historian*,
special issue, vol. 9 (Winter/Spring 1990).
San Pedro, Enrique, S.J. "La Iglesia en Cuba." *Ideal* 18, no. 256 (1989): 57–60.
Santana, Maydel. " 'Salva a Cuba,' piden cubanos a Virgen." *El Nuevo Herald*, 9 September
1993, 1A, 9A.
Santiago, Ana. "Thousands of Cuban Exiles Gather to Pay Tribute to Island's Patron Saint."
Miami Herald, 9 September 1993, 8B.
Schlereth, Thomas J. *Cultural History and Material Culture: Everyday Life, Landscapes,
and Museums*. Ann Arbor: UMI Research Press, 1990.
———, ed. *Material Culture: A Research Guide*. Lawrence: University Press of Kansas,
1985.
Sciorra, Joseph. "Yard Shrines and Sidewalk Altars of New York's Italian Americans." In
Perspectives in Vernacular Architecture, III, ed. Thomas Carter and Bernard L.
Herman, 185–98. Columbia: University of Missouri Press, 1989.
Scully, Vincent, Jr. *Architecture: The Natural and the Manmade*. New York: St. Martin's,
1991.
———. *Modern Architecture*. New York: George Braziller, 1967.
Sheskin, Ira M. "The Jews of South Florida." In *South Florida: Winds of Change*, ed.
Thomas D. Boswell. Prepared for the Annual Conference of the Association of
American Geographers. Miami, 1991.
———. *The Synod Survey Summary Report: The Archdiocese of Miami*. Miami:
Archdiocese of Miami, 1986.
Short, Margaret I. *Law and Religion in Marxist Cuba: A Human Rights Inquiry*. New
Brunswick N.J.: Transaction Publishers, for the North-South Center, University
of Miami, 1993.
Shostak, Marjorie. *Nisa: The Life and Words of a !Kung Woman*. Cambridge: Harvard
University Press, 1981.
Smith, Jonathan Z. *Map Is Not Territory: Studies in the History of Religions*. Chicago:
University of Chicago Press, 1978.
———. *To Take Place: Toward Theory in Ritual*. Chicago: University of Chicago Press,
1987.
Smith, Theophus H. *Conjuring Culture: Biblical Formations of Black America*. New York:
Oxford University Press, 1994.
Soja, Edward. *Postmodern Geographies: The Reassertion of Space in Critical Social
Theory*. New York and London: Verso, 1989.
Sollors, Werner, ed. *The Invention of Ethnicity*. New York and Oxford: Oxford University
Press, 1989.
Sopher, David E. *Geography of Religions*. Englewood Cliffs, N.J.: Prentice-Hall, 1967.

Sosa, Juan. "Devociones populares: Santa Bárbara y San Lázaro." *Cuba diáspora* (1976): 101–3.

―――. "Popular Religiosity and Religious Syncretism: Santería and Spiritism." *Documentaciones sureste* 4 (March 1983): 14–26.

―――. "La Santería: A Way of Looking at Reality." M.A. thesis, Florida Atlantic University, 1981.

―――. "La Santería: The Lucumí Traditions of the Afro-Cuban Religions." M.Th. thesis, St. Vincent dePaul Seminary, 1972.

Sperber, Dan. *Rethinking Symbolism*. Trans. Alice L. Morton. Cambridge: Cambridge University Press, 1975.

Steele, James Williams. *Cuban Sketches*. New York: G. P. Putnam's Sons, 1881.

Stevens-Arroyo, Anthony M. *Cave of the Jagua: The Mythological World of the Taínos*. Albuquerque: University of New Mexico Press, 1988.

―――. "Latino Catholicism and the Eye of the Beholder: Notes toward a New Sociological Paradigm." *Latino Studies Journal* 6 (May 1995): 22–55.

―――. "The Persistence of Religious Cosmovision in an Alien World." In *Enigmatic Powers: Syncretism with African and Indigenous People's Religions among Latinos*, ed. Anthony M. Stevens-Arroyo and Andres I. Pérez y Mena, Program for the Analysis of Religion among Latinos Studies Series, no. 2. 113–35. New York: Bildner Center for Western Hemisphere Studies, 1995.

Stevens-Arroyo, Anthony M., and Ana María Díaz-Stevens, eds. *An Enduring Flame: Studies on Latino Popular Religiosity*. Program for the Analysis of Religion among Latinos Studies Series, no. 1. New York: Bildner Center for Western Hemisphere Studies, 1994.

Suchlicki, Jaime. *Cuba: From Columbus to Castro*. Washington: Pergamon-Brassey's, 1990.

―――. *Historical Dictionary of Cuba*. Metuchen, N.J.: Scarecrow Press, 1988.

"Sumario de la encuesta de la reflexión Cubana en la diáspora." *Ideal* 20, no. 261 (1992): 4–5.

Tafuri, Manfredo, and Francesco Dal Co. *Modern Architecture*. Trans. Robert Erich Wolf. New York: Harry N. Abrams, 1979.

Tames, Robert. "The Americans on Their Travels." *Harper's New Monthly Magazine* 31 (June 1865): 57–63.

Taves, Ann. *The Household of Faith: Roman Catholic Devotions in Mid-Nineteenth-Century America*. Notre Dame: University of Notre Dame Press, 1986.

Tebeau, Charlton W. *Synagogue in the Central City: Temple Israel of Greater Miami*. Coral Gables, Fla.: Temple Israel, 1972.

Testé, Ismael. *Historia eclesiástica de Cuba*. 3 vols. Burgos: Editorial El Monte Carmelo, 1969.

Thomas, Hugh. *The Cuban Revolution*. London: George Weidenfeld and Nicolson Limited, 1986.

Thompson, Richard H. *Theories of Ethnicity: A Critical Appraisal*. Contributions in Sociology, no. 82. Westport, Conn.: Greenwood, 1989.

Thompson, Robert Farris. *Face of the Gods: Art and Altars of Africa and the African Americas*. New York: Museum for African Art; Munich: Prestel, 1993.

―――. *Flash of the Spirit: African and African-American Art and Philosophy*. New York: Vintage Books, 1983.

Tiele, C. P. "Religions." In *Encyclopedia Britannica*, 9th ed., vol. 20, 358–71. New York: Charles Scribner's Sons, 1886.

Torre, Monseñor Teodoro de la. *Félix Varela: Vida ejemplar*. Miami: Padre Félix Varela Foundation, n.d.

"Transcripción del documento original de Juan Moreno." In *La Virgen de la Caridad: Patrona de Cuba*, ed. Mario Vizcaíno. Colección: Cultura Cubana; Miami: Instituto pastoral del sureste, 1981.

Tremols, José. *Historia de la devoción de la Virgen de la Caridad*. Miami: Album de America, [1962?].

Tuan, Yi-Fu. "Geopiety: A Theme in Man's Attachment to Nature and Place." In *Geographies of the Mind: Essays on Historical Geosophy*, ed. David Lowenthal and Martyn J. Bowden, 11–39. New York: Oxford University Press, 1976.

———. *Space and Place: The Perspective of Experience*. Minneapolis: University of Minnesota Press, 1977.

———. *Topophilia: A Study of Environmental Perception, Attitudes, and Values*. Englewood Cliffs, N.J.: Prentice-Hall, 1974.

Turner, Victor. *The Forest of Symbols*. Ithaca: Cornell University Press, 1967.

———. *From Ritual to Theater*. Performance Studies Series. New York: PAJ Publications, 1982.

Turner, Victor, and Edith Turner. *Image and Pilgrimage in Christian Culture: Anthropological Perspectives*. New York: Columbia University Press, 1978.

Tweed, Thomas A. "Asian Religions in America: Reflections on an Emerging Subfield." In *Religious Diversity and American Religious History: Studies in Traditions and Cultures*, ed. Walter Conser and Sumner Twiss. Athens: University of Georgia Press, forthcoming.

———. "An Emerging Protestant Establishment: Religious Affiliation and Public Power on the Urban Frontier in Miami, 1896–1904." *Church History* 64 (September 1995): 412–37.

———. Introduction to *Retelling U.S. Religious History*, ed. Thomas A. Tweed, 1–23. Berkeley: University of California Press, 1997.

"20,000 at Stadium Mass in Honor of Blessed Virgin." *The Voice*, 11 September 1964, 15.

Tyson, Ruel W., Jr. Introduction to *Diversities of Gifts: Field Studies in Southern Religion*, ed. Ruel W. Tyson Jr., James L. Peacock, and Daniel W. Patterson, 3–20. Urbana: University of Illinois Press, 1988.

Tyson, Ruel W., Jr., James L. Peacock, and Daniel W. Patterson, eds. *Diversities of Gifts: Field Studies in Southern Religion*. Urbana: University of Illinois Press, 1988.

Underwood, John. "Exiles Pray for End of Tyranny." *Miami Herald*, 9 September 1961, 1A, 2A.

Valdés Domínguez, Fermín. "La Virgen de la Caridad." *Patria* (New York), 9 June 1894.

Van Gennep, Arnold. *The Rites of Passage*. Trans. M. B. Vizedom and G. L. Caffee. 1909. Reprint, Chicago: University of Chicago Press, 1960.

Varela, Félix. "Address to Protestants." *Catholic Observer*, 15 December, 22 December, 29 December 1836, 12 January 1837.

Varona Guerrero, Miguel Ángel. *La guerra de independencia de Cuba*. 3 vols. Havana: Editorial Lex, 1946.

Vega, María. "No teman, la tormenta va a pasar." *La Voz Católica*, 23 September 1994, 10.

Vidal, Jaime R. "The American Church and the Puerto Rican People." *U.S. Catholic Historian* 9 (Spring 1990): 119–35.

Villaronda, Guillermo. "Plegaria por Cuba." *Bohemia*, Edición de la libertad, part 3, vol. 51, no. 5 (1 February 1959): 35–70.

Villaverde, Alberto, S.J. *Santa María, Virgen de la Caridad del Cobre*. 2nd ed. San Juan, Puerto Rico: Publi-RIN, 1994.

Viñas, Carmelo, and Ramón Paz, eds. *Relaciones histórico-geográfico-estadísticas de los pueblos de España: Hechas por iniciativa de Felipe II, Reino de Toledo*. Vol. 2, part 1. Madrid: Consejo superior de investigaciones científicas, 1951.

La Virgen de la Caridad en Miami. Pamphlet. Miami: Ermita de la Caridad, n.d.

Vizcaíno, Mario, ed. *La Virgen de la Caridad: Patrona de Cuba*. Colección: Cultura Cubana; Miami: Instituto pastoral del sureste, 1981.

Wallace, Caroline L. *Santiago de Cuba before the War; Or Recuerdos de Santiago*. New York and London: F. Tennyson Neely, 1898.

Walsh, Bryan O. "Cuban Refugee Children." *Journal of Inter-American Studies and World Affairs* 13 (July–October 1971): 378–415.

———. "Cubans in Miami." *America*, 26 February 1966, 286–89.

———. "The Spanish Impact Here: How the Archdiocese Is Meeting the Challenge." *The Voice*, 18 July 1975, 1A–3A.

Walsh, Michael. *Dictionary of Catholic Devotions*. San Francisco: Harper San Francisco, 1993.

Washington, Joseph R., Jr., ed. *Jews in Black Perspectives: A Dialogue*. Rutherford, N.J.: Fairleigh Dickinson University Press, 1984.

Weiss, Joaquín E. *La arquitectura colonial cubana: Siglos XVI/XVII*. Havana: Editorial letras Cubanas, 1979.

———. *La arquitectura colonial cubana: Siglo XVIII*. Havana: Editorial letras Cubanas, 1979.

White, O. Kendall, Jr., and Daryl White, eds. *Religion in the Contemporary South: Diversity, Community, and Identity*. Southern Anthropological Society Proceedings, no. 28. Athens: University of Georgia Press, 1995.

Whoriskey, Peter. "A Matter of Style." *Miami Herald*, 17 October 1993, 1B, 5B.

Williams, Peter W. "Religious Architecture and Landscape." In *Encyclopedia of the American Religious Experience*, ed. Charles Lippy and Peter W. Williams. New York: Scribner's, 1988.

Williams, Raymond Brady. *Religions of Immigrants from India and Pakistan: New Threads in the American Tapestry*. Cambridge and New York: Cambridge University Press, 1988.

———, ed. *A Sacred Thread: Modern Transmission of Hindu Traditions in India and Abroad*. Chambersburg, Pa.: Anima Publications, 1992.

Wills, David W., and Albert J. Raboteau. "Rethinking American Religious History: A Progress Report on 'Afro-American Religious History: A Documentary Project.'" *Council of Societies for the Study of Religion Bulletin* 20 (September 1991): 57–61.

Wilson, Stephen, ed. *Saints and Their Cults: Studies in Religious Sociology, Folklore, and History*. Cambridge: Cambridge University Press, 1983.

Wind, James P. *Places of Worship: Exploring Their History*. Nashville: American Association for State and Local History, 1990.

Wind, James P. and James W. Lewis, ed. *American Congregations: New Perspectives in the Study of Congregations*. Vol. 2. Chicago: University of Chicago Press, 1994.

Wolf, Eric R., ed. *Religion, Power, and Protest in Local Communities: The Northern Shore of the Mediterranean*. Berlin and New York: Mouton, 1984.

Wolff, Janet. *The Social Production of Art*. 2nd ed. New York: New York University Press, 1993.

Wright, Irene A. "Nuestra Señora de la Caridad del Cobre (Santiago de Cuba), Nuestra Señora de la Caridad de Illescas (Castilla, España)." *Archivos del folklore Cubano* 3, no. 1 (January–March 1928): 5–15.

———. "Our Lady of Charity: Nuestra Señora de la Caridad del Cobre (Santiago de

Cuba), Nuestra Señora de la Caridad de Illescas (Castilla, Spain)." *Hispanic American Historical Review* 5 (1922): 709–17.

Wright, John K. *Human Nature in Geography: Fourteen Papers, 1925–65.* Cambridge: Harvard University Press, 1966.

Young, Robert J. C. *Colonial Desire: Hybridity in Theory, Culture, and Race.* London and New York: Routledge, 1995.

Zimdars-Swartz, Sandra L. *Encountering Mary: Visions of Mary from La Salette to Medjugorje.* New York: Avon Books, 1992.

———. "The Marian Revival in American Catholicism: Focal Points and Features of the New Marian Enthusiasm." In *Being Right: Conservative Catholics in America*, ed. Mary Jo Weaver and R. Scott Appleby. Bloomington: Indiana University Press, 1995.

Index